Eufrasia Burlamacchi

Illuminating Women Artists: Renaissance and Baroque

The series *Illuminating Women Artists* launches at a critical moment in contemporary culture. It marks a significant intervention within the broader movement underway among scholars, museums, collectors and the wider world of cultural heritage to make evident and contextualise historically the contributions of women artists. As such, the books, each written by a leading specialist in the field of art history, will appeal to audiences from the academic sphere to the general public. Beautifully illustrated, the volumes collectively offer an unprecedented visual contextualisation of the lives and works of their subjects, to whom in some cases a monograph has yet to be dedicated.

Books in the sub-series *Illuminating Women Artists: Renaissance and Baroque* critically reappraise the lives and works of female artists in Europe from the fifteenth to the early eighteenth centuries. Many of the women represented by the volumes were celebrated professional artists in their own eras, yet their names and works have not been passed down continually in the history of art. As the first series dedicated to correcting this omission, the books interweave established conclusions with new discoveries to reframe how women's artistic production is approached and understood.

Eufrasia Burlamacchi

LORETTA VANDI

GETTY PUBLICATIONS

LOS ANGELES

In memory of Kristi Burman (1958–2008)

"Les perfections de Dieu sont celles de nos âmes, mais il les possède sans bornes: il est un océan, dont nous n'avons reçu que des gouttes [. . .] L'ordre, les proportions, l'harmonie nous enchantent, la peinture et la musique en sont des échantillons; Dieu est tout ordre, il garde toujours la justesse des proportions, il fait l'harmonie universelle: toute la beauté est un épanchement de ses rayons."

—Gottfried Wilhelm Leibniz
Essais de Théodicée, Préface

Published in the United States of America by Getty Publications, Los Angeles
1200 Getty Center Drive, Suite 500
Los Angeles, California 90049-1682
getty.edu/publications

Distributed in the United States and Canada by the University of Chicago Press

Printed in China

ISBN 978-1-60606-956-1
Library of Congress Control Number: 2024945784

Published simultaneously in the United Kingdom by Lund Humphries
Originated by Lund Humphries
Huckletree Shoreditch
Alphabeta Building
18 Finsbury Square
London EC2A 1AH
UK
lundhumphries.com

Copy edited by Julie Gunz
Project managed and designed by Crow Books
Set in Adobe Caslon Pro

Front cover: Eufrasia Burlamacchi, *Initial E, Hybrid*, Gradual MS 2649, f.58v, c.1530, tempera and gold leaf on parchment, 14.5 × 14.5 cm (5 ¾ × 5 ¾ in), Biblioteca Statale, Lucca

Back cover: Eufrasia Burlamacchi, *Initial V, Virgo gloriosa semper—St. Cecilia with Book and Palm Frond*, Antiphonary MS 4, f.91v, c.1513, tempera and gold leaf on parchment; folium 54.2 × 38.5 cm (21 ⅜ × 15 ⅛ in); initial 13 × 13 cm (5 ⅛ × 5 ⅛ in), Dominican convent, California

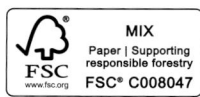

Contents

Series Foreword

The series *Illuminating Women Artists: Renaissance and Baroque* was conceptualised at a pivotal moment in contemporary life, when the call to dismantle structural bias was taking on a new urgency. As social justice movements, such as #MeToo, #BlackLivesMatter, and #TransLivesMatter, exposed assumptions about gender, race, and sexual identity, academic research has been infused with a new energy around these topics. Although approaches to, and even the very applicability of, identity categories as they are defined today vary in regard to the past, early modernity and the contemporary moment share a desire to contend with the power structures that have repressed individuals and groups, albeit in historically distinct ways. Books in *Illuminating Women Artists* advance a specific aspect of this study – the feminist academic enterprise – by making evident various ways that early modern women of the fifteenth through eighteenth centuries negotiated, and sometimes resisted, structural constraints in the sphere of the visual arts.

The series is indebted to feminist art-historical studies produced from the beginning of the 1970s that aimed to disrupt the traditional academic focus on early modern male artists by writing their female counterparts into the discipline of art history. These and other scholarship also began to investigate

gender norms in the Renaissance and Baroque, which created different conditions for women and men who sought to practice art as professionals or amateurs. Societal limitations disadvantaged most women (and some men) who aspired to a life in the visual arts. For example, girls were excluded from the formal apprenticeship system through which most male artists were trained, and therefore they sought informal instruction, often from male relatives. Women practitioners who married and became mothers generally experienced a lapse in artistic production while they attended to the responsibilities that came with these roles. On the other hand, fathers sometimes supportively promoted their daughters as artists, which also aggrandised the family and improved its financial standing through patronage and sales.

This series considers early modern women artists within their social, cultural, temporal, and geographic contexts. These female artmakers worked in a period when a literary defence of women's merits began to challenge the patriarchal misogynist ideas that sought to suppress women and their potential. Some women artists may have been aware of this incipient feminism or have visually voiced related issues in their art. But the female artists represented by the series also identified with the social structures of their place and time. These structures, prominent among them gender and class, contributed to shaping their identities and to forming their conceptions about others. While women challenged normative structures in important ways (some more overtly than others), they also were acculturated into dominant cultural attitudes and thus complicit in supporting social hierarchies of class and race. Renaissance and Baroque women artists themselves derived from a spectrum of social classes – artisan, merchant, professional, or patrician. Membership in these classes made it possible for some women artists to have servants or even to enslave persons who contributed to their households. This practice reduced their own domestic obligations and freed time for artmaking, but in turn contributed to reinforcing existing systems of social stratification regarded as the norm.

Some gendered conditions with which female artists contended did not necessarily impede their success, but, even when women's artistic production was critically acclaimed, it was often evaluated according to gender stereotypes. Yet, certain women independently challenged, and circumvented or broke, restrictive gender protocols to enable prolific art production. In the process, they revised those protocols and influenced the history of art. Some established their own professional studios and trained pupils, both female and male, who in turn established themselves as professionals in workshops of their own. Others produced large bodies of work as amateurs, and some rendered porous the boundaries between these two statuses by bridging them. Still others produced works for members of communities to which they belonged, such as professed nuns in enclosed convents, or for personal reasons, such as to have in their possession a portrait of a family member. Some worked under contract for patrons, producing images for prestigious European courts and churches, where their art came under the eyes of the public. These women in the aggregate produced works that varied widely in subject, including both sacred and secular themes, and in artistic media. Represented in the latter category were the familiar forms of sculpture, painting, and printmaking, and also other ways of artmaking that were valued more highly in the past than they are in the present, including papercutting, embroidery, and weaving.

Five decades of sustained research have transformed our understanding of early modern women artists. *Illuminating Women Artists: Renaissance and Baroque* takes stock of this work through books that offer state-of-the-question analyses of their subjects. These peer-reviewed volumes variously interweave established conclusions with new discoveries investigated through emerging modes of analysis to reframe our understanding of the lives, artistic production, and works of art by European women. Together the books reveal the varied ways in which women of the fifteenth through the seventeenth centuries skilfully and often successfully navigated restricting gender norms to stake out productive lives as artmakers and develop innovative approaches to the works they produced. The volumes offer an unprecedented contextualisation of the lives and works of their subjects, to whom in some cases a monograph has not previously been dedicated.

Marilyn Dunn, Loyola University Chicago
Andrea Pearson, American University, Washington, DC
April 2021

Acknowledgements

I wrote my first article on Eufrasia Burlamacchi 18 years ago, but my discovery of her achievements dates back to 2004. While studying incunabula of Girolamo Savonarola's sermons and treatises in the Biblioteca Statale at Lucca, I came across a book by Innocenzo Taurisano, OP, reporting that at the beginning of the sixteenth century, two Dominican Observant convents were founded in Lucca – San Domenico and San Giorgio – both following Savonarolan reform. There I also found that among the sisters of San Domenico, one in particular – Eufrasia – was renowned for her distinguished ability in writing, singing and illuminating manuscripts. Chance had it that the same library was the repository of three manuscripts, the two-volume Gradual 2649–50 and Ritual 1984. Marco Paoli, the former director of the Biblioteca Statale, attributed to Eufrasia the illumination of the two-volume Gradual, while the two miniatures of MS 1984 were assigned to another nun who followed Eufrasia's style.

Casting around for more information, at the Archivio Storico Diocesano in Lucca I met Massimiliano Coli, a scholar of Lucchese ecclesiastical history, who alerted me to the existence of five manuscripts, written, notated and illuminated by Eufrasia, in a conventual archive in California. He also advised me to consult the multivolume Chronica of the San Domenico convent, no longer in Lucca: in the 1920s it emigrated, along with the few nuns who remained, to the monastery of Santa Maria del Sasso at Bibbiena, near Arezzo. When in July 2020 I was eventually able to see the Chronica at Bibbiena, Sister Bernadetta Giordano, the learned librarian with whom I exchanged some calls during the 2000s, was no longer there. Actually, neither librarian nor archivist welcomed me at Santa Maria del Sasso. Rather, a thoughtful volunteer, Giuseppe Masini, helped me during a two-day tour de force to collect all the documents concerning the history of San Domenico, the original Bull instituting the new convent, signed by Pope Alexander VI in 1501, included.

I should like to thank first and foremost Kristi Burman, whom I met in 2006 at the International Medieval Congress at Leeds, and I missed too early in 2008, for inviting me to present the first results of my research on Eufrasia at a seminar in the Art History Department of Umeå University in Sweden. In 2007 she published 'The Eternal Flame. Eufrasia Burlamacchi and Savonarolan Art in the Lucchese Convent of San Domenico' in a small essay collection, my first written contribution to the history of this intriguing Dominican sister.

Sections of this work have been presented at some seminars and lectures, as in March 2008 at Lucca (Biblioteca Statale) and in July 2008 at Dublin (Trinity College). I discussed my new findings on

Eufrasia in two conferences at Florence, in October 2013 (*Artiste nel chiostro*, Jane Fortune Annual Conference, Convent of the Santissima Annunziata) and in October 2018 (*The Colours of Paradise*, Jane Fortune Annual Conference, San Marco Library). I should like to thank the organisers and all those who attended, and particularly those who offered comments and suggestions.

After the publication of two short entries, the first in 2018 (in Giovanna Murano, ed., *Autographa ii.1. Donne, sante e madonne (da Matilde di Canossa a Artemisia Gentileschi)*) and the second in 2021 (for the blog *Art Herstory*, 20 September 2021), I set out to write this book, which underwent many changes thanks to Marilyn Dunn and Andrea Pearson, the series editors of *Illuminating Women Artists* for Lund Humphries; to the acquisitions editor, Erika Gaffney, who never spared pertinent questions, comments and encouragement; and to the two anonymous reviewers who offered a detailed critical analysis of my manuscript.

The scholarship on nuns in Renaissance Italy seems to expand daily, yet some scholars have been to me truly inspirational: Sheila Barker, Mary Garrard, Megan Holmes, Kate Lowe, Ann Roberts, Sharon Strocchia, Anabel Thomas, Catherine Turrill Lupi and Gabriella Zarri. I should like to acknowledge the contribution of Pavlos Jerenis, who offered insights on Catholicism and Reformation, spirituality and interpretation of the Sacred Scripture. Also, I should express special thanks to Prioress Sister Carla Kovack of a Dominican convent in California for the permission to publish the miniatures of the five choir books illuminated by Eufrasia for the San Domenico convent; to the Tavolozza Foundation for the grant that supported the publication of the book; and to Anna Pagnini, for her untiring help in improving my photographs. As ever, my greatest debt lies with archivists, librarians – especially Dr Monica Maria Angeli, director of the Biblioteca Statale, Lucca – and fellow historians and art historians, but also with the nun chroniclers of San Domenico and with Eufrasia, scribe, illuminator and singer, who made my project possible.

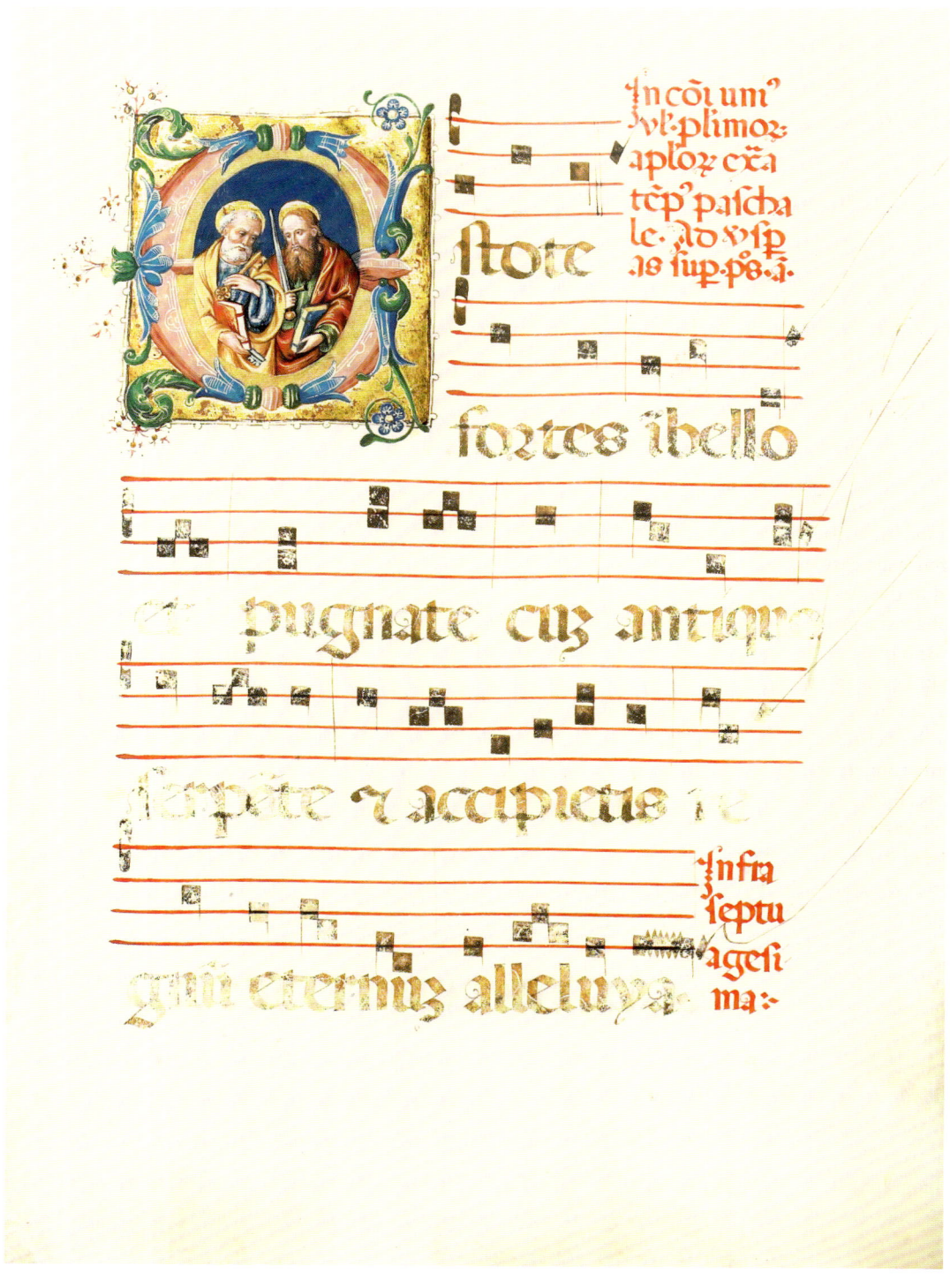

1   Eufrasia Burlamacchi, *Initial E, Estote fortes in bello – The Saints Peter and Paul*, Antiphonary MS 4, fol.132ʳ, *c.*1513, tempera and gold leaf on parchment, folium 54.2 × 38.5 cm (21⅜ × 15⅛ in), initial 13 × 12.8 cm (5⅛ × 5 in), Dominican Convent, California

Preface

No artistic biography of Eufrasia Burlamacchi (1478–1548) exists, despite her status as a highly talented early modern artist.[1] The reasons for this historical negligence are easy to single out as they are mainly related to the seeming dearth of documents and the type of art she produced. Eufrasia was a Dominican sister who practised the art of illumination. She was based in Lucca in the first quarter of the sixteenth century, in the Observant convent of San Domenico which she helped to found in 1502.

Some comparisons might be made to Plautilla Nelli (1524–88), another Dominican sister in the convent of Santa Caterina da Siena, who became a renowned painter in Florence. Nelli, however, was able to connect the spiritual and secular worlds, engaging herself with Florentine aristocrats and literary circles. In all probability, she was acquainted with artists like Agnolo Bronzino (1503–72) and connoisseurs such as Benedetto Varchi (1503–65). Also, her spiritual orientation was seemingly shared by Florentine households. She marketed her paintings outside the convent to Florentine noblemen and noblewomen; especially the latter may have favoured Nelli's art.[2]

A biography devoted to Eufrasia must acknowledge that, during her artistic development, she had neither encounters nor meetings, neither travels nor direct experiences with the artistic world of her time. Here the names of both Artemisia Gentileschi (1593–after 1654)[3] and Giovanna Garzoni (1600–1670)[4] come to mind. Even though they worked a century later, both promoted themselves through travels, meetings and discussions, facing competition in a world hardly favourable to women in search of social and artistic recognition.

Conventual environments were different realities entirely. Nevertheless, though apparently definable as secluded places with a strict system of control, they were not secluded enough to impede the circulation of ideas and artworks that elicited, from the nuns, reactions in the religious as much as in the artistic fields. Although we are accustomed to painting and sculpture produced by lay artists who worked for an art market supported by private patrons, clerics and state institutions, from the late fifteenth century onward, nuns contributed to the development of that market. As the example of Sister Plautilla Nelli demonstrates, nuns' output was the product of a culture of art that flourished within convents, grounded in a tradition that privileged specific religious subjects and specific techniques.

The flourishing of this tradition in Italy has been recently studied by scholars who have mainly focused on convents in Florence, Pisa, Rome, Venice, Bologna and Milan, grounding their research on conventual chronicles, devotional texts, liturgical manuscripts and artworks.[5] Some light also has been shed on instances of Italian conventual art from the point of view of clients, as in the Dominican convent of Santa Caterina da Siena in Florence, where the nuns produced paintings, sculptures, figurines and reliefs for distribution outside of their community. Questions about the customers' identity, the reasons for the high esteem in which they held these objects and the degree of kinship that may have prompted the acquisition of such works are also valid for all the convents of the early modern period, the Dominican convent of San Domenico in Lucca included.[6]

In the convents, craftwork was an important part of the nuns' communal life since they were expected, following scriptural guidelines, to avoid idleness. The tasks they variously accomplished were spinning, weaving, sewing, writing, illuminating manuscripts and making lace. These practical and 'honest' occupations were subservient to spiritual activities, like praying, meditating, reading and singing. The products of the nuns' workshop were sold, contributing to the convent's annual income together with other pecuniary resources such as dowries, donations, legacies, agricultural sales and property rentals. On other occasions, artistic products, generally belonging to what is sometimes called the 'minor arts', were exchanged between different convents. Only from the middle of the sixteenth century is there evidence for the production of painting and sculpture that was sold or given as gifts. Members of the religious orders, but also lay individuals or families, admired how the convents treated devotional subjects, especially Jesus, Mary, the Christ Child, saints and angels. Originality was not the primary focus, since images produced for and by monastic environments were valued for their devotional efficacy. They had to inspire meditation and prayer 'by inducing emotional empathy'.[7]

Eufrasia was an expert in illuminating manuscripts, a proficiency that did not pass unnoticed at her time, but all the sixteenth-century information concerning her art belongs to conventual records, destined to remain within a limited and self-referential history. In the first quarter of the sixteenth century, there was no art biographer and painter like Giorgio Vasari (1511–74) creating the category of women artists, so there was no one to comment upon and connect Eufrasia's illumination to larger artistic realities. Her work, contrary to Sister Plautilla Nelli's painting, had to wait until the nineteenth century to be placed in its proper art-historical frame.

The first mention of Eufrasia as an illuminator is in Vincenzo Marchese's study on Dominican artists published in 1846, followed in 1914 by Innocenzo Taurisano, OP, in his book on the Dominicans in Lucca.[8] It is to the latter's merit to have recorded the four Antiphonaries (books collecting the choral parts for the Divine Office, that is the public service of praise and worship) and one Gradual (a book collecting all the musical items of the Mass) illuminated by Eufrasia when they were still with the nuns of San Domenico in Lucca. Shelf marked MSS 1, 2, 3, 4 and 5, they are now preserved in the archive of a Dominican convent in California. Two miniatures published by Taurisano – *The Saints Peter and Paul*, MS 4, fol.132ʳ (fig.1) and *Saint Dominic*, MS 5, fol.152ʳ – paved the way for the reconstruction of Eufrasia's artistic corpus. In 1977 Marco Paoli connected them with the miniatures in the two-volume Gradual, now MSS 2649 and 2650 in the Biblioteca Statale at Lucca, written, notated and decorated by Eufrasia from 1527 to *c*.1532 for the Lucchese Dominican monastery of San Romano.[9]

In 1996 Gerardo Mansi, in his book on Lucchese aristocrats, devoted a short passage to her illumination when he treated the Burlamacchi family.[10] In 2002, Mark Gregory D'Apuzzo again took up the topic of 'Eufrasia Burlamacchi' in a few lines of an essay on the Savonarolan nuns in

Tuscany; in 2007, he devoted two detailed entries to the two-volume Gradual MSS 2649–50, published in the catalogue for the exhibition *Italian Women Artists from Renaissance to Baroque*, organised by the National Museum of Women in the Arts in Washington, DC.[11] On this occasion the American public became acquainted with two miniatures by Eufrasia, in addition to artworks by already known artists such as Caterina Vigri, Properzia de' Rossi, Plautilla Nelli, Sofonisba Anguissola, Lavinia Fontana, Fede Galizia, Artemisia Gentileschi, Giovanna Garzoni and Elisabetta Sirani.

A more extensive treatment of Eufrasia's illumination, though confined to the five manuscripts described by Taurisano, was provided by Ileana Tozzi in 2005. The eulogistic tone of Tozzi's essays does not clarify, however, how Eufrasia's work participated in the development of early modern Italian art.[12] In 2008 Ann Roberts reported Eufrasia's activity as a scribe and illuminator in the context of Dominican women and Renaissance art.[13] In 2013 Marilyn Dunn found for Eufrasia the appropriate environment within the 'convent creativity', grounded on literacy and knowledge of both liturgy and notation. In addition, Dunn attributed to Eufrasia familiarity with and re-elaboration of the Tuscan miniature tradition, exhibiting 'an aesthetic sophistication' not always present in other nun-miniaturists of her time.[14] In 2023 Alexa Greist, in a short entry on manuscript illumination in the catalogue for the exhibition *Making Her Mark*, insisted on Eufrasia's ability to portray saints to establish a connection with the viewer, without facing the issues of other kinds of connection with the inner and outer environments.[15] This, however, is the path the present author has followed since 2007, placing Eufrasia within her religious, social and artistic environments, emphasising her contribution to both illumination and art in general in the sixteenth century.[16] But why is it only recently that Eufrasia's work has received sustained attention? Social and cultural preconceptions concurred in placing her and many other nuns who specialised in illumination apart from the mainstream artistic development and so outside the canon of art history.

In 1982, Svetlana Alpers contributed an article to the essay collection *Feminism and Art History: Questioning the Litany*, edited by Norma Broude and Mary D. Garrard, pointing at the problem of how to rewrite art history to account for women's production. She was disappointed by the exhibition *Women Artists: 1550–1950* held in New York in 1976 and organised by Linda Nochlin and Anne Sutherland Harris. She noticed that there were no specific features distinguishing a female from a male painter and, moreover, only oil painting was exhibited. She rightly complained about the absence of medieval and Renaissance illuminated manuscripts, tapestries and other objects. This was the field of women religious of the early modern era, but it has received relatively little attention because it was small in scale (manuscript illumination and embroidery), impermanent in material (textile, wax and papier mâché), occasional in purpose and marginal because of limited inventiveness in iconography, style and technical treatment.

Alpers was aware of the existence of familiar psychological terms that early modern Italian commentators appended to northern European art as suitable to women. Also, by extension, she was aware that those commentators assigned the Italian art of the same period exclusively to male artists, who, instead of adapting themselves to the world, tried to seize it and make it their own. She was right in believing that the sexual designation 'to want to possess meaning is masculine, to experience presence is feminine' was not biologically but culturally determined. The strategy Alpers suggests is not to insist that 'women be written into art history, but that art history itself – specifically its notions of what a work of art is, how it functions in society, and how we understand it – be rewritten'.[17]

No fewer than 43 years have elapsed since the publication of Alpers's contribution, and yet the issue remains unsolved. If painting and painting alone allows women artists to vie with men, degrading other artistic productions to 'servility' to the 'major arts', then no art history could be rewritten. I do not deny that the criterion of quality that goes beyond the all-justifying concept of function must always be present; but if we wish to write an art history encompassing as many women artists as possible, then even illumination must be included, distinguishing its historical from its art-historical value. The former will have room also for simple book decoration; the latter will include manuscripts decorated according to high standards of design, composition and colouring.

Instead of searching for the 'female hand' as if it were a value in itself, it is better to evaluate women artists according to what they produced within their social and cultural environments. In the Renaissance, the making of art did not depend as much on individual emotional experience as on 'conventions, schemata, or systems of notation, which have to be learned or worked out, either through teaching, apprenticeship, or a long period of individual experimentation'.[18] Making art grew within institutions that supported it with the necessary instruments for its development. In the San Domenico convent, the propensity of Eufrasia for art was encouraged, and her responsibility in conveying the correct religious meaning increased with the complexity of the tasks assigned to her. In the end, Eufrasia's illuminations were not only a beautiful series of religious images to be looked at; rather, they were instances of a spiritual investment that would have long-lasting effects on the production of additional images by nuns of the ensuing centuries and on the attitudes towards the inner relationship between images and words in the texts used within convents.

Introduction

A Multifaceted Artist

This monograph is devoted to the illumination of Eufrasia Burlamacchi, who lived and expressed her artistic talent in the Observant convent of San Domenico at Lucca (fig.2). She was a determined and active woman, well before her move from the San Nicolao Novello convent, where she professed in the 1490s, to the new convent of San Domenico to whose foundation she eagerly contributed. As a woman, she could not participate in the political and social life to which her male relatives – her father, three brothers and many uncles and cousins – were accustomed, but she acquired significance as a historic figure. In historical terms, unlike for many unnamed or unknown women religious who contributed to the artistic culture of the Church, there are extensive records, both direct and indirect, about Eufrasia such that one can tell her individual story. Also, she may be considered representative of a group of women artists whose stories have been lost.

Eufrasia was one of the interpreters of a spiritual reform that found in illumination an outlet for manifesting its values. The nuns of the San Domenico convent formed a sisterhood, whose communal understanding of the rules and of the meaning of the Sacred Scripture had the goal to establish and keep Christian harmony. The images they placed around them – mainly wooden crucifixions and Madonna with Child reliefs – and those represented in the manuscripts, contributed to this harmony. From its foundation in 1502, not by one but by 14 fervent female followers of the Dominican preacher Girolamo Savonarola (1452–98), the convent of San Domenico in Lucca became an important centre of Savonarola's spiritual heritage through the sixteenth century.

This heritage related to the Observant movement of the 1450s, which aimed to give new life to monastic organisations, especially to houses of the Franciscan and Dominican orders. It stressed foundational ideals of monastic discipline – such as simplicity of life, poverty and spiritual renewal – already promoted in Florence by Pope Eugene IV through the 1430s and by his successor Nicholas V.[1] However, the Observant movement, a complex phenomenon, was not a novelty of the fifteenth century. The female Dominican Observant movement in Italy started in 1385, when Chiara Gambacorta (c.1362–1420) founded the convent of San Domenico in Pisa, where strict enclosure was enforced.[2] Gambacorta was a follower of Catherine of Siena (1347–80), who was not an 'Observant' woman since she did not belong to any religious order, but she advocated for the renewal of the Church.[3]

The Observant reform Savonarola championed in the 1490s did not differ in substance from the

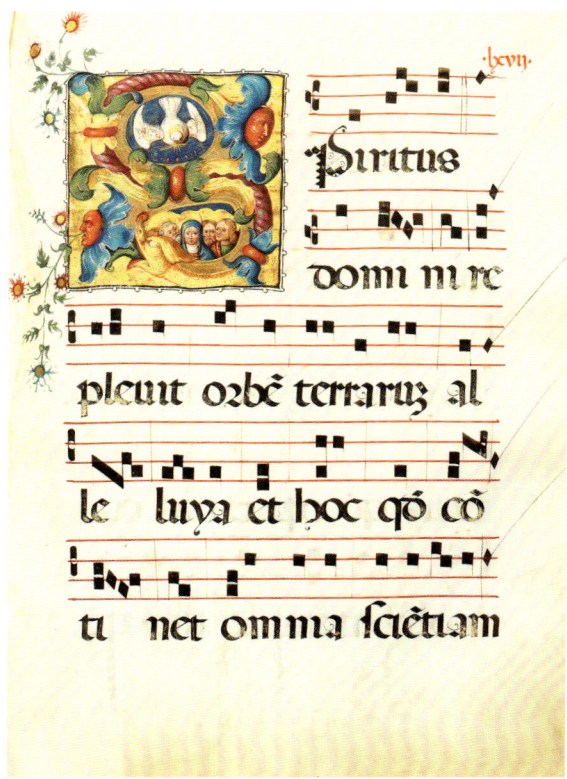

2   Eufrasia Burlamacchi, *Initial S, Spiritus Domini –
Pentecost*, Gradual MS 5, fol.67ʳ, *c.*1515, tempera and gold
leaf on parchment, folium 54.2 × 38.5 cm (21⅜ × 15⅛ in),
initial 14 × 13 cm (5½ × 5⅛ in), Dominican Convent,
California

was not lucrative at the beginning; it was always
subservient to the nuns' intercessory role manifested
through prayers, moving within the spiritual realm,
considered to be superior to the material world.

When the Lucchese sisters settled in the new
convent in 1502, Savonarola had already been dead
for four years. Had he had the chance to live longer
and see Eufrasia's output – four Antiphonaries
and one Gradual for the San Domenico convent,
another Antiphonary for San Martino Cathedral
and the two-volume Gradual for the San Romano
monastery – he would have appreciated her work.
Her artistic contributions demonstrate that the
Renaissance idea of the artist as interested in aspects
of reality, exemplified by, for example, Leonardo da
Vinci (1452–1519), had further possibilities by moving
the focus from the natural world to the cultural and
supernatural contexts.

In Eufrasia's manuscripts, figures, both humble
and charged with energy; ornament, both naturalistic
and abstract; and chant, in its simplest forms, all
interact in book decoration. This was a privileged
field in which a great variety of formal and chromatic
experiments, excluded from other forms of art,
could be realised. Illumination was indeed freer
from naturalistic constraints, from the direct study
of anatomy and natural light, than painting, and
especially in ornament one could invent and develop
forms and choose colours with no limitations
imposed by the subject and composition. In her
eclectic works, Eufrasia treated the 'architectural'
elements of the letters – the vertical, horizontal,
oblique and semicircular bars – according to various
metamorphoses. The pliability of this 'architecture'
to the expressive needs of religious meaning is
Eufrasia's most original contribution to Renaissance
ornament and, accordingly, to the history of
Renaissance illumination.[5]

With a few exceptions to be discussed below,
Eufrasia did not have direct access to artworks, but
she must have been aware that nuns produced work

previous one apart from being more radical in
prescribing the nuns various sorts of renunciation
– food, personal and communal property, artistic
activity – with the aim of promoting spiritual self-
determination and endurance in their religious choice.
In regard to artistic activity, in a sermon Savonarola
delivered on 10 May 1495, he censured the large-scale
and lucrative production of embroidery and music in
the convent of Le Murate in Florence.[4] By contrast,
the convent art produced in San Domenico at Lucca

of varying quality that fell roughly into two groups. The first expressed devoutness in a simple and untrained style. Here, the images made by Blessed Caterina Vigri, Sister Dorotea Broccardi, Sister Angela de' Rabatti or the German Nonnenarbeiten come to mind (fig.3).[6] The second manifested the same devoutness through a highly sophisticated style. This book focuses on the latter, on the conditions that enabled Eufrasia, through knowledge of, and experimentation with, drawing and colour, composition, treatment of space, and proportions, to arrive at high levels of artistic proficiency and pursue a style related to professional illuminators and artists of her era.[7] At the same time, she never changed the traditional fifteenth-century iconography derived from the Sacred Scripture, limiting her inventiveness to the ornamental apparatuses.

In Eufrasia's illumination, we witness the encounter of ideas from the external world with those accepted in female religious communities, an encounter that can be reconstructed through some primary sources referring to her. Noteworthy passages in the first three tomes of the Chronica of the San Domenico convent, now in the monastery of Santa Maria del Sasso at Bibbiena, Arezzo, refer to her participation in the foundation of the new religious institution; the process of her piecemeal artistic achievements under the Prioress Sister Petra Cenami; and her religious career soberly and precisely expressed in her necrology, penned on 2 January 1548. To these texts must be added a 'colophon' of sorts in her hand, now lost, but providentially transcribed in 1914 by the Dominican scholar Innocenzo Taurisano. Finally, there are the eight manuscripts she wrote, notated and illuminated from c.1505 to c.1532.

The first who were interested in recording both the religious and the artistic accomplishments of Eufrasia were two contemporary nun-chroniclers in the convent of San Domenico, the first, Sister Hilaria Cenami (1457–1537), writing in 1502 and 1527, and the second, who remains anonymous, in 1548. In these

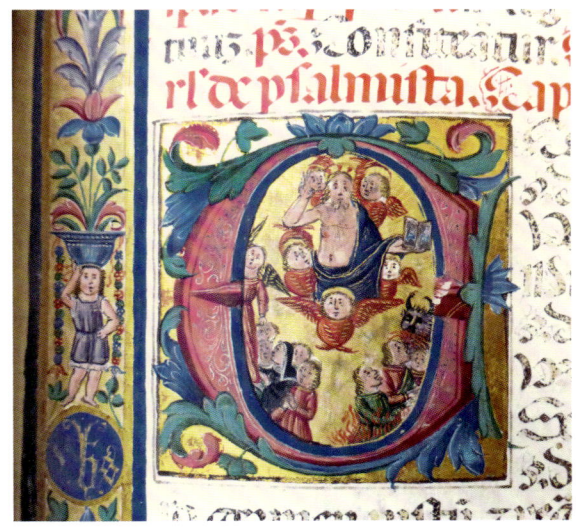

3 Angela di Antonio de' Rabatti, *Initial E, Last Judgement*, Breviary, MS Conv. Soppr. 90, fol.7ʳ, 1518, tempera and gold leaf on parchment, 4.2 × 3.8 cm (1 ⅝ × 1 ½ in), Biblioteca Medicea Laurenziana, Florence

texts, tendencies, expectations and attainments can be discovered through a careful and patient reading. Sister Hilaria, who wrote the proem to the first tome of the Chronica in 1502, set an epical pace for the historical development of the convent. By borrowing and aptly modifying some passages from the Sacred Scripture – Genesis, Luke, John and Paul – and making recourse not to 'what they [the nuns] had heard but according to what they had seen with their eyes, had looked upon and had touched with their hands', she chose a powerful frame in which, instead of patriarchs, a group of matriarchs gave direction to religious history. Eufrasia, who belonged to the group that founded the new convent, is described in the proem of the Chronica as the youngest of these matriarchs.[8]

In 1527 the same Sister Hilaria wrote the life of the first prioress of San Domenico, Petra Cenami, in the third tome of the Chronica. There, she included

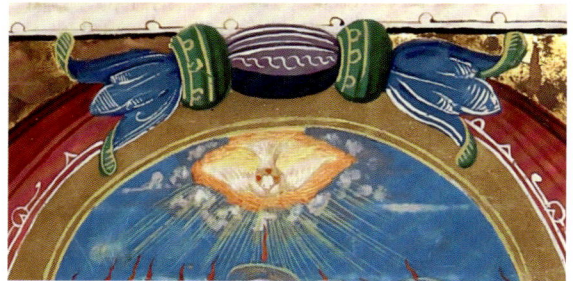

4 Eufrasia Burlamacchi, *Initial S, Pentecost*, Gradual MS 2650, fol.99ʳ, *c*.1532, tempera and gold leaf on parchment, 18.6 × 18.6 cm (7⅜ × 7⅜ in), detail, Biblioteca Statale, Lucca

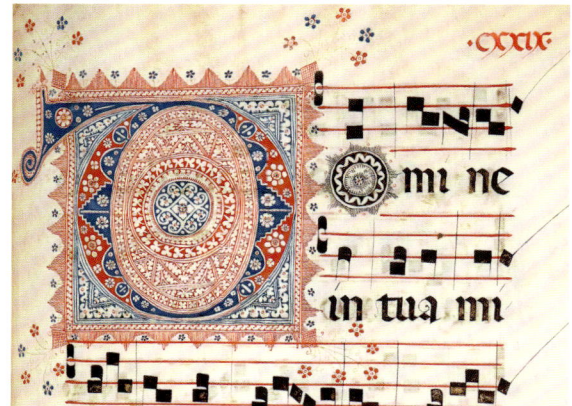

5 Eufrasia Burlamacchi, *Initial D, Domine*, Gradual MS 2650, fol.129ʳ, *c*.1532, tempera and ink on parchment, 15.5 × 15.2 cm (6⅛ × 6 in), Biblioteca Statale, Lucca

important references to Eufrasia's illumination, namely, the kind of books she transcribed, notated and illuminated upon the prioress' request, and the beautiful results she attained in her miniatures. In 1548, a different, anonymous nun wrote Eufrasia's necrology in the Chronica's second tome, adding elements that go beyond the formulaic expressions regarding patience, devoutness and endurance, specifically emphasising Eufrasia's artistic proficiency.

The anonymous nun wrote neither of Eufrasia's favourite colours nor of her compositions but rather of the beautiful execution of her miniatures. To this appreciative evaluation, one should add a meaningful feature of her technique, which can be described by the term '*sprezzatura*' (fig.4). Usually interpreted as nonchalance or easiness in executing a demanding work, *sprezzatura* is here intended as a blending of precision and speed to attain a balanced composition tending to grace, as enumerated in Chapter 7.

Eufrasia, a multifaceted artist, manifested these features in sacred scenes and portrayals of saints, still-life compositions and fanciful motifs, re-elaborating a large variety of models, a rather surprising attainment since she lived in a cloistered convent. She depicted illusionistic figures, using tempera as if it were oil. Also, she constructed with tempera and coloured inks monumental initial letters with complex ornamental patterns that, being an accomplished singer (*cantrix*),

complement the notes she transcribed in eight large size choir manuscripts (fig.5).

Moreover, she updated and re-elaborated what arrived at the convent without the strictures that Giorgio Vasari saw in the art of Sister Plautilla Nelli.[9] In his words:

The best works from Plautilla's hand are those she has copied from others, wherein she shows that she would have done marvellous things if she had enjoyed, as men do, advantages for studying, devoting herself to drawing and copying living and natural objects. [. . .] The truth of such an opinion is proved by this, that in her works the faces and features of women, whom she has been able to see as much as she pleased, are considerably better than the heads of the men.[10]

Eufrasia did not look to nature directly for inspiration. What interested her belonged to the realm of art: painting, sculpture and illumination as much as decorative arts, with a sensibility rather close to what Matteo Civitali (1436–1501), the most important Lucchese painter-sculptor of the fifteenth century, attained especially in the 1480s and 1490s.[11]

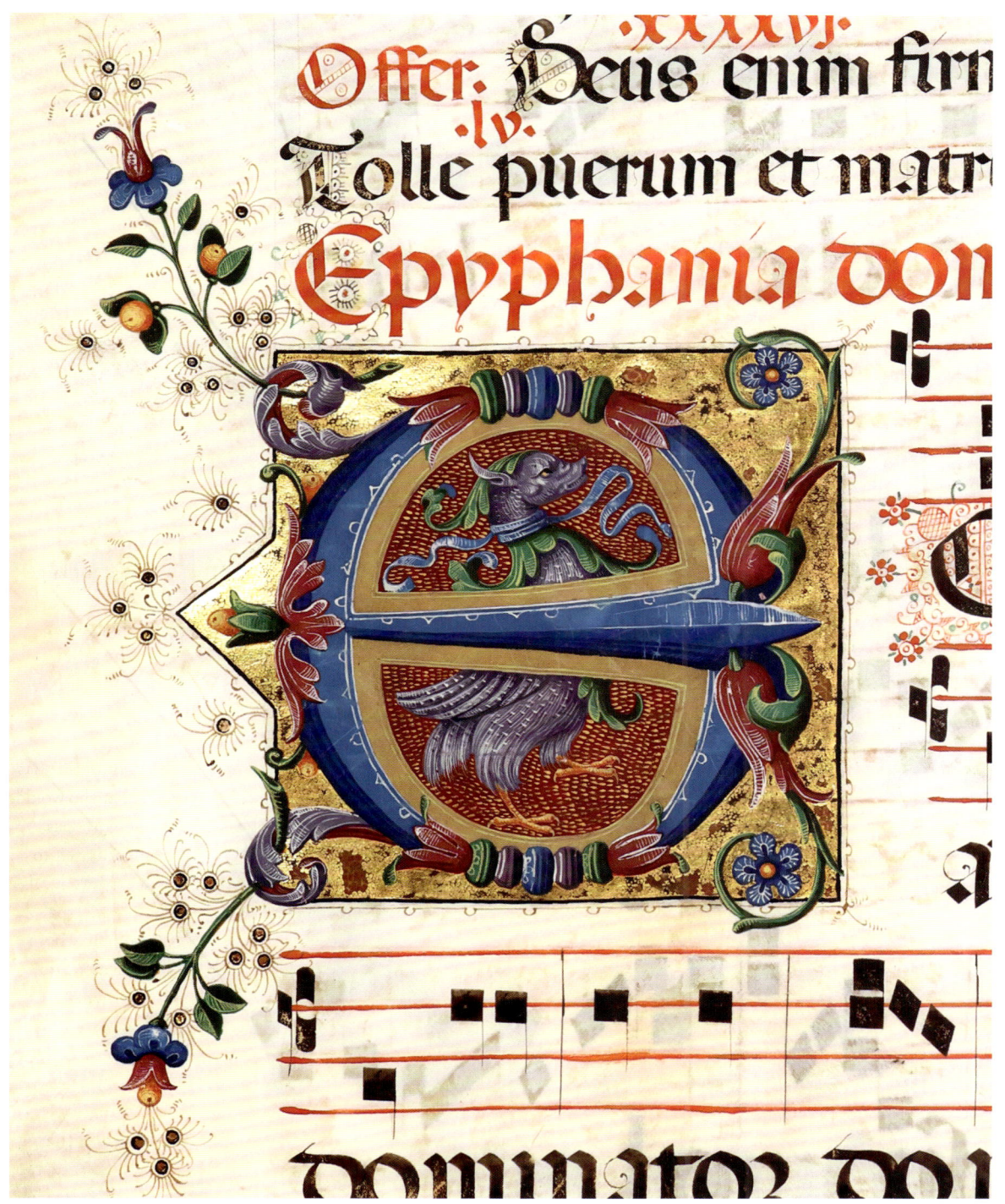

6   Eufrasia Burlamacchi, *Initial E, Hybrid*, Gradual MS 2649, fol.58ᵛ, *c*.1530, tempera and gold leaf on parchment, 14.5 × 14.5 cm (5¾ × 5¾ in), Biblioteca Statale, Lucca

She created illusionistic forms endowed with delicacy as well as plasticity that remind us also of the paintings by Fra Filippo Lippi (1406–69). Lippi, renowned for his altarpieces and frescoes of religious subjects, borrowed from Masaccio (1401–28) figures depicted in sculptural fashion, while the works by Giovanni da Fiesole, better known as Fra Angelico (c.1400–1455), were examples of how to use warm and limpid colours, toned down with shading.[12]

Within a convent of strict enclosure, where the rules were seemingly rigorously applied and observed, Eufrasia learned how to see, compare, select and elaborate enthralling images that belong to illumination only because they are within manuscripts. All these activities, made possible by the circulation in the convent of drawings, prints and manuscripts as will be discussed below, allowed Eufrasia's illumination to undergo a progressive change. From the simplicity and delicacy of the figures in the first five manuscripts for her convent, which are especially close to the art of the Florentine painter Antonio del Ceraiolo (*fl. c.*1500–1527), whose works likely came to be known to her through drawings, she moved to fanciful and colourful subjects, directly influenced by the works in Lucca of the Florentine illuminator Giuliano Amadei (c.1425–96).[13] His miniatures, as we will see, opened new horizons for Eufrasia through the encounter of Florentine and Roman art with Lucchese illumination. Antiphonary MS 14 for the San Martino Cathedral in Lucca, which Amadei left unfinished in 1496, was taken up by Eufrasia after 1515 and brought successfully to completion.

In the two-volume Gradual for the monastery of San Romano in Lucca, Eufrasia infused figures and ornament with a new gamut of colours and style. Some artistic solutions, for example the importance given to the sfumato effects, which created an atmosphere of naturalness through the delicacy of lights, likely came from the works of Fra Bartolomeo (1472–1517), displayed in the Cathedral of Lucca. Also,

some features of Michelangelo (1475–1564), such as the rendition of monumental figures characterised by energetic gestures, are particularly evident, the latter probably made known to her by the painting of the Lucchese Agostino di Francesco Marti (1482–1544), who travelled to Rome in the first decades of the sixteenth century, becoming acquainted with the frescoes of the vault of the Sistine Chapel, which he reproduced in drawings.[14]

The multifaceted illumination of Eufrasia is a balanced blend of simplicity of forms, variety of colours and a sense of essentiality that increases the visual appeal of the images, together with fanciful inventions, as is the case of the grotesques. They belong to a typology of ornament widespread in the Renaissance after the rediscovery of the Domus Aurea, a palace complex built in Rome at the order of the Roman Emperor Nero, where acanthus scrolls, candelabra, festoons, cornucopias, phytomorphic and zoomorphic hybrids and masks are intertwined in frescoes.[15] Eufrasia always resisted excessive variety of forms by means of ornamental rules (fig.6) and never abandoned her faith in 'materiality', expressed through images of sculptural appearance.

Finally, she lived her artistic experience within a community. Her proficiency led her to instruct her younger sisters in faith in order to establish a convent workshop that operated until the late nineteenth century, no longer producing manuscripts but paintings, sculptures and church implements. This long and inspired religious enterprise lasted until 1892, when the Dominican sisters were obliged to leave the convent of San Domenico as the Commune of Lucca transformed it into a tobacco factory. In the same year the nuns bought a small convent in Lucca, which they eventually abandoned in 1927 to move to Santa Maria del Sasso at Bibbiena.[16] The manuscripts written, notated and illuminated by Eufrasia still speak to us of a shared system of values and show us that art addresses imagination in its visual and aural components.

I

Childhood and Relatives

Eufrasia was born in 1478 in Lucca, a walled city in the north-west of Tuscany (fig.7), which has kept even today some of its medieval architectural features. During her childhood, adolescence and early maturity, the political situation of the city was marked by its seemingly good order, while Florence was characterised by the turmoil following the expulsion in 1494 of Piero de' Medici (1472–1503), the reforms of Girolamo Savonarola discussed above, his death in 1498 and its aftermath.[1]

Two temporary residents of Lucca, Ortensio Lando (c.1512–53) and Aonio Paleario (1503–70), scholars influenced by the theologian and reformer Erasmus of Rotterdam (1466–1536),[2] appreciated the stability of the city's oligarchic government.[3] The Republic appeared to be solidly grounded on the good relationships between the secular and the religious powers. The former comprised two institutions: the General Council of the People, whose members had a yearly capacity and exerted the deliberative and legislative powers, and the Council of Elders (*Anziani*), ten in number, ruling for a bimester and presided over by a Gonfalonier of Justice, who exerted the executive power. The latter

was represented by the bishopric, the canonries, the convents, the monasteries and the congregations.[4] Both Lando and Paleario saw in the relationship of the Lucchese aristocracy with the Church, through 'religious piety, civic harmony and political freedom', the true components of an ideal city.[5]

Beyond the rhetorical appreciation, other factors granted Lucca an apparent stability. After the expulsion in 1430 of the Lord Paolo Guinigi (1376–1432) and the restoration of the Republic, no further political changes took place.[6] The 50-year league with Florence, stipulated in 1441, was renewed in 1482 for another 30 years. After the death of Lorenzo the Magnificent in 1492 and Piero de' Medici's ascension to power, Lucca faced the arrival in the city of the rivalrous Charles VIII of France (1470–98) on his way to conquer the Kingdom of Naples. After Piero de' Medici offered Sarzana, Motrone, Pietrasanta and Pisa to the King as a sign of his fidelity, the people of Florence reacted and in 1494 expelled the Medici family.

The year 1494 was less momentous for Lucca than for Florence. Charles VIII's invasion was hardly the symbol and precursor of change, leading Lucchese society instead to become less dynamic and more conventional.[7] Nevertheless, the city, eager to keep its independence and to regain its former territories, applied a policy of great moderation that also affected

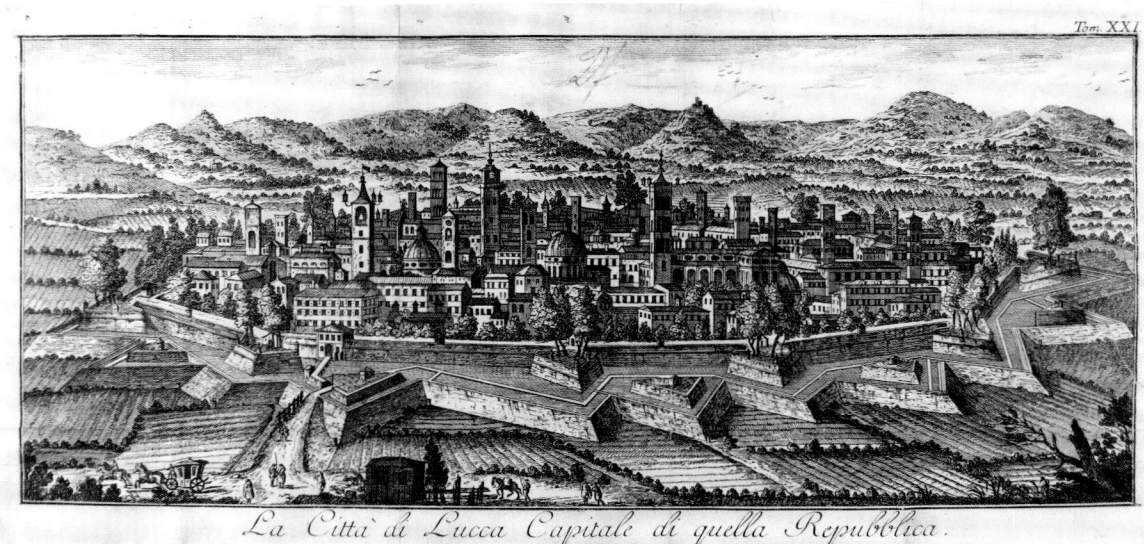

La Città di Lucca Capitale di quella Repubblica.

7 Anonymous engraver, *Lucca Cityscape from Saint Peter's Gate*, Lucca – El. ii/27, 1757, burin, 16 × 37.2 cm (6 ¼ × 14 ⅝ in), Biblioteca Statale, Lucca

cultural matters. If in the sixteenth century the Florentine governing Signoria absorbed politically and culturally all the cities of Tuscany, Lucca alone – small and tending to present itself even smaller – miraculously kept its independence thanks to a policy of oscillation rather than of balance, showing fidelity and paying large sums of money to both Emperor Charles V (1500–1558) and King Francis I (1494–1547).

While a certain degree of conventionality is detectable in political terms, in the religious field Lucchese society was anything but conventional, manifesting a great unrest within Catholicism, touching as much its popular as its aristocratic components.[8] Eufrasia, her family and her relatives belonged to this wide and tumultuous religious current that led to the foundation in Lucca of a new Observant convent in 1502 under the aegis of Savonarola's reform. This new religious institution was an important presence within a network of initiatives in Lucca aiming at a general renewal of conventual life, and Eufrasia participated in various fashions, ranging from administrative engagements to artistic productions, from writing and illuminating manuscripts to the organisation of chant for the liturgy and the Divine Office.

THE BURLAMACCHI-TRENTA FAMILY

In her early years, Eufrasia lived in a wealthy, politically engaged, religiously committed and culturally advanced family. The Burlamacchi, who boasted a twelfth-century ancestry, moved from the small centre of Avane, in the Valdiserchio, to Lucca. In the second half of the thirteenth century the city, in the wake of Florence, witnessed the formation of two factions within the Guelf party: the first, called the Black Guelfs, championed the Obizzi family and was supported by the popular party; the second, called the White Guelfs, championed the Antelminelli family. Since 1278, the Burlamacchi had been described as White Guelfs.

At the beginning of the fourteenth century, after the assassination of the Black Guelf Obizzone degli Obizzi, and the strife that ensued between Black and White Guelfs, the former prevailed, together with the popular party.[9] In 1308, it approved a Statute containing a list, called *De cerna potentium* (On the Separation or Distinction of the Powerful), with the injunction that all the noble families and their relatives had to abandon Lucca, since they belonged to the White Guelfs. The Burlamacchi were on the list.[10] They departed, but later returned when in 1317 Castruccio Castracani (1281–1328) was elected Captain General by the Elders and the General Council of Lucca.[11] The family regained their wealth through trade with France, Flanders and England, while their civic importance was re-established thanks to capacities as Elders and Gonfaloniers in the government of the Republic.[12]

Eufrasia's mother, Costanza di Giovanni di Girolamo Trenta (*c.*1448–*c.*1515), belonged to one of the oldest noble families of Lucca. One of her relatives, Stefano Trenta, had been Bishop of Lucca (1448–77). Some years earlier (1413–16), a leading sculptor in Lucca, Jacopo della Quercia (*c.*1374–1438), had completed their family sepulchre in the church of San Frediano.[13] Costanza's family was involved with conventual growth in Lucca as well, insofar as on 24 January 1501 her brother Alderico Trenta, with Girolamo Franciotti and Baldassarre Montecatini, bought the building where Sister Petra Cenami and her 13 companions, including Eufrasia, were to move from the San Nicolao Novello convent on 5 April 1502 to found San Domenico.[14] Chiara, Alderico Trenta's daughter and Eufrasia's cousin, on 28 June 1502 had the privilege to be the first novice to receive the dress of the order in San Domenico. She also had a second privilege: 'after serving God for three years, nine months and four days', on 31 March 1506 she passed away, an event that the nun-chronicler described in the convent's necrology by adding that she was 'the first to receive the dress in the convent of Jerusalem

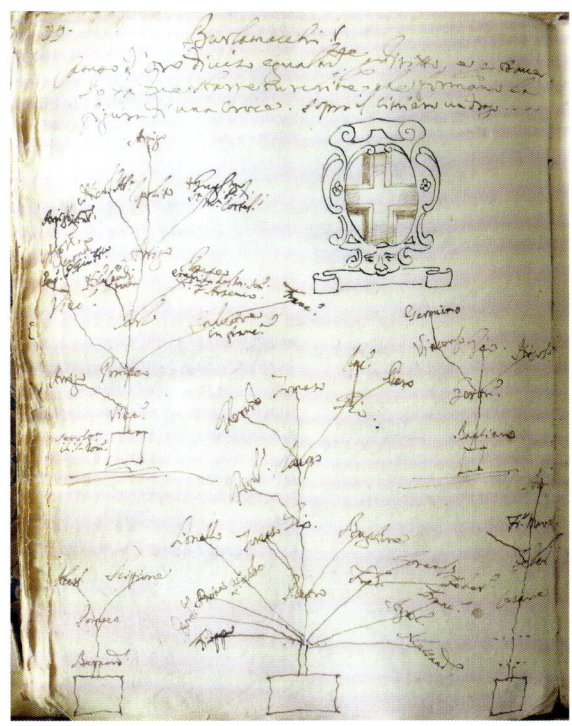

8   Bartolomeo Beverini, Burlamacchi Family, Coat of Arms and Genealogical Trees, in 'Memorie storiche e familiari di Lucca', MS 2965, c.99 (fol.56ᵛ), seventeenth century, ink drawing on paper, 38 × 25 cm (15 × 9 ⅞ in), Biblioteca Statale, Lucca

[that is, Heaven] where with no defects she serves her longed-for spouse'.[15]

Eufrasia's father, Giovanni di Michele Burlamacchi (1439–1506), had a long and important ancestry that Lucchese scholars reconstructed between the sixteenth and eighteenth centuries (fig.8). A renowned merchant, he was ten times elected Elder, an office held for two months per year; his terms began in 1473 (July–August) and ended in 1491 (May–June).[16] Although Giovanni Burlamacchi was wealthy enough to endow at least one of his two daughters with the required dowry

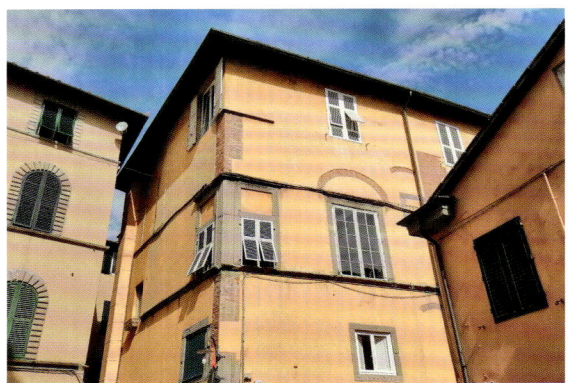

9   The 'Casa grande' of the Burlamacchi family, fifteenth–
    sixteenth centuries, Lucca

for a marriage, he decided to place both sisters in the convent to keep the family patrimony for his three sons, Tommaso, Girolamo and Vincenzo.[17] This action on Giovanni's part reflects a vivid preoccupation of the noble families of Italy in this era: to sustain their lines through the production of male heirs, who could ostensibly increase their civic and economic power.

Eufrasia lived with her family until 1490, when she entered the Dominican convent of San Nicolao Novello in Lucca mentioned above. Her sister Gabriella (1462–1534) had already entered San Nicolao Novello in 1474. Apart from the few visits Eufrasia and her mother may have paid to Gabriella, always taking place within the restrictions imposed by enclosure, the two sisters properly met only when Eufrasia entered the convent, which she abandoned in 1502 to join the first group of nuns at the new convent of San Domenico, where she produced art until c.1532.[18]

THE 'CASA GRANDE'

The civic power of an Italian family at this time was also symbolised by their main residence in the city.

The Burlamacchi family owned a series of houses in Lucca – they never mentioned them with the term 'palazzo' (palace) but used 'domus magna' or 'Casa grande' (large house), or simply 'casa' – in the district (*terziere*) of San Paolino. As the material centre of domestic life, the 'domus magna' and the 'familia' had become one and the same thing. For the affluent citizens of Lucca, their palace was the visible sign of the family's historical unity that they tried to preserve for future generations.[19] The 'Casa grande' of the Burlamacchi, where Eufrasia was born in 1478, is still standing, occupying a large block (fig.9).

Undoubtedly, this building will hardly satisfy the architectural taste of one accustomed to fifteenth-century Florentine palaces – Medici, Rucellai, Strozzi, Tornabuoni – with their *all'antica* paraphernalia. With its severe and essential, if not simplistic and even old-fashioned, elements, this Lucchese palace exemplifies the idea that wealth must not be manifested in architecture nor through other forms of public display. In fact, in the external walls of the Burlamacchi's 'large house', one sees no trace of columns or piers that reproduce the ancient orders; not even large windows or 'modern' ornament. This 'palace', simple and severe, features three levels distinguished by unadorned horizontal bands, windows of middle size, and the Burlamacchi coat of arms. Such an unpretentious but monumental civic presence was shared by almost all early modern Lucchese aristocrats, even the most affluent. In Eufrasia's case, it remained a point of reference within her walled city (fig.10), even 12 years after she had left it.

An episode on 5 April 1502 demonstrates the strong ties Eufrasia kept with her family at the 'Casa grande'. At 8 am, a group of eight nuns, accompanied by three 'wise men', left the San Nicolao Novello convent in Lucca, 'and their dowries', to found a new one in the same town. With the approval of Pope Alexander VI, San Domenico would be a convent in which they could 'live the strictest observance'. Although previously assured that they would be

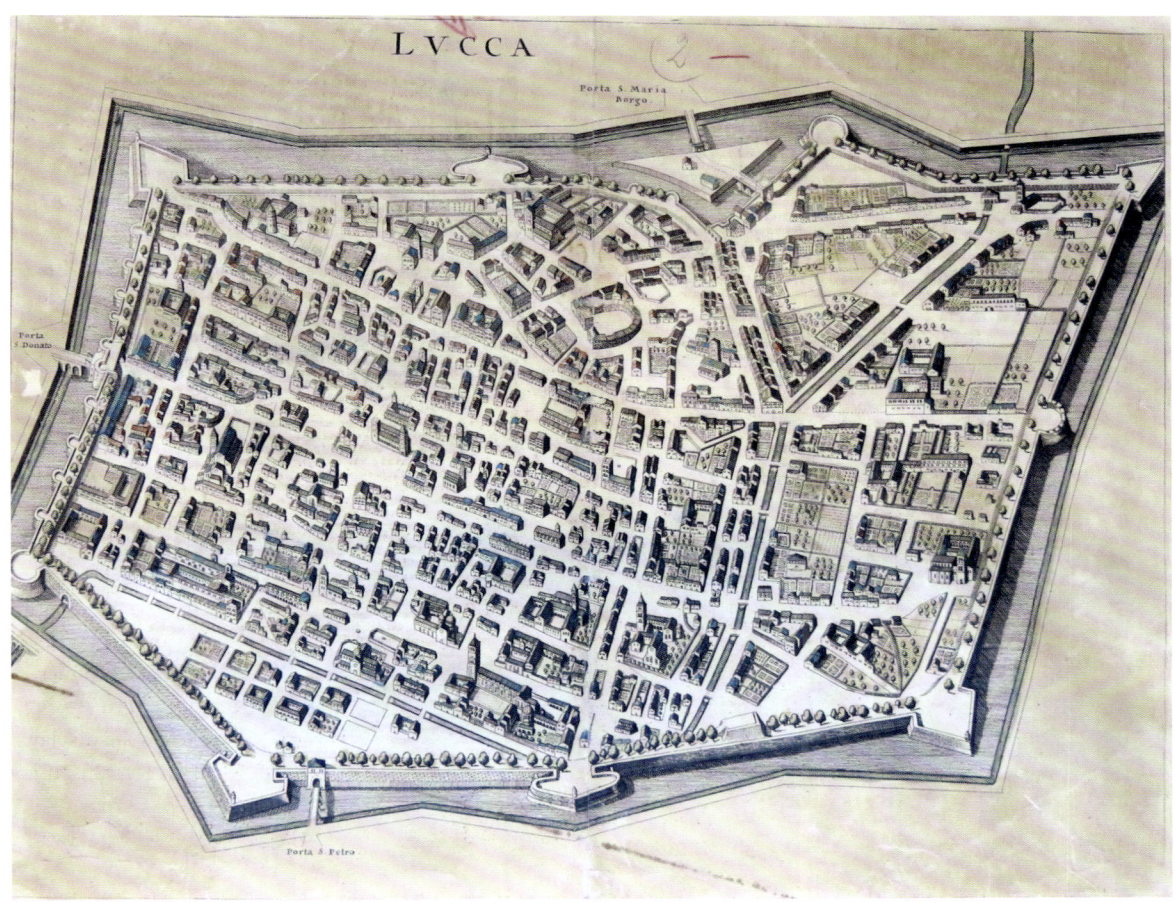

10   Anonymous engraver, *Map of the City of Lucca*, El. ii/2, second half of the sixteenth century, engraving, burin and
     watercolour, 40.3 × 50.4 cm (15 ⅞ × 19 ⅞ in), Biblioteca Statale, Lucca

among the selected nuns to found the new convent, Gabriella and Eufrasia were left behind. After recovering from their disappointment, they noticed a sign from Providence. 'It happened that the door of the San Nicolao Novello convent, because of a certain cause, was opened' so that the two sisters, 'seeing the opportunity', left the building hand in hand and entered 'the courtyard where was the house of the convent's servant', close to the church. From there, accompanied by the servant, they reached the house of their parents.[20]

As was customary for noble families, the Burlamacchi did not abandon their daughters, even after they had become nuns. Since a noble cause justified the girls' flight, at 10 am Gabriella and Eufrasia, with their father, mother and three brothers, joined the group who had left San Nicolao Novello two hours earlier. From that moment onward, they lived according to Savonarola's monastic reform. The first new convent was in a palace formerly belonging to the nobleman Francesco Minutoli. Having quickly increased in number, the nuns moved into a second new convent on 15 May 1513, constructed in accordance with the plans of Simone del Pollaiolo, called il Cronaca (1457–1508), a follower of Savonarola,[21] in the large garden once belonging to Gabriella's and Eufrasia's paternal aunt, Isabecta Burlamacchi (1442–c.1498).[22] The convent of San Domenico underwent modifications and enlargements through the centuries, and ended its days in the 1890s when it was transformed, as mentioned above, into a tobacco factory.

RELATIVES TO BE REMEMBERED OR FORGOTTEN

The Burlamacchi family had a long political history in Lucca. Of the 25 recorded generations, the position of Elder has been held 300 times by a Burlamacchi.[23] However, if many members illustrated the family's success in political and religious matters, the actions of a few may have detracted from its lustre were it not for the efforts of the merchant Gherardo di Gherardo Burlamacchi (1522–90) who, in his 'Ricordi' ('Memoirs') written around 1584, listed the most serious crimes perpetrated by those members, adding explanations and justifications.[24]

One of the members who brought honour to the family was Eufrasia's cousin Filippo Burlamacchi (1465–1519), who played an important role in the religious community of Lucca as much as in Eufrasia's life. Born to Pietro and Angela di Paolino Bernardini, Filippo, after some years spent in Florence to secure the development of his father's trade enterprises, became a Dominican friar on 18 March 1499 in San Romano at Lucca, with the name of Fra Pacifico. From 1512 to 1517 he was confessor to the San Domenico convent in Lucca. It is likely that Fra Pacifico offered some advice to Eufrasia when she was writing, notating and illuminating the five manuscripts now in California.[25]

By contrast, the actions of two members, belonging according to Gherardo Burlamacchi 'to the few instances of which to be ashamed while in the great families there are many of various sorts', cast a shadow on the family's distinction.[26] The first was the notary of the family, Ser Giovanni Burlamacchi (1490–1550), who was condemned to life as a galley-rower for complicity in a homicide committed by his son Giuseppe in 1541.[27] The second was Eufrasia's cousin Francesco, born in 1498, who became Gonfalonier of Lucca in 1546. He was beheaded on 14 February 1548 in Milan, upon the accusation of having conspired against the Medici. Since he was convinced that the Medici wished to annex all Tuscany to the principate, he imagined a federation of Tuscan cities each with an independent republican government. His final aim was the 'Christian peace' granted by Emperor Charles V, which would have reformed the Church from the many abuses and varieties of opinion.[28]

This singular conception of social, political and religious renewal had in its background the message of Savonarola, including the purification of the Church and a more inner and personal religiosity. This religious attitude excluded all conventional ceremonies since Christ's grace alone could save the soul, while in political matters the State had to be a republic. Most likely Francesco learned of these ideas through his tutor, his uncle Fra Pacifico Burlamacchi, who was not a simple Dominican but one of the most ardent followers of Savonarola. He knew Savonarola's claim that 'divine things go slowly, with great strength and many contradictions' and the Ferrarese friar's idea about the importance of human will in matters of faith.[29] Through the news brought to the convent by her relatives, Eufrasia followed the events of her cousin Francesco's life until his arrest, but she never learned of his beheading on 14 February 1548 since she had already passed away on 2 January of the same year.

2

A Walled Adolescence and Womanhood

BEFORE THE FOUNDATION OF SAN DOMENICO

Eufrasia did not live quietly within Catholicism. She was caught between two reforms, the Savonarolan and the Lutheran, that, for some time, shared certain views about the interpretation of the Sacred Scripture and the role of rituals in the faithful's life. She embraced Savonarola's reform but witnessed with concern the diffusion of Lutheran reform in Lucca and among some of her relatives.

The translations of the books of Martin Luther (1483–1546) from Latin into Italian appeared when the author was still alive, but none of the editions preserved bears his name.[1] This is the case with the first dated Italian translation of Luther's small book on the explanation of the Ten Commandments, the Credo and the Paternoster, printed in Venice in 1525.[2] In fact, the circulation of Luther's texts became illegal in Italy in 1520, after the publication by Pope Leo X of the Bull *Exsurge Domine*, prescribing the destruction by fire of all his books, present and future.[3] The papal prohibition notwithstanding, Luther's ideas on religion kept circulating in Italy; in Lucca they were spread especially among merchants and aristocrats, and later others favourably received them.[4]

In the margins of some late fifteenth- and early sixteenth-century printed books of Girolamo Savonarola's sermons and treatises, now held at the Biblioteca Statale in Lucca, it is not rare to find comments, written by Lucchese readers, directly referencing the main topics of the Lutheran reform.[5] Some scholars believe that the positive reception in Italy of Luther's religious claims was not an unprecedented phenomenon because it had been anticipated by Savonarola's ideas. However, Savonarola did not aim to subvert the Catholic hierarchy or intervene to modify rituals; rather, he strove to change behaviours that did not conform to the message of Christ, which he tried to convey by means of his sermons until 1498.[6]

In January 1492, Savonarola was invited to preach in various places at Lucca. He delivered a series of sermons, of which the first eight were in San Martino Cathedral, the ninth was in the government palace before the Elders, the tenth was in the church of the Dominican monastery of San Romano, and the last two were in the Dominican convent of San Nicolao Novello.[7]

Eufrasia attended Savonarola's sermons in San Nicolao Novello when she was a 14-year-old novice (fig.11).[8] Some notes for these sermons have remained in the margins of fol.6ᵛ of Savonarola's

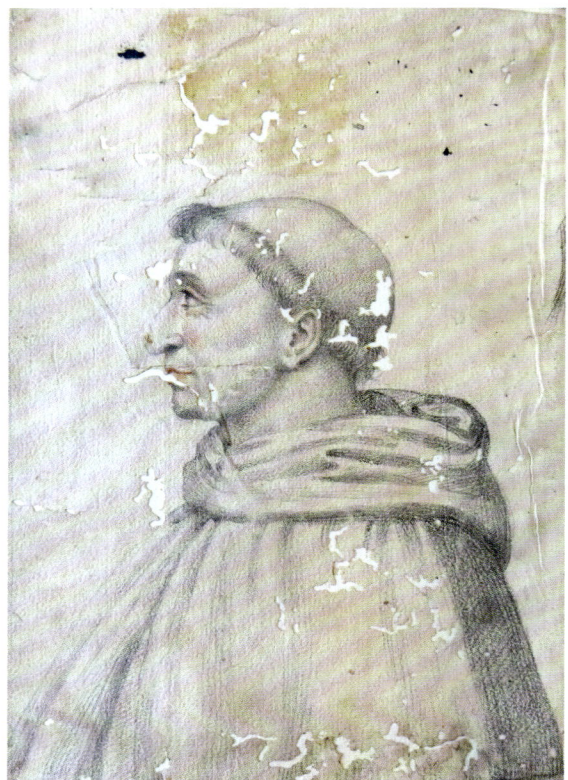

11 Anonymous artist, 'Fra Girolamo Savonarola', in Serafino Razzi, *Vita del Padre Fra' Girolamo Savonarola – Epistole*, MS 2415, drawing on the back of the frontispiece, second half of the sixteenth century, black and rose pencil on paper, 18.3 × 12.9 cm (7¼ × 5⅛ in), Biblioteca Statale, Lucca

breviary – referring to Psalm 44:7–10, Psalm 132:1 and Genesis 32:23–32 – that help to reconstruct their content and to understand their influence on Eufrasia.[9] Psalm 44, about righteousness and anointment by God, is particularly suitable to nuns. Verse 10 reads: 'Hearken, O daughter, and consider, and incline thine ear; forget also thine own people, and thy father's house.'[10] For an Observant convent, unity was essential for enduring the strict behaviour

required by the reform. This spiritual condition is described in Psalm 132:1:

> Behold, how good and how pleasant it is for brethren to dwell together in unity.
> It is like the precious ointment upon the head, that ran down upon the beard, even Aaron's beard: that went down upon the skirts of his garments.
> As the dew of Hermon, and as the dew that descends upon the mountains of Zion: for there the Lord commanded the blessing, even life for evermore.

This psalm, a favourite biblical passage of Savonarola's and one he often commented upon, also became a *lauda*, written by the Florentine Dominican Fra Luca Bettini (1489–1527), and, after Savonarola's death, the song identifying his supporters, the *Piagnoni* (Weepers).[11] The long passage from Genesis on which Savonarola based a sermon for the nuns at San Nicolao Novello – about Jacob's fight with the angel of the Lord – evoked faith, trust, endurance, moral strength and final reward.

When Savonarola preached at Lucca, he had already modified the manner of delivering his sermons in order to make them affect his audience and elicit the response he sought. He was aware of the difference between reading and listening to a sermon, as he aptly remarked in a note in the margins of his breviary where, writing a panegyric for the Dominican Vincent Ferrer (1350–1419), he stated that 'his sermons are written but they are like a shadow in comparison with the living voice'.[12] One should consider Savonarola's living voice as what he and his contemporaries believed to be the unfailing instrument to successfully convey religious content and inspire faith. It should come as no surprise that the series of sermons he preached publicly in Lucca left a deep impression on its citizens since Savonarola had become a 'powerful preacher' after adopting a prophetic style of speech.[13] Also, Savonarola assured Lucchese citizens that had not Florence been elected by God for the renovation of the Church, such a light would have been cast on their city.[14] The influence of Savonarola's preaching at Lucca can be recognised in the foundation and development of religious institutions.

'OUR OWN CONVENT, AT LAST!'

According to the Pseudo-Burlamacchi, a biographer of Savonarola once believed to be Eufrasia's cousin Fra Pacifico,[15] the most visible sign of the Ferrarese friar's preaching in Lucca was the foundation of two Observant convents, San Domenico in 1502, to which Eufrasia had fled, and San Giorgio in 1520.[16] However, the years that elapsed between the delivery of the sermons in Lucca and the foundation of the two convents suggest that the two religious initiatives were not prompted by Savonarola's direct influence alone. True, those years might have been used for reflection and planning, but they were too many for keeping alive in the nuns the freshness of their first inspiration.

Modern commentators, such as Domenico Di Agresti and Massimiliano Coli, no longer rely on the Pseudo-Burlamacchi's interpretation. They insist on the role played by Savonarola's followers, the friars of the San Marco monastery in Florence, as preachers and confessors to the Lucchese Dominican nuns.[17] After Savonarola's death at the stake on 23 May 1498, some of those friars moved of necessity to San Romano in Lucca, among them Jacopo di Sicilia, Bartolomeo da Faenza, Antonio d'Olanda and Nicolò Michelozzi. In the Chronica of San Romano, begun in 1525 by the Ferrarese Fra Ignazio Manardi, the Dominican history of the monastery is divided into two sections, before and after Savonarola's appearance. The new Dominicans who embraced poverty were opposed to the rich and hardly commendable friars of the late fifteenth century.[18] Di Agresti also added that while by the middle of the sixteenth century the monasteries

of San Marco at Florence and San Domenico at Fiesole, under powerful political pressure, were obliged to abandon the last signs of the Savonarolan reform, in some convents in Florence, Prato and Lucca, by contrast, it continued to flourish.[19]

For women in religious orders, like Eufrasia, the tenets of Savonarola's reform had exclusively disciplinary connotations. They expressed a need for the nuns to lead a common life, adopt a more severe monastic rule and turn their convents into communities observing strict enclosure.[20] The underlying principle of female monasticism, as it turned increasingly inward on itself, was 'the need to live with one heart, one soul, and one will in order to thrive as a self-governing institution'.[21] In female Dominican environments, even those outside Lucca, it was known that the cult of Savonarola was deeply rooted in the Lucchese convent of San Domenico where Eufrasia resided. The 'Codice Savonaroliano', now in Perugia, records:

> In the city of Lucca there is a monastery called San Domenico under the care of the reverend fathers of San Romano, reformed by the reverend father Fra Girolamo Savonarola of Ferrara, to whom the whole monastery was very affectionate and since its inception the nuns have paid him the highest veneration, exerting themselves with much devotion to his doctrine and celebrating each year his feast with as much spiritual joyfulness as they showed in other solemnities. The first mothers of the monastery bequeathed to their young daughters their affection and devotion to Savonarola.[22]

The last sentence of the Perugia 'Codice Savonaroliano' stresses the importance of continuity through imitation. This concept, one of the touchstones of the worthiness of historical recollections, was also invoked by the San Domenico nun-chronicler Sister Hilaria Cenami, discussed in the Introduction above, at the outset of her

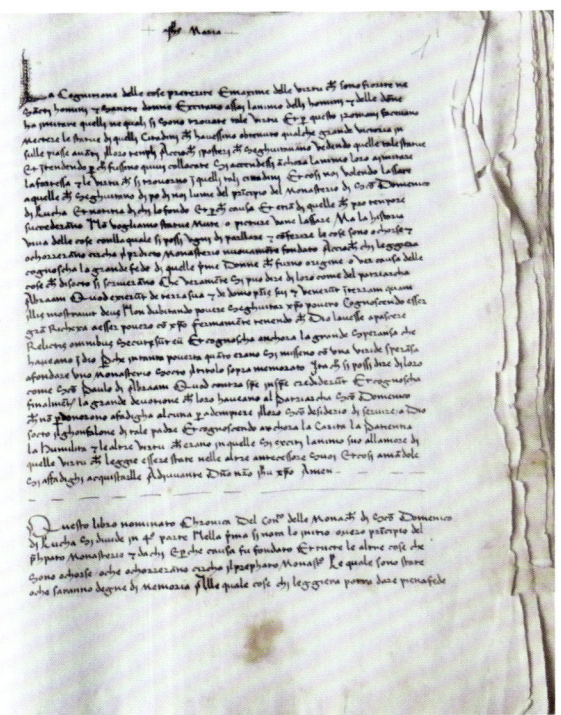

12 Sister Hilaria Cenami, *The Proem*, 'Chronica' of the San Domenico Convent, t.i, fol.1ʳ, 1502, black ink on paper, 32 × 22 cm (12 ⅝ × 8 ⅝ in), Archivio del Monastero di Santa Maria del Sasso, Bibbiena, Arezzo

narration (fig.12). How she valued the foundation of the Observant convent is manifested by treating its history as if it were a heroic enterprise. Her argument unfolds with the general appreciation of the past and particularly of the virtues of male and female saints. In so doing, she acknowledges the civic role of imitation of past virtues, a role the ancient Romans advanced through images, including placing statues of virtuous men before their temples. Nonetheless, it is not the visual arts that Sister Hilaria insists upon but rather written records, the only ones able to convey the 'living history of the

things with which one could entertain a dialogue on the facts that occurred and will occur in regard to the monastery'.[23]

To justify the convent's foundation as a heroic enterprise, the nun-chronicler chose one scriptural passage from Genesis 12:1 that served her purpose to present the nuns who founded San Domenico convent as contemporary matriarchs by aligning their actions with scripture that emphasised patriarchal activity and authority. In this passage, the Lord addresses Abraham, telling him: 'Get thee out of thy country, and from thy kindred, and from thy father's house, unto a land that I will shew you.' Coherently with her aim of making known to the reader the 'great faith inspiring those first Women who were the origin or the cause of the events that will be written below', Sister Hilaria modified the tense of the narration from the future to the past and substituted the plural – the nuns – for the singular – Abraham: 'They got out of their country and of the house of their father and arrived at the land that God showed them.'[24]

The nuns who on 5 April 1502 abandoned neither their homeland nor the house of their relatives but San Nicolao Novello in Lucca, a convent that did not adhere to strict enclosure, declared their faith in Savonarola's reform by embracing poverty. Quoting Luke 5:11, 'they forsook all, and followed him' – this time Sister Hilaria modified part of the verb, substituting *secutae sunt* for *secuti sunt* – knowing that only through poverty and relying on God's help, the nuns could follow Christ. Poverty, however, was supported by hope, qualified through its symbolic colour – green – and a reference to Saint Paul, who spoke of Abraham as 'that who against hope believed in hope' (Epistle to the Romans 4:18). This confidence in God's help led to the construction of the new convent, which also was a sign of the nuns' devotion to Saint Dominic.[25]

Within this new place, a new community started to take shape. What could not be developed outside the convent in terms of family ties and exchanges was carried forward within the conventual walls, where an enlarged female family, metaphorical and real, took shape.[26] The case of the Burlamacchi sisters is instructive, for it points to connections of kinship that were often found among nuns in a convent at this time. Sister Gabriella and Sister Eufrasia were first-degree cousins of Sister Christina (1451–1535) and Sister Hilaria, two of the seven daughters of Caterina Burlamacchi, their father's sister.[27] They also became aunts and began to know their nieces, daughters of their brother Girolamo, for the first time when they entered the convent, Costanza (1509–44) on 23 November 1523 and Barbara (1515–79) on 6 January 1530.[28] Sister Barbara, an acknowledged talented *cantrix*, was the only one among all the Burlamacchi women in the convent of San Domenico who, in 1570, had the privilege to be elected prioress.[29]

Three other nieces, Isabetta, Maria and Antonia, daughters of Gabriella's and Eufrasia's brother Vincenzo, never met their aunts since both had already passed away when the three young Burlamacchi entered the convent in 1549 and 1555. On 24 February 1549, one of them, Isabetta (1536–1613), became Sister Eufrasia, a name that honoured Eufrasia senior who had died on 2 January 1548. Although Sister Eufrasia junior did not follow in her aunt's artistic path, she shared with her an 'extended and sounding voice, highly proficient in chant and all the ceremonies'.[30] In addition, other cousins, three Burlamacchi and six Trenta women, lived with Gabriella and Eufrasia in the same convent.[31] Although Florentine prelates had objected to the factionalism that sometimes arose from clustering kin in the same convent, no such evidence has come to light for San Domenico in Lucca.[32]

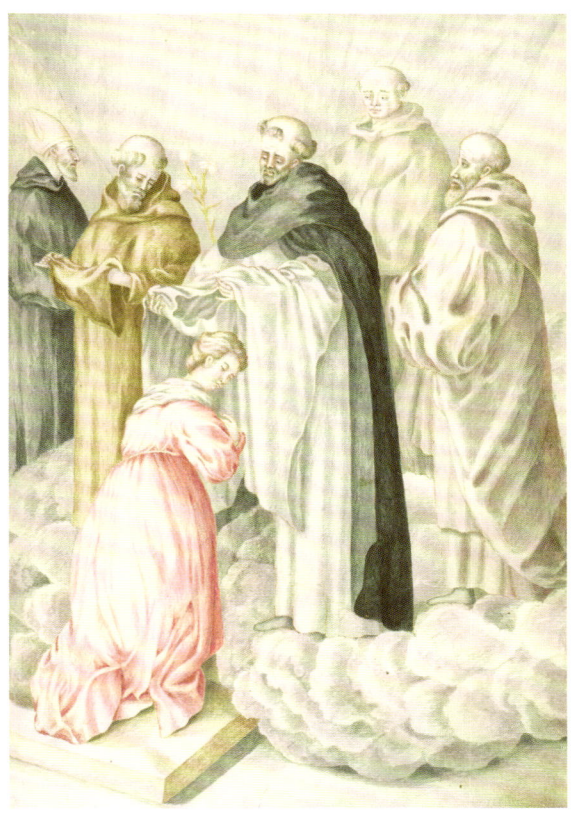

13 Anonymous artist, *Saint Dominic Dressing a Novice with Four Fathers of the Order*, 'Terrilogio del Monastero di San Domenico', Enti Religiosi Soppressi, MS 2498, fol.vi[r], 1702, pencil and watercolour on paper, 43 × 30 cm (16 ⅞ × 11 ¾ in), Archivio Storico Diocesano, Lucca

CONVENTUAL CAREER

Although she was elected neither prioress nor sub-prioress, Eufrasia had an outstanding career within the convent, lasting almost 45 years. After the dressing (*vestitio*) (fig.13), the profession and the veiling (*velatio*) – the customary liturgical vestiture of the Dominicans as specified in the *Constitutiones sororum ordinis praedicatorum* – she held a series of important and influential positions in the convent: she became scribe and illuminator, the choir's first singer (*cantrix*), treasurer (*camarlinga*), syndic, the nun responsible for the Rota (*rotaria*)[33] and, with her sister Gabriella, one of the life members of the Council of the Wise Mothers (*Consiglio di madre*).[34]

While the prioress remained the chief officer during her two-year term, her decisions were guided by this formal advisory council of 11 or 12 senior nuns. Their role was to develop a larger communal agenda in accord with the prioress and the convent syndic and to make a careful and critical examination of the proposals from the syndic before submitting them to the full chapter. This important group within the convent made decisions on religious and economic issues, as happened with a particularly sensitive case in 1529.[35] Sixteen-year-old Magdalena, daughter of Ser Urbano Franciotti, had entered the convent on 24 November 1527. On 29 May 1529 the sisters sent her back to her father with her dowry and ten ducats more since most of the Wise Mothers, Eufrasia among them, understood from 'some probable signs' that she was unhappy living in the convent.[36] The dismissal of a novice was rare, and it was especially painful for the community. Importantly, the decision preserved the inner order. The Council of the Wise Mothers kept its prerogatives until the changes imposed in 1563 by the Tridentine Council, which favoured an administrative style present in male-run ecclesiastical institutions.

These changes limited, but did not abolish, self-governance since nuns maintained a certain autonomy in administrative matters.[37] The relative independence of the nuns in Eufrasia's lifetime supported their engagement with forms of art, including patronage decisions regarding both architecture and art, which was not uncommon in Renaissance convents, and what happened at San Domenico confirmed the value of art for devotional aims.

3

Matters of Dependence and Autonomy

It is often asserted that conventual communities provided women with environments conducive to creative endeavours.[1] However, these environments had also their negative aspects, since opportunities for study were obviously far more limited for women in enclosure than for either daughters of artists, such as Artemisia Gentileschi, or noble women (*gentildonne*) living at home, such as Sofonisba Anguissola (1532/5–1625) and her sisters.[2] Yet life without men did not necessarily mean an artistic life without male instruction or influence. This was the case of Sister Zita Fatinelli (1628–51) of the San Domenico convent.[3]

Even if well beyond Eufrasia's time and likely an exception, Zita's propensity for drawing was encouraged by both her father and the prioress of San Domenico. She copied complex compositions from prints, which, in the nun-chronicler's opinion, attained excellent results.[4] To support her inclination, the prioress hired an expert and discreet painter, one of the most famous of the city, whose name the nun-chronicler does not report. The training took place in the presence of other nuns, and, in a few months, Sister Zita progressed in an outstanding manner, due as much to her great attitude as to her willingness to become a proficient artist.[5]

Sister Zita's artwork raises a question regarding the complex prints she reproduced. Apart from showing that the images were not created after nature, one could ask whether the prints were already in the convent, or had she brought them with her from home? If they were already in the convent, they would have been the common patrimony of sacred images used as models by previous nun-artists. If they were brought by Sister Zita, they belonged to the few things – including a breviary and a small crucifix – that the nuns were allowed to bring with them from home to keep in their cell. The issue of prints also concerns Eufrasia, as we will see later.

What kind of training would have been necessary for Eufrasia to have illustrated the series of choir books introduced above – five for her own convent, one for San Martino Cathedral and two for the monastery of San Romano – in a reasonable time? She had lived in the palace of her parents until 1490, where she might have received rudimentary training. After that year, when she was 12 years old, she entered the San Nicolao Novello convent, where her sister Gabriella, sixteen years her elder, had already become a professed nun. By this time, she might have made drawings that supported the writing and illustration of these manuscripts. However, no record exists that could testify to the presence either of a male instructor or of a nun-illuminator in San Nicolao Novello. Thus, before starting the analysis and assessment of Eufrasia's artworks, I will consider what happened in the convent of San Domenico in Pisa,

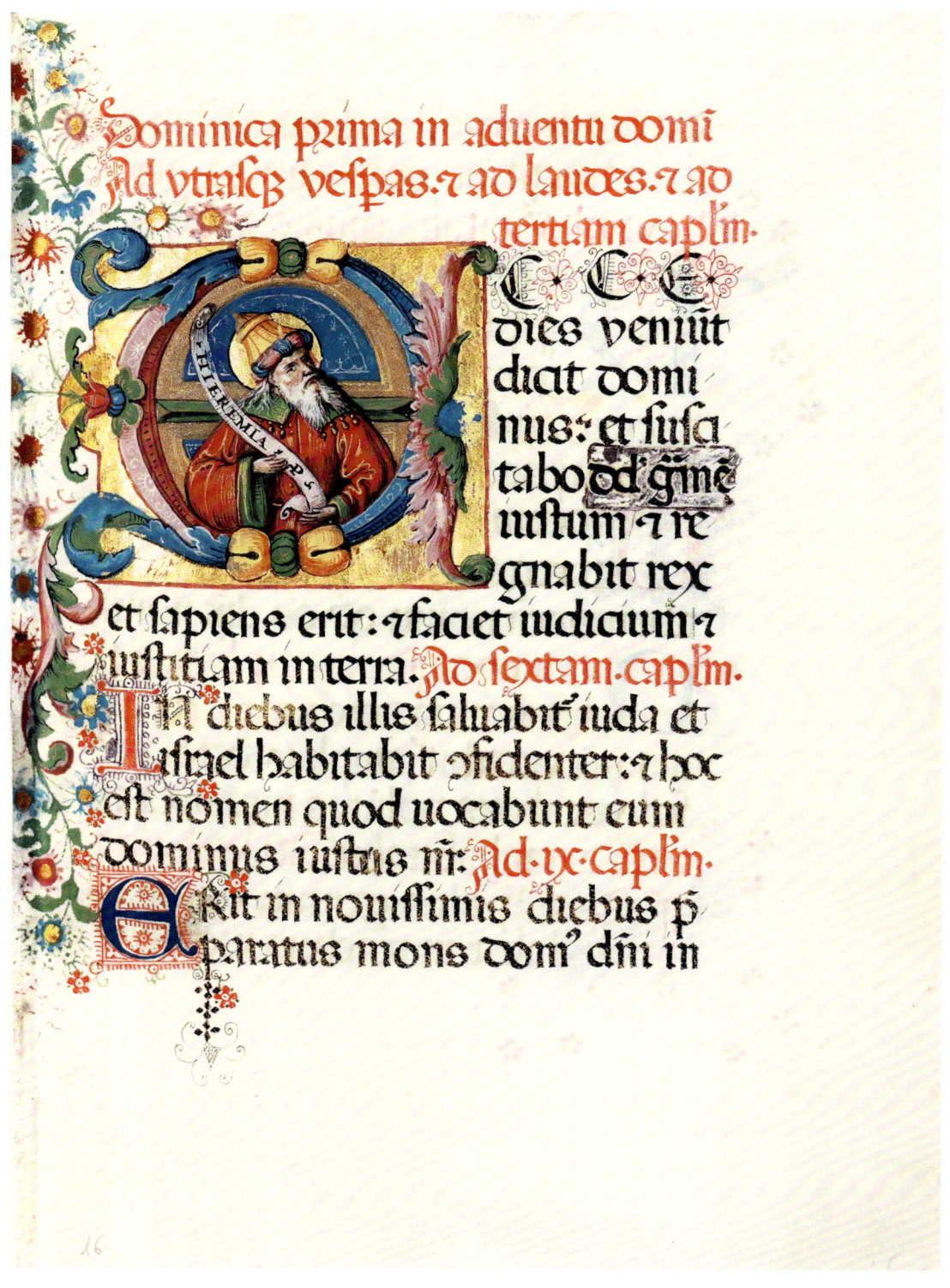

Dominica prima in aduentu domi
Ad vtrasqz vespas. 7 ad laudes. 7 ad
tertiam caplm.
Ecce
dies veniūt
dicit domi
nus: et fusi
tabo dd gñe
iustum 7 re
gnabit rex
et sapiens erit: 7 faciet iudiciūm 7
iustitiam in terra. Ad sextam caplm.
IN diebus illis saluabit iuda et
Israel habitabit cōfidenter: 7 hoc
est nomen quod uocabunt eum
dominus iustus nr. Ad ix caplm.
ERit in nouissimis diebus p
paratus mons dom' dñi in

14 Attributed here to Benedetta Arnolfini, *Initial E, Ecce dies veniunt – The Prophet Jeremiah*, Ritual MS 1984, fol.16ʳ, c.1500, tempera and gold leaf on parchment, folium 26 × 19 cm (10 ¼ × 7 ½ in), initial 6.8 × 7.6 cm (2 ⅝ × 3 in), Biblioteca Statale, Lucca

seen by some scholars as the primary source for the diffusion of illumination in San Domenico in Lucca.

SISTER BENEDETTA ARNOLFINI FROM PISA

In the fifteenth century the Observant convent of San Domenico in Pisa was among the most important institutional patrons of altarpieces in the city. Turino Vanni (*c.*1348–after 1438), Bicci di Lorenzo (*c.*1373–1452), Benozzo Gozzoli (1420–97), Paolo Schiavo (1397–1478) and an unknown Flemish artist all worked for the nuns. They were active patrons who, in addition to fame and value, selected the artists on the basis of politics, location, vicinity and previous family contacts.[6] This had been the case for Turino Vanni and Bicci di Lorenzo; Benozzo Gozzoli may have been recommended either by the friars of Santa Caterina in Pisa or by the bishop of the city, while Paolo Schiavo was hired through the intermediation of one of the convent's factors.[7] In what way did the works of these artists influence the nun-miniaturists of the Pisan convent? This question concerns us since the nuns could not rely, as male artists did, on a normal training outside the convent, which comprised years of apprenticeship in the master's workshop, learning to draw, prepare colours and create compositions, but also studying works made by other artists displayed in churches.

The issue of artistic influence in the San Domenico convent in Pisa was seemingly solved in the first decade of the twentieth century: no painter need have influenced the Pisan nuns directly because illumination had been brought there by the Florentine Dominican Giovanni Dominici (1356–1419). The topic had also a sequel: since two nuns left San Domenico in Pisa in 1502 to bring the 'Observance' to San Domenico in Lucca, one of them might have been trained in art and brought models to teach illumination to her sisters in faith. This is the story all modern commentators rehearsed in the wake

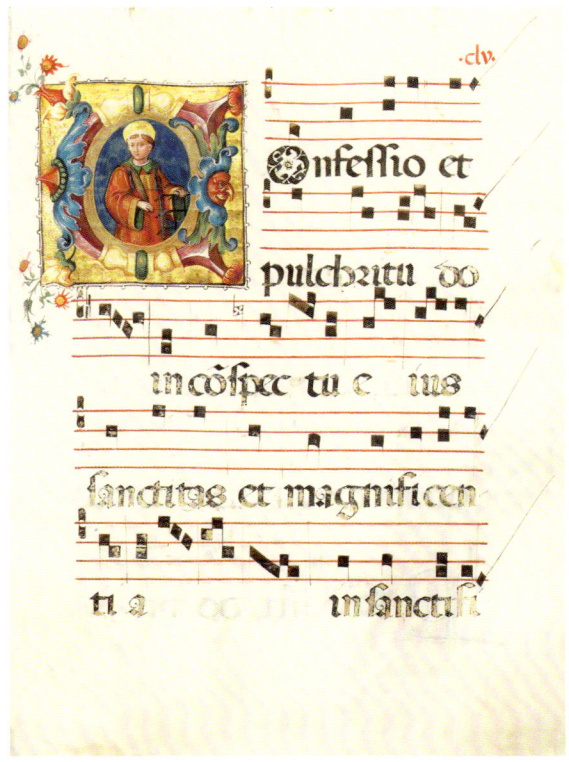

15　Eufrasia Burlamacchi, *Initial C, Confessio et pulchritudo – Saint Lawrence*, Gradual MS 5, fol.155ʳ, *c.*1515, tempera and gold leaf on parchment, folium 54.2 × 38.5 cm (21 ⅜ × 15 ⅛ in), initial 14 × 13 cm (5 ½ × 5 ⅛ in), Dominican Convent, California

of Innocenzo Taurisano, who first proposed it in 1914. He stated that it had been Sister Benedetta Arnolfini (d.1515), one of the miniaturists in the convent of San Domenico in Pisa, who taught Eufrasia the art of illumination.[8]

This is the occasion to free Eufrasia from the oft-repeated story of her complete artistic dependence on Sister Benedetta's illumination (fig.14). One may consent that initial stylistic influences cannot be denied, but in Eufrasia's artistic training they made up just a limited part that she promptly modified by

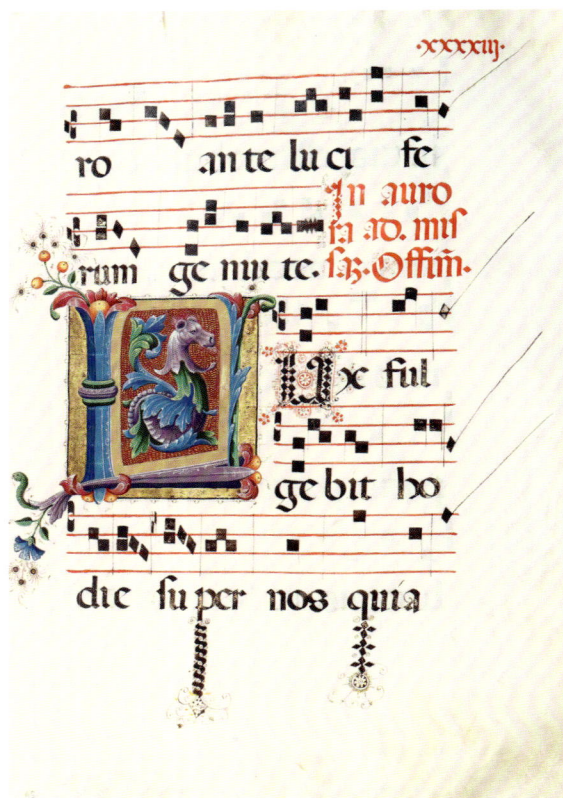

16 Eufrasia Burlamacchi, *Initial L, Lux fulgebit hodie –
Hybrid and Acanthus Leaves*, Gradual MS 2649, fol.45ʳ,
c.1530, tempera and gold leaf on parchment, folium
59.3 × 43.2 cm (23 ⅜ × 17 in), initial 14.7 × 14 cm
(5 ¾ × 5 ½ in), Biblioteca Statale, Lucca

blending them with various models from painting,
illumination, drawings, prints, woodcuts, plaquettes
and coats of arms which did not come from the
convent in Pisa but rather from Florence and Lucca
(fig.15). Furthermore, this is also the occasion to
assign Eufrasia the role of chief illuminator she
objectively deserves in the scriptorium of the San
Domenico convent as much as a place within the
history of illumination outside the conventual

walls. A careful look at the documents will help to
disentangle the matter and best support my claims.

In the Chronica of the San Domenico convent,
Sister Benedetta Arnolfini is mentioned on three
occasions: when she moved from the San Domenico
convent in Pisa to the homonymous religious house
in Lucca; when she transcribed a book of collects
(short prayers said during the Mass); and, with her
death, in her necrology, written on 3 September 1515.[9]
On fol.5ᵛ of t.i of the Chronica, Sister Hilaria Cenami
wrote a momentous statement:

> Since all things of the greatest importance should
> have good and solid beginning on which all future
> things will be built, we felt the need to be helped
> by some learned nuns well conversant with the holy
> Observance of the glorious father Saint Dominic.

The convent of San Domenico in Pisa had acquired
the fame to be 'redolent' (*odorifero*) with sanctity.[10] Its
founder, the Blessed Chiara Gambacorta, and another
sister, Blessed Maria Mancini (d.1430), whose remains
caused miracles, contributed to this fame.[11]

Although a document issued in Bologna on 5 April
1502 by the Dominican Master General Vincenzo
Bandelli (1435–1507) mentions four Lucchese nuns,
namely 'Agneti, Benedicta, Christina and Raphaela
de Luca',[12] who left San Domenico of Pisa to join
the new group, after three months only two nuns –
Sister Agnese and Sister Benedetta – arrived at the
San Domenico convent in Lucca, at 1 am.[13] In the
Chronica of the Lucchese convent no mention is made
of four nuns, and never are the names of Christina and
Raphaela, who belonged to the Burlamacchi family,
recorded. What most likely happened was that the
two sisters, both elderly, either changed their minds,
passed away or their names were simply omitted in
the conventual records of Pisa after 1502 as much as
in those of Lucca, which start in 1502.[14] At any rate,
although the expression 'well conversant with the holy
Observance' may have also encompassed the teaching

of illumination by Sister Benedetta, there are no explicit statements in the documentary sources. If one considers, instead, the Lucchese artistic reality, many documents show how the scriptorium of San Martino Cathedral since the eleventh century had been a centre for illumination, developing a variety of iconographic and stylistic solutions to problems this type of painting posed for artists.[15]

Regarding the book of collects written by Sister Benedetta – no mention is made of whether it was decorated – a long passage in the Chronica of San Domenico, devoted to the lives and deeds of the prioresses, is revealing. The nun-chronicler reports that Prioress Petra Cenami, during her long tenure of 23 years, from 1502 to 1505 and 1507 to 1527, furnished the inner and the outer church with paintings, sculptures and low reliefs. At that time

> were written and decorated by Sister Eufrasia Burlamacchi four antiphonaries, one gradual, one hymnal, one *de venite* [book containing the invitations of the Matins for the various feasts of the year], also a psalter with no notes, one of Calends, and one collects, while another book of collects had been previously written by Sister Benedetta Arnolfini, all of good parchment.[16]

The nun-chronicler paid great attention to Eufrasia's achievements. She carefully listed the different kinds of books she wrote and illuminated, and commented on the quality of the parchment, with Sister Benedetta mentioned at the end and not regarding illuminations.

As to Sister Benedetta's necrology, even here the nun-chronicler offers no hints to her proficiency in illumination. In Eufrasia's necrology, by contrast, her ability is once again clearly remarked upon, not only by listing the illuminated books to sing the Divine Office 'in large letters with the notes, chapter headings, and miniatures very beautiful, that is three Antiphonaries, a Gradual, a Psalter, and a Collects',

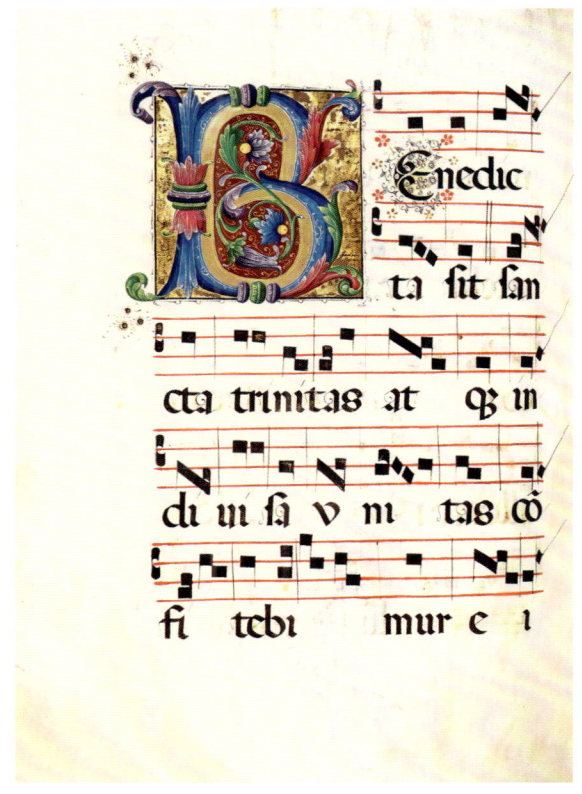

17 Eufrasia Burlamacchi, *Initial B, Benedicta sit sancta trinitas – Flowers and Acanthus Leaves*, Gradual MS 2650, fol.120ᵛ, *c*.1532, tempera and gold leaf on parchment, folium 60.5 × 43.3 cm (23 ⅞ × 17 in), initial 15.3 × 14.5 (6 × 5 ¾ in), Biblioteca Statale, Lucca

but also by expressing an aesthetic judgement, perhaps one of the first evaluations, even if general, of this sort about illumination (figs 16–17).[17]

I do not deny that Sister Benedetta was a talented artist, and I attribute to her the decoration of MS 1984 described below. But if she had been an expert in illumination, why was this distinguished ability passed over in silence? If it were an omission, this is even more remarkable since the nun-chroniclers

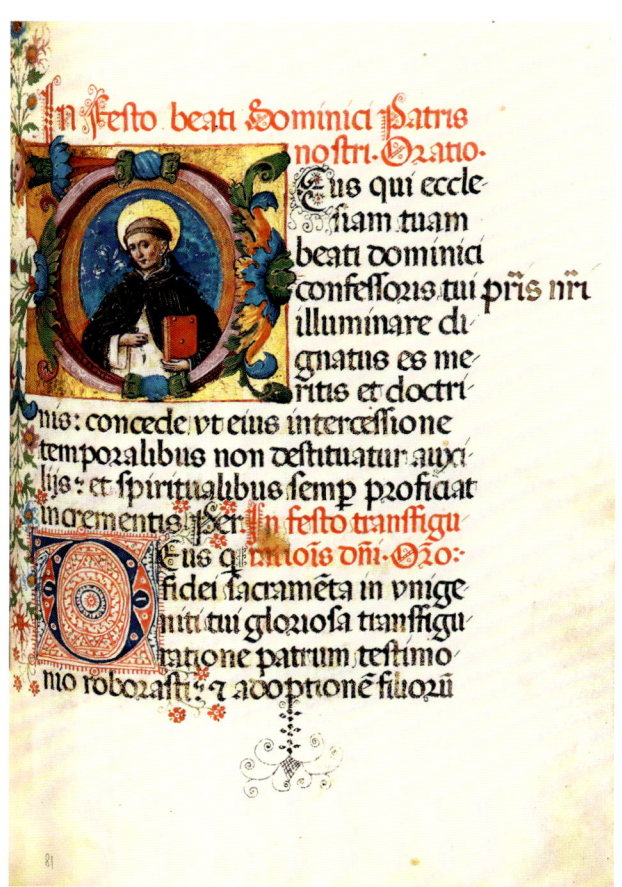

18 Attributed here to Benedetta Arnolfini, *Initial D, Deus qui ecclesiam tuam – Saint Dominic*, Ritual MS 1984, fol.81ʳ, *c.*1500, tempera and gold leaf on parchment, folium 26 × 19 cm (10 ¼ × 7 ½ in), initial 7.2 × 8 cm (2 ⅞ × 3 ⅛ in), Biblioteca Statale, Lucca

19 Eufrasia Burlamacchi, *Initial G, Gaude felix parens – Saint Dominic*, Antiphonary MS 3, fol.218ᵛ, *c.*1510, tempera and gold leaf on parchment, folium 54.2 × 38.5 cm (21 ⅜ × 15 ⅛ in), initial 14.2 × 14 cm (5 ⅝ × 5 ½ in), Dominican Convent, California

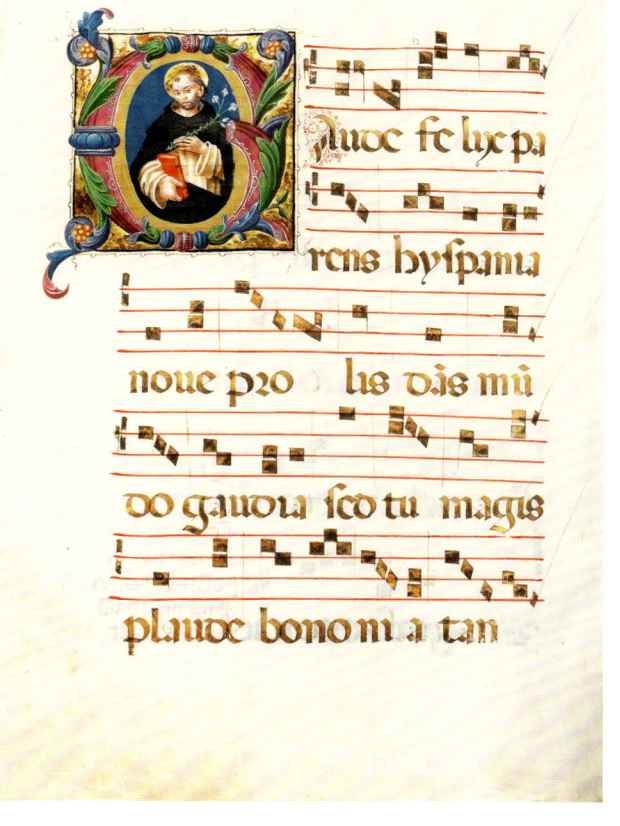

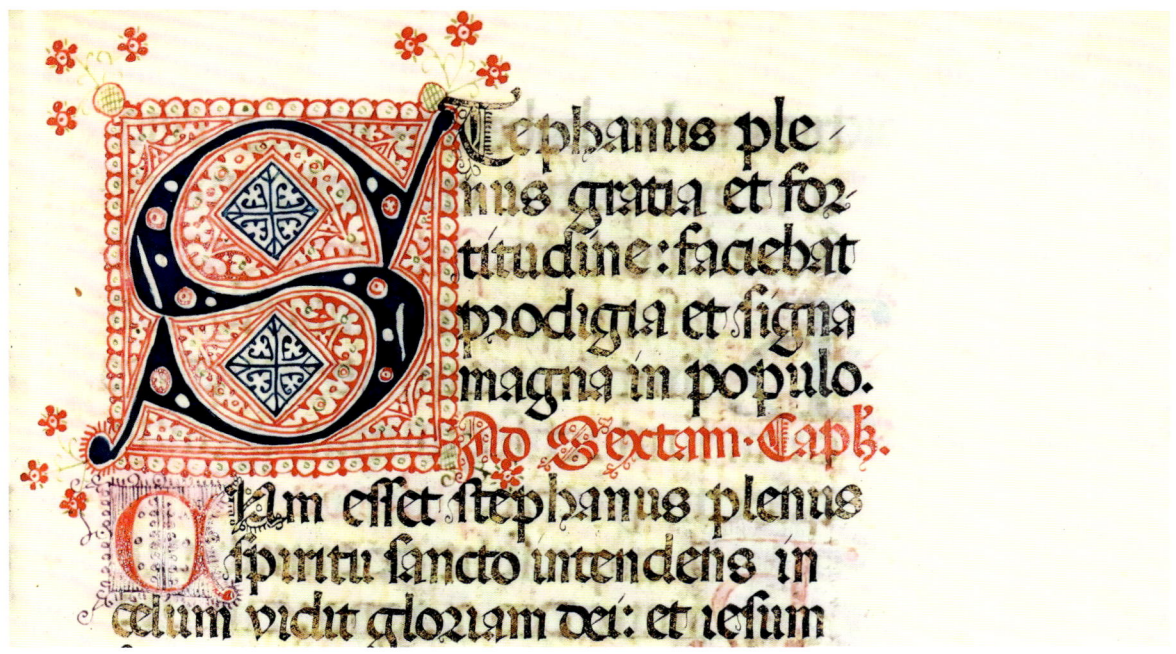

20 Attributed here to Benedetta Arnolfini, *Initial S*, Ritual MS 1984, fol.23ʳ, *c*.1500, tempera and ink on parchment, 6 × 6 cm (2 ⅜ × 2 ⅜ in), Biblioteca Statale, Lucca

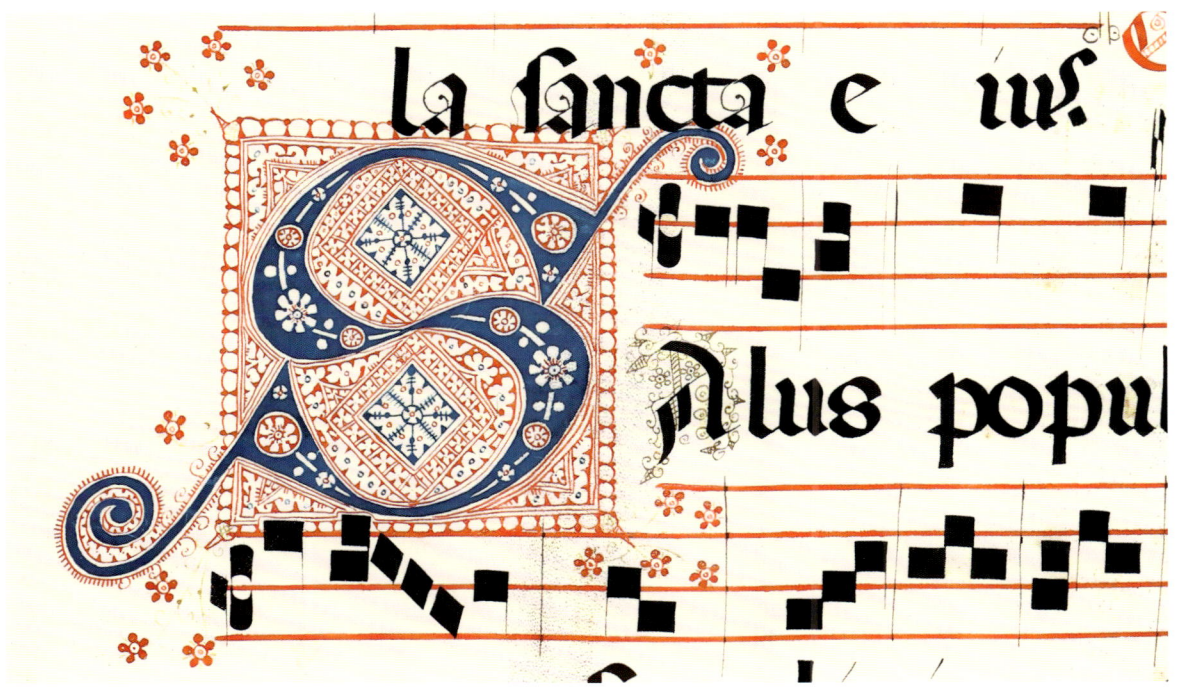

21 Eufrasia Burlamacchi, *Initial S*, Gradual MS 2650, fol.227ᵛ, *c*.1532, tempera and ink on parchment, 12.5 × 12 cm (4 ⅞ × 4 ¾ in), Biblioteca Statale, Lucca

who wrote about the lives of the nuns in the San Domenico convent unfailingly recorded every kind of artistic production, including painting, statues, terracotta and stucco reliefs, fabrics, liturgical implements and crowns for the Virgin and the saints made of gold and silver threads.[18] The probable solution is to be found in the nun-chroniclers' intentions. As described above, Eufrasia belonged to the first group of nuns who founded the new Observant convent. For this reason, the nun-chroniclers may have wished to emphasise her 'foundational' contribution 'from within' – and not 'from without' – to the establishment of an artistic tradition in the San Domenico convent in Lucca.

According to the life of Prioress Petra Cenami, it seems that by 1527 Eufrasia had accomplished ten manuscripts, the two-volume Gradual for San Romano included. In her own necrology, however, only six manuscripts are listed: 'three Antiphonaries, a Gradual, a Psalter, and a Collects'.[19] In the second record, the number of manuscripts attributed to Eufrasia has been dramatically reduced. This noteworthy discordance cannot be explained, as Mark Gregory D'Apuzzo argued, by suggesting that the nun-chronicler referred to another series of illuminated books.[20] Rather, it seems more logical to consider that different authors wrote the records: the nun-chronicler who wrote Eufrasia's necrology on 2 January 1548 was not the same person who penned Sister Petra Cenami's life in 1527.

The manuscripts for the Mass and the Divine Office were necessities that a newly founded convent had to obtain. Yet, Eufrasia's recorded output did not cover the range of texts required by the Dominican liturgy. The 14 specified texts needed by a community comprised an ordinary, martyrology, collects, processional, psalter, breviary, lectionary, antiphonary, gradual, pulpitary, conventual missal, epistolary, evangeliary and a missal for the minor altars.[21] Although the manuscripts produced by Eufrasia fell into some of these categories, the convent must

have acquired others by different means or, perhaps, Eufrasia and other nuns produced additional volumes that were never written about and were lost over time.

RITUAL MS 1984 FOR SAN DOMENICO, *c.*1500

MS 1984, a Ritual (a book of all the services not contained in the missal that a priest or deacon may perform) that once belonged to the convent of San Domenico, features two figural illuminations, one of the prophet Jeremiah (fig.14 above) and the other of Saint Dominic (fig.18). It also includes many penwork initials.[22] These initials are clearly connected to a lengthy decorative tradition that went back to the thirteenth century, and they are like the ones in the manuscripts decorated by Sister Eufrasia. Yet, the two figural miniatures differ considerably from the manner of rendering the human body that is recognisable in her other works, in the gamut of colours and the distribution of light and shade. The figures of Jeremiah and Saint Dominic in the Ritual feature minute facial traits, a gentleness, suppleness and attention to the folds, made more precise with subtle yellow lines.

These features are absent in Eufrasia's work (fig.19). Even the acanthus leaves, the flowers, the roundels and the form of the letters, although showing some similarities, do not present the lithe plasticity nor the sculptural sense of materiality that defined Eufrasia's style from the beginning of her artistic career. Jeremiah and Dominic are more 'Florentine' or even 'Pisan' in style than 'Lucchese'. Thus, these two portrayals may not be the work of Eufrasia but rather of a nun acquainted with those artistic traditions.

I attribute here the miniatures and the ornamental letters of Ritual MS 1984 to Sister Benedetta Arnolfini (fig.20). If Benedetta received training in writing and illuminating manuscripts in the San Domenico convent in Pisa – of which no examples have been preserved – she may have made this small book there and brought it from Pisa to San Domenico in Lucca when she moved. The Ritual includes a section for the ceremony for the profession and veiling of the nuns, that is, when the novice, usually a year after her dressing, made her final vows as a nun. I suspect that Benedetta wished to have it available for use at the time of the convent's foundation, together with the books for the Mass and the Divine Office. It was, so to speak, a functional book that she knew would be needed very soon after her arrival.

However, the two miniatures of MS 1984 could not provide a full gamut of iconographic models upon which Eufrasia could have relied to illuminate the books for the Mass and the Divine Office she produced. To arrive in a reasonable time at mastering both figures and ornamentation (fig.21) in the series of choir books for her own convent, Eufrasia certainly had a more general acquaintance with illumination and other forms of art that led her to become the chief illuminator in San Domenico until around 1532. In such a capacity, at the beginning of the 1520s Eufrasia likely taught several nuns in the art of ornamentation and probably figural illumination as well. Some of these sisters resided at San Domenico, while others came from San Giorgio, the second Observant convent referred to above. Among the former, it is recorded that Sister Agnesa Castrucci (1506–81), who entered San Domenico in 1522 at 16 years of age, since 'she knew to write large letters and solmization, she wrote the Office of Saint Agnes Martyr and other things we sing in specific sheets for every nun'.[23] Among the latter, Sister Alessandra Guidiccioni moved from San Giorgio to the San Domenico convent, where she remained for three years to learn to write 'large letters, to practise solmization and to illuminate books; later, she wrote three large and beautiful books for the Divine Office' for her own convent.[24]

4

An Eclectic Blend of Acanthus Leaves, Flowers and Monsters

In the previous chapter, I stated that Eufrasia had a general acquaintance with illumination and other forms of art. From among the miniatures of the various manuscripts that belonged at her time to the San Martino Cathedral and to the church of San Frediano, and which I believe she knew through family connections, discussed in Chapter 1, she likely would have chosen for inspiration only those examples she considered to express sacred meaning through three-dimensional forms in both figures and ornament.[1] At the same time, her choices also comprised layout, composition, form of the initials, colours and technique. Let us consider some examples of Eufrasia's selective attitude.

MARTINO DI BARTOLOMEO

The set of five late fourteenth-century Graduals for the San Martino Cathedral, now numbered 1, 7, 8, 9 and 10 (Archivio Storico Diocesano, Lucca), which include the chants for the Mass, integrated the Cathedral's liturgical books of the eleventh, twelfth and thirteenth centuries.[2] Anna Rosa Calderoni Masetti attributed both the miniatures and the ornamental apparatuses to Spinello Aretino (c.1350–1410), who lived and worked in Lucca in the second half of the fourteenth century.[3] Recently, other art historians have substituted the

Sienese Martino di Bartolomeo (c.1365/70–1435) for Spinello. Martino was an illuminator who privileged bright and contrasting colours, showing attention to details and to the narrative aspects of the image within the letter (fig.22).[4] He represented the acanthus leaves either long and synthetic or just curling around themselves. Eufrasia, by contrast, conferred to the leaves weight and naturalness, with no insertion of fanciful motifs.[5] The most marked differences reside in the conception of the body: slender and almost weightless in Martino, monumental and plastic in Eufrasia. Although they were precious evidence of the activity of a prolific illuminator, apart from the rendition of the initial letters as monumental compositions endowed with space, a feature she may have appreciated, Eufrasia did not reproduce in the scriptorium of San Domenico the illumination of these late fourteenth-century manuscripts.

The same cannot be said for the manuscripts illuminated in the last decades of the fifteenth century, an initiative likely to be ascribed to the Bishop Stefano Trenta. One of his relatives, the wealthy merchant Lorenzo di Francesco Trenta, had in the early fifteenth century commissioned a missal from the Master of Jean de Boucicaut's famous Book of Hours. Now MS 3122 in the Biblioteca Statale, Lucca, this missal later passed on to Bishop Trenta.[6] For San Martino Cathedral, he ordered two manuscripts around 1470–75,

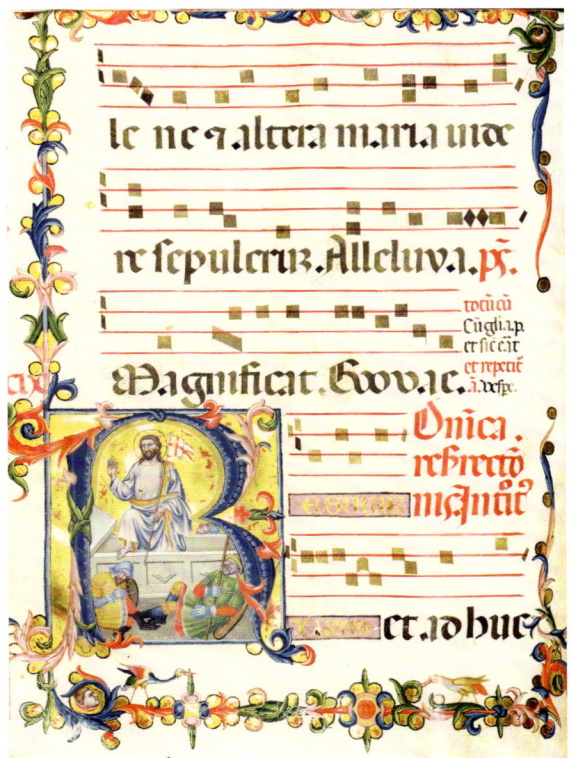

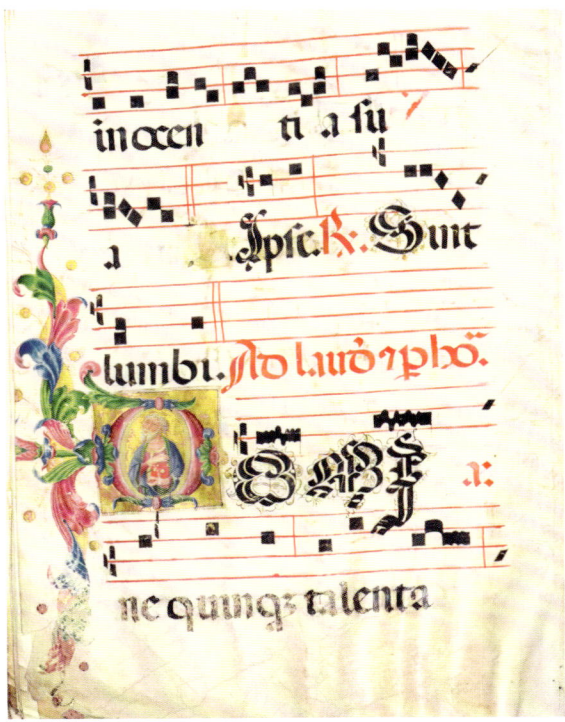

22 Martino di Bartolomeo, *Initial R, Resurrexi et adhuc tecum sum – Resurrection*, Gradual MS 9, fol.89ᵛ, *c*.1395, tempera and gold leaf on parchment, folium 60 × 44 cm (23 ⅝ × 17 ⅜ in), initial 18.5 × 18 cm (7 ¼ × 7 ⅛ in), Archivio Storico Diocesano, Lucca

23 Entourage of Matteo Civitali and Baldassarre di Biagio, *Initial D, Domine quinque talenta – Saint with Book*, Antiphonary MS 2, fol.84ᵛ, 1471–7, tempera and gold leaf on parchment, folium 59.5 × 45 cm (23 ⅜ × 17 ¾ in), initial 15 × 15 cm (5 ⅞ × 5 ⅞ in), Archivio Storico Diocesano, Lucca

the Common of Saints MS 2 and the Antiphonary MS 6, written and decorated in the workshop of the Lucchese Baldassarre di Biagio del Firenze and both bearing the coat of arms of the Trenta family, which comprises three ox heads.

BALDASSARRE DI BIAGIO DEL FIRENZE

Among the illuminators operating in Lucca whose works Eufrasia must have known is Baldassarre di Biagio del Firenze (*c*.1425–*c*.1484), a painter-miniaturist whose biography and work have recently been reconstructed. Son of Biagio, a weaver expert in drapes and velvets, Baldassarre may have had at his disposal a large variety of drawings for fabric. To update his art, in 1454 he moved to Florence 'for some of his occupations'. Far from being an innovator, Baldassarre can be best described as a translator in more affordable terms of iconographic and stylistic solutions, first and foremost of Filippo Lippi and, also, of Pesellino (*c*.1422–57), Alesso Baldovinetti (c.1427–99) and Andrea del Castagno (c.1421–57). His eclectic art was not an exception but instead conforms to norms in Lucca.[7]

Collaborator of the painter-sculptor Matteo Civitali, Baldassarre ran his own workshop, which produced Antiphonaries MSS 2 and 6 for San Martino Cathedral. In both manuscripts, the artist and his collaborators followed three main contrasting figural paths: the first comprises heavy and short figures, with large hands, cheeks and eyes; the second encompasses especially female figures, slender and elegant, with thin and elongated fingers; the third regards the naturalistic ornament surrounding the letters, where the leaves possess volume and thickness constructed through heavy chiaroscuro that finds direct correspondence in the folds of the mantles worn by the saints (fig.23).

Eufrasia seems to have been acquainted with these solutions, which she adopted especially in the five manuscripts in California, as in MS 5, fol.103ᵛ (fig.24). Here, heavy acanthus leaves sprout from double red and blue cornucopias, ending with yellow and red fruits, emphasising softness in stark contrast with metallic rigidity. But even the metal objects seem to be pliable to their function, which is to form the initial S of 'Scio'.

The Antiphonaries MSS 4 and 5 for the same cathedral were commissioned by the *Operario* Domenico Bertini (c.1417–1506), the head administrator of the Opera of San Martino Cathedral from 1484. His coat of arms – a cock with a spike – was represented in 1484 in a naturalistic bas-relief by Civitali in the cornice of the *Tempietto del Volto Santo* in San Martino (fig.27).[8] A naturalistic cock and a spike also appears in MS 4, fol.94ᵛ, in the frieze which surrounds Saint Regolo enthroned, within a small quadrilobed medallion.[9] It seems that Eufrasia had the occasion to look at fol.94ᵛ of MS 4 and to adapt the emblem to her artistic purposes, as in Antiphonary MS 14, fol.15ᵛ (fig.26) and in Gradual MS 2650, fol.40ᵛ (fig.25), in which the fanciful aspects of the composition prevail.

GIULIANO AMADEI

If Eufrasia selected some elements of Baldassarre di Biagio's illumination, such as the structure of human bodies and the heavy acanthus leaves, for her first enterprise in the same set of choir books and in the manuscripts that followed, she also carefully studied and re-elaborated the illumination of the Florentine Giuliano Amadei. A Camaldolese monk and later prior of the Abbey of Santa Maria d'Agnano near Arezzo, Amadei too, like Baldassarre di Biagio, was an eclectic artist. After his initial training in Florence in the 1440s in the environment of Fra Angelico, he became a collaborator of Piero della Francesca (c.1412–92) in the *Polittico della Misericordia* in Sansepolcro, Arezzo.[10] Once in Rome in the 1460s, he worked for the papal Curia during the papacies of Pius II Piccolomini (1458–64), Paul II Barbo (1464–71), Sixtus IV Della Rovere (1471–84) and Innocent VIII Cybo (1484–92), illuminating around 30 manuscripts, both religious and secular.[11]

In Rome, Amadei remained faithful to Fra Angelico and Piero della Francesca in the depiction of figures. Regarding ornament, he demonstrated a clear sensitivity towards all kinds of patterns in representations of cornucopias, acanthus leaves and fruits, and multicoloured scrolls with festoons and garlands. This ornamentation was inspired by the frescoes of Sandro Botticelli (1445–1510) and Pietro Perugino (c.1448–1523) in the Sistine Chapel and by Pinturicchio (c.1452–1513). Amadei was especially interested in a repertoire of grotesques that he employed in both religious and secular texts. This ancient fanciful ornament owes its name to a fruitful mistake: when some parts of the Emperor Nero's Domus Aurea were unearthed in the fifteenth century, they were believed to be grottoes and for this reason the ornamental motifs found in them were called grotesques.[12] Amadei also represented monsters forming the body of the initial letters that reappear in the manuscripts he decorated in

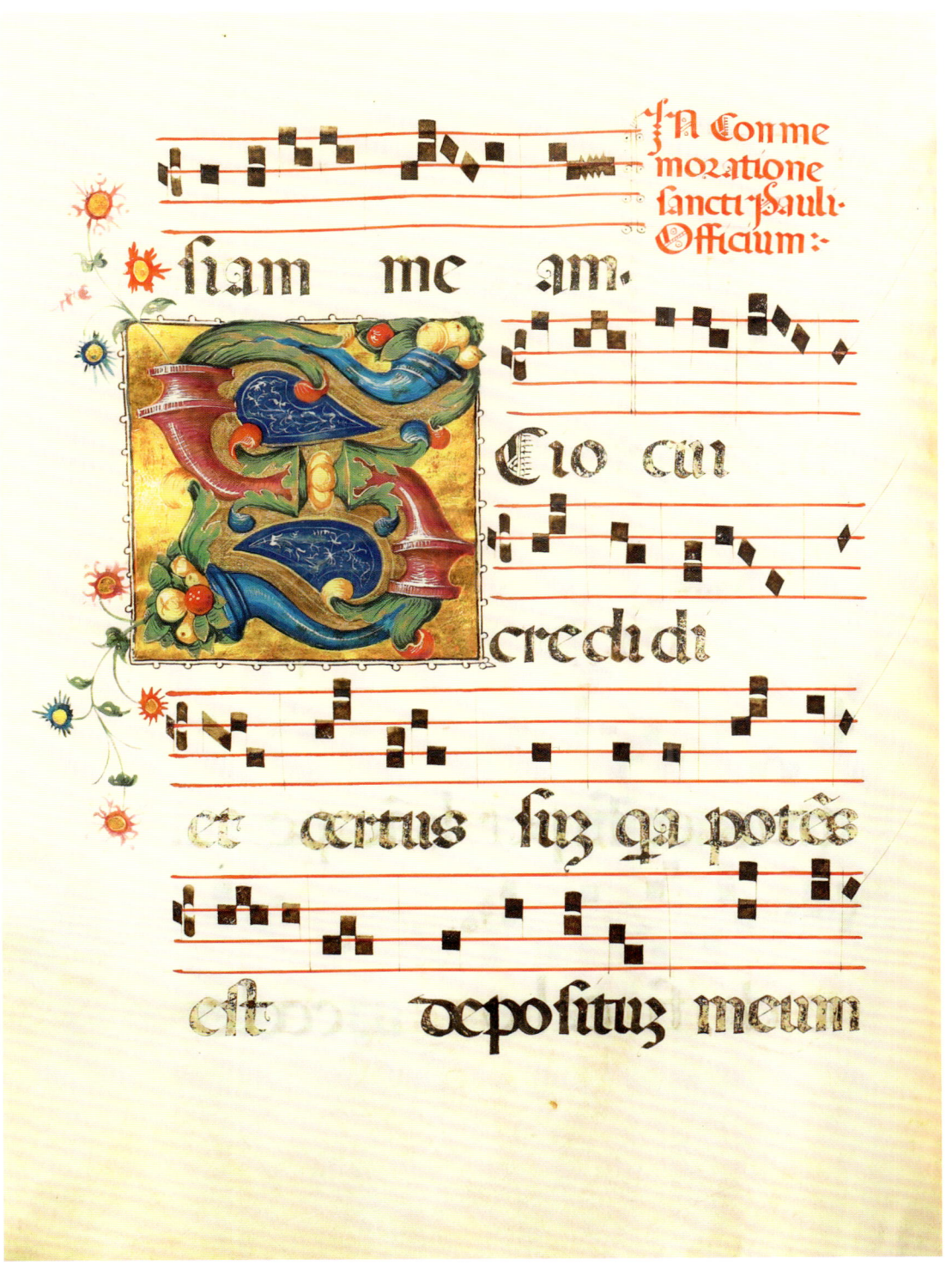

24 Eufrasia Burlamacchi, *Initial S, Scio cui credidi – Cornucopias, Fruit and Acanthus Leaves*, Gradual MS 5, fol.103ᵛ,
   c.1515, tempera and gold leaf on parchment, folium 54.2 × 38.5 cm (21 ⅜ × 15 ⅛ in), initial 14 × 13 cm (5 ½ × 5 ⅛ in),
   Dominican Convent, California

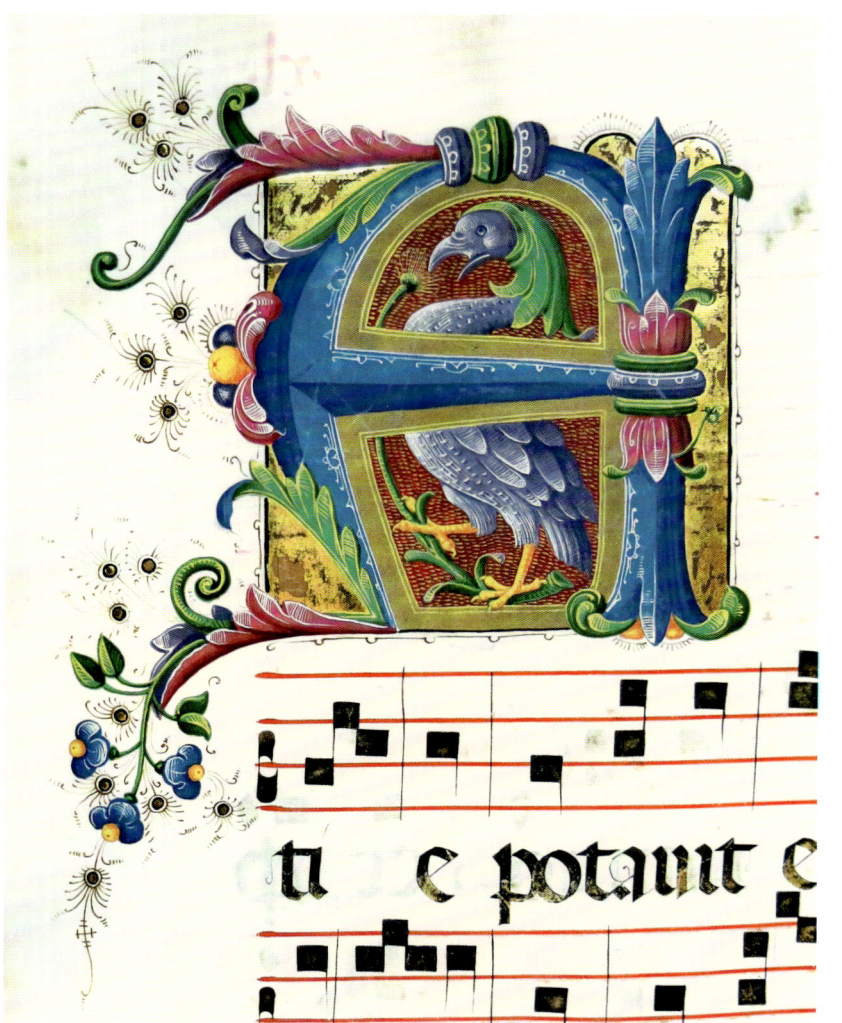

25 Eufrasia Burlamacchi, *Initial A, Cock and Spike*, Gradual MS 2650, fol.40ᵛ, *c.*1532, tempera and gold leaf on parchment, 14.5 × 14.5 cm (5¾ × 5¾ in), Biblioteca Statale, Lucca

26 Eufrasia Burlamacchi, *Initial A, Angelus domini – Cock and Spike*, Antiphonary MS 14, fol.15ᵛ, *c.*1515–20, tempera and gold leaf on parchment, 14.5 × 12.5 cm (5¾ × 4⅞ in), Archivio Storico Diocesano, Lucca

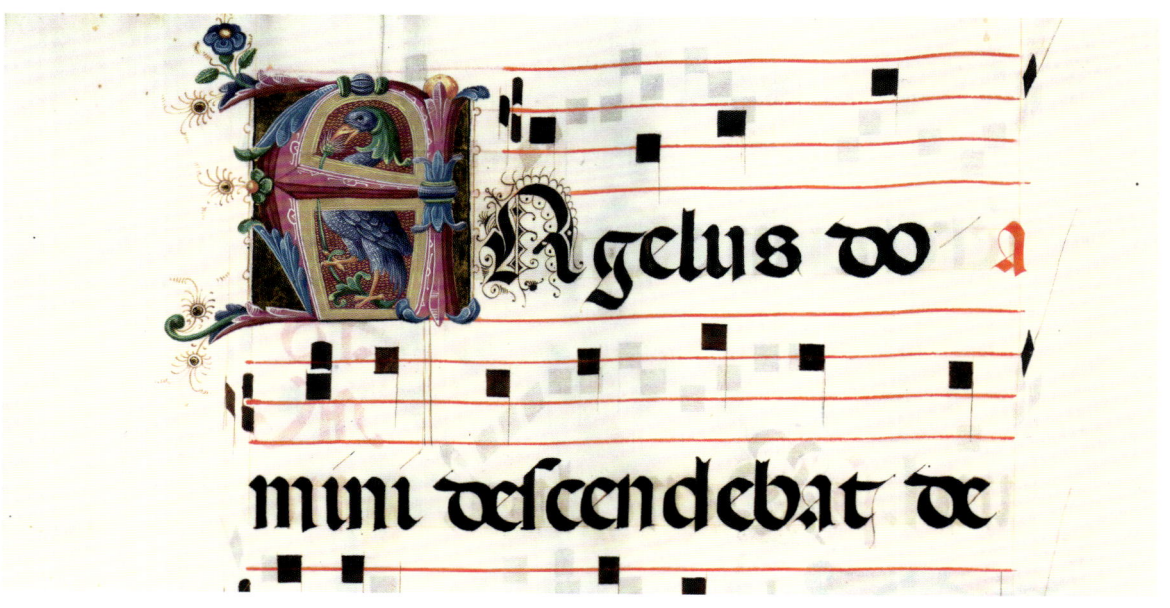

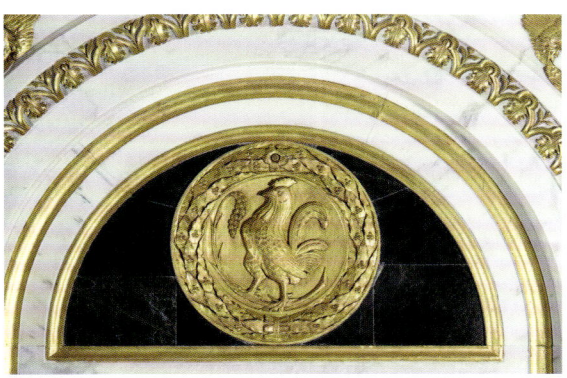

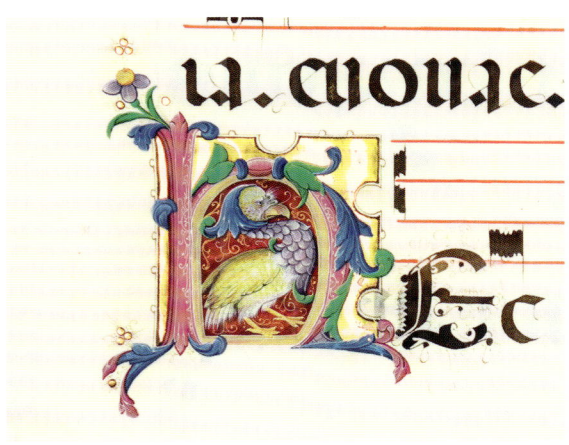

27 Matteo Civitali, *Cock and Spike, Medallion with the Coat of Arms of Domenico Bertini*, *Tempietto del Volto Santo*, 1484, gilded Carrara marble, diameter 50 cm (19 ⅝ in), Cattedrale di San Martino, Lucca

28 Giuliano Amadei, *Initial H, Hec locutus – Hybrid*, Antiphonary MS 16, fol.87ᵛ, *c*.1495, tempera and gold leaf on parchment, 6 × 5 cm (2 ⅜ × 2 in), Archivio Storico Diocesano, Lucca

Lucca, as in the Hymnary MS F for the church of San Frediano, *c*.1496.[13]

Amadei's move from the Abbey of Santa Maria d'Agnano to Lucca may have depended on economic factors. In a 1491 brief, Pope Innocent VIII gave Amadei permission to leave the monastery 'to illuminate and with his earnings to cover the many debts he had accumulated', likely issuing from the poor administration of his abbey.[14] Once in Lucca, he continued to reproduce his ornamental repertory featuring hybrids, acanthus leaves and flowers (fig.28) in the manuscripts for San Martino Cathedral, Antiphonaries 11, 13, 16 and 17 commissioned by Domenico Bertini.

EUFRASIA'S RESPONSE

Eufrasia drew inspiration from some of Amadei's ornamentation, yet with remarkable precision and inventiveness in modifying her model for an important enterprise for San Martino Cathedral: the

decoration of Antiphonary MS 14, left unfinished by Amadei, who died in 1496. MS 14 has no sacred scenes; its ornamental letters are filled with a great variety of animals, fruits and flowers (fig.29). Eufrasia reproduced for this manuscript some initials Amadei created for other projects, such as the hybrid with tongue and 'skirt' of acanthus leaves in Antiphonary MS 16, fol.35ʳ (fig.30). Yet, she turned towards bright colours, suppleness in the rendition of leaves, elegance in shapes and a great variety of ornamental subjects.

Eufrasia completed the decoration for MS 14 in *c*.1520 under the patronage of her relative, Jacopo Burlamacchi (d.1556), another overseer of the Cathedral.[15] As with the previous overseers, Jacopo was concerned with the patronage of the Cathedral's manuscripts. An unfinished manuscript may have been a problem, and his handing over of MS 14 to Eufrasia for completion should not be seen as a strange initiative. On the contrary, apart from familial connections, Eufrasia's fame as an illuminator may

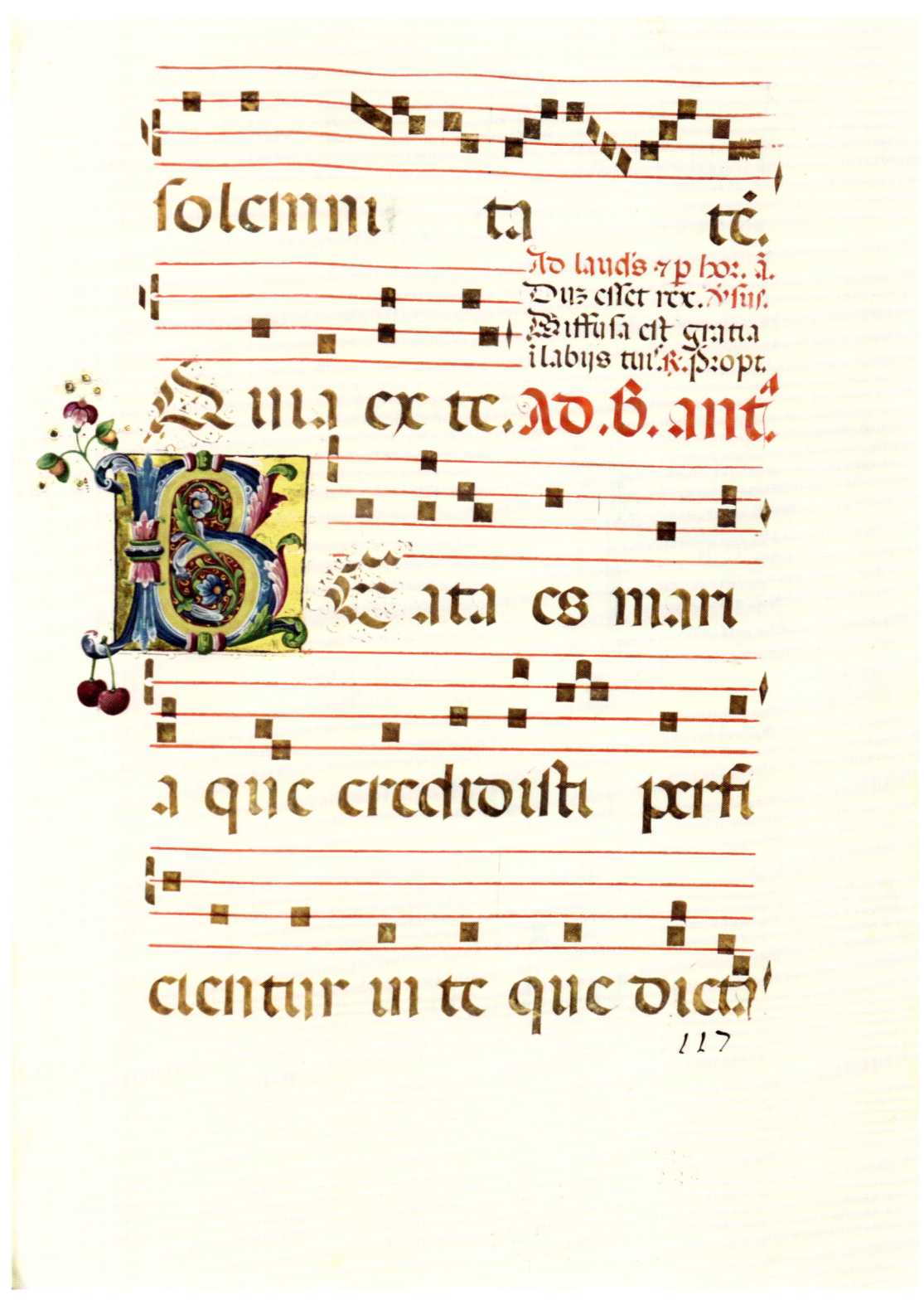

29 Eufrasia Burlamacchi, *Initial B, Beata es Maria – Flowers, Fruit, Acanthus Leaves and Two Cherries*, Antiphonary MS 14, fol.117ʳ, *c.*1515–20, tempera and gold leaf on parchment, folium 62 × 44.5 cm (24⅜ × 17½ in), initial 14.5 × 12.5 cm (5¾ × 4⅞ in), Archivio Storico Diocesano, Lucca

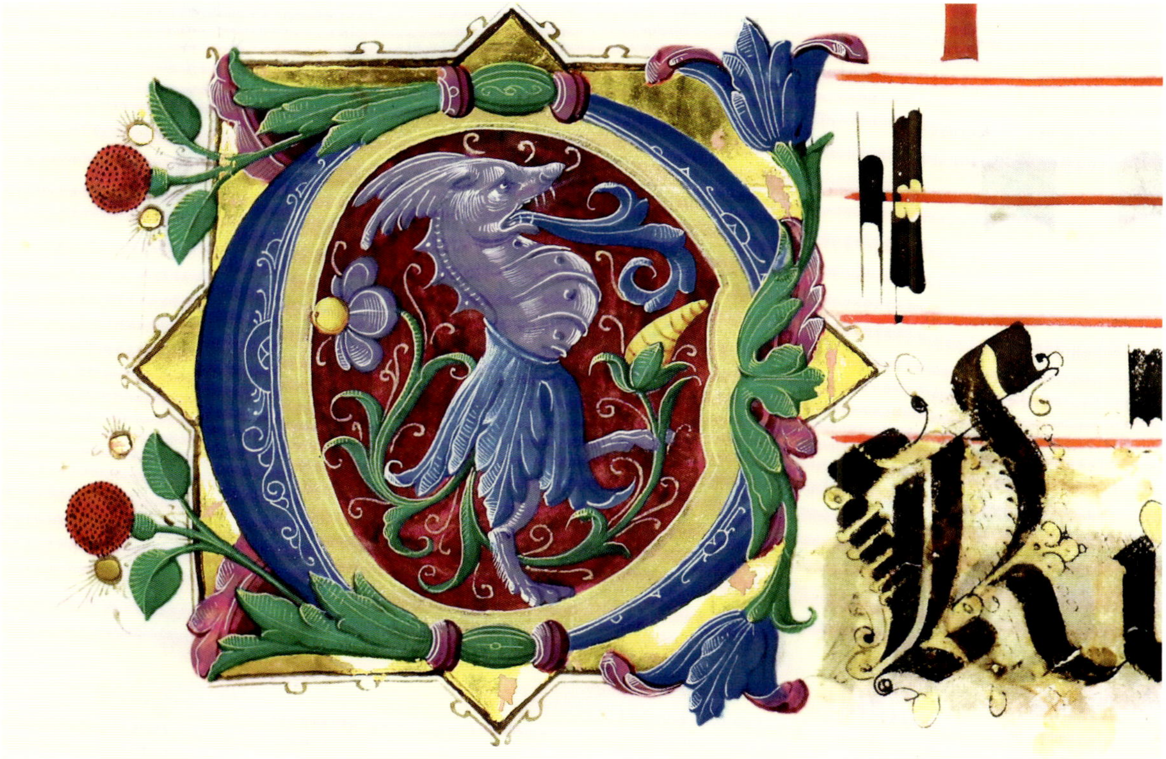

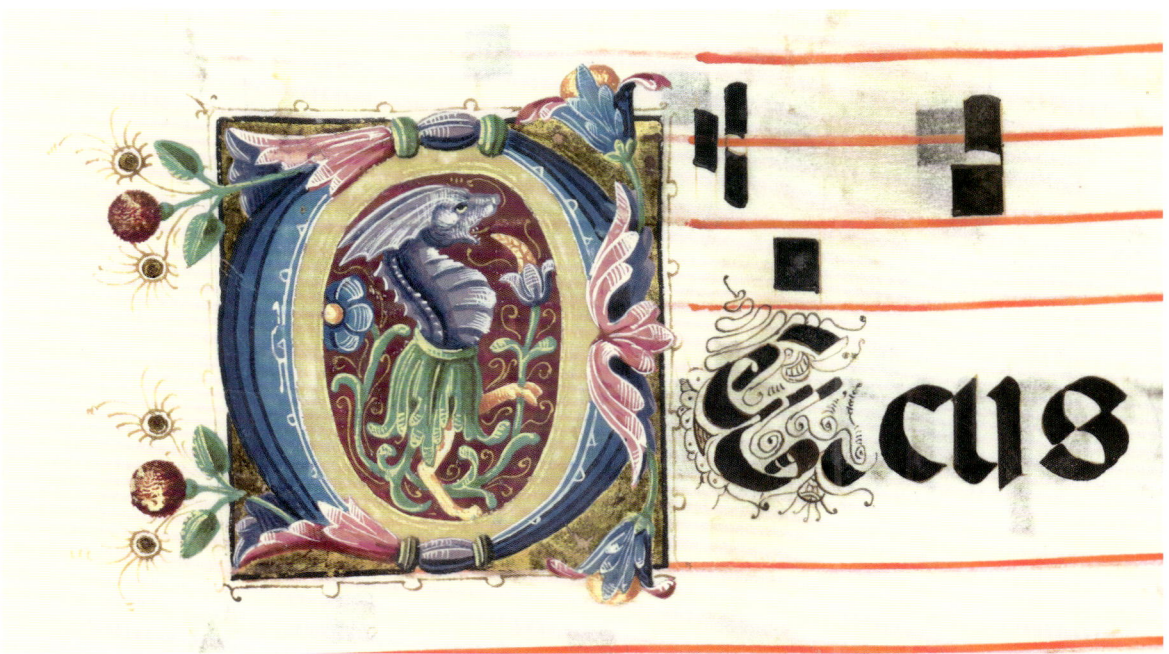

30 Giuliano Amadei, *Initial C, Crucem sanctam – Hybrid*, Antiphonary MS 16, fol.35^r, *c.*1495, tempera and gold leaf on parchment, 6 × 5 cm (2 ⅜ × 2 in), Archivio Storico Diocesano, Lucca

31 Eufrasia Burlamacchi, *Initial D, Decus magis – Hybrid*, Antiphonary MS 14, fol.56^r, *c.*1515–20, tempera and gold leaf on parchment, 7 × 5 cm (2 ¾ × 2 in), Archivio Storico Diocesano, Lucca

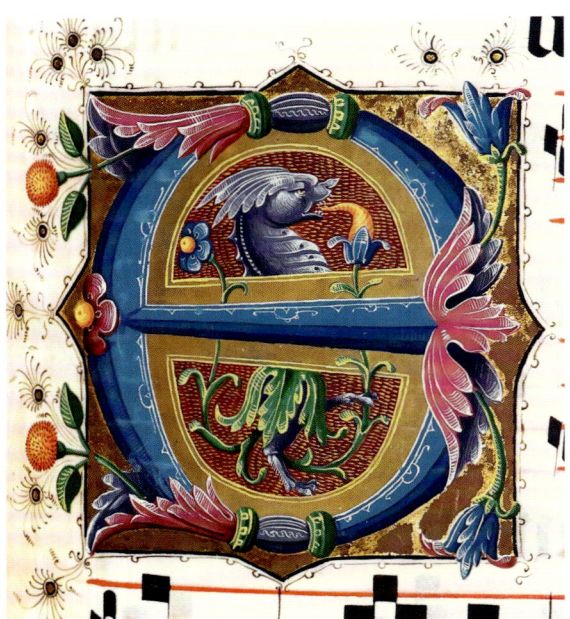

32 Eufrasia Burlamacchi, *Initial E, Exaudi domine vocem meam – Hybrid*, Gradual MS 2650, fol.92ʳ, *c.*1532, tempera and gold leaf on parchment, 15 × 14.5 cm (5⅞ × 5¾ in), Biblioteca Statale, Lucca

have already been acknowledged within religious and secular environments. In fact, in *c.*1515 she had completed the five manuscripts for her convent, an enterprise that may have granted her the opportunity to intervene in a manuscript for San Martino, the most important church of Lucca.

Eufrasia's direct observation of the art of Giuliano Amadei enriched her iconographic repertory and suggested some important changes in her technique. On fol.56ʳ of MS 14 (fig.31), Eufrasia, looking at the fanciful animal created by Amadei on fol.35ʳ of MS 16 (fig.30), did not change the hybrid in profile with its open mouth, the flower on the left or the plant on the right. Likely due to the small size of the initial, she diminished the energy of the animal while retaining many of the details of Amadei's model. In *c.*1532 Eufrasia re-elaborated again the same decorative model on fol.92ʳ of Gradual 2650 for the monastery of San Romano (fig.32). This time, she had plenty of space at her disposal, but she did not reproduce the hybrid, playing freely with both foreground and background. Within the ornamental 'stage', two flowers occupy the middle zone, solving a visual issue connected to the compression of space provoked by the horizontal bar of the initial E. In the end, rather than privileging the fanciful features of the hybrid, Eufrasia made the letter E the true protagonist of the folium. The bars of the E – with their mauve and azure acanthus leaves and yellow fruits that resemble the berries of the strawberry tree – and also the hybrid, become sculptural thanks to the subtle variations of blue, an effect produced by light seemingly coming from the upper part of the page.

5

A Blessed Hand, Expert in Colour, Ornament and Chant

ANTIPHONARIES MSS 1, 2, 3 AND 4 FOR SAN
DOMENICO, *c*.1505–13

Around 1505, Eufrasia undertook the largest of
her artistic enterprises. She wrote, notated and
illuminated five manuscripts, MSS 1, 2, 3, 4 and 5, four
Antiphonaries and one Gradual, that are now in a
Dominican convent in California. She received this
commission from her prioress, Sister Petra Cenami,
to provide the community with books for the Divine
Office and the Mass in San Domenico (fig.33).[1] These
manuscripts were kept by the Dominican nuns even
after the convent's suppression in 1892, escaping the
confiscations of manuscripts, paintings and sculptures
perpetrated once in 1806 with the Napoleonic
suppressions and a second time in 1866 after the
unification of Italy.[2] The nuns still had the volumes in
the Capucine convent they bought in 1892 at Lucca,
where in 1914 Innocenzo Taurisano saw and described
them with appreciative words.[3] But in 1927, when the
nuns moved from Lucca to the Santa Maria del Sasso
monastery at Bibbiena, near Arezzo, the five choral
books were no longer in their possession, as we will
see below.

The most exhaustive analysis of the five choir
manuscripts, although unpublished, is by Bernard
M. Rosenthal, dated 15 May 1991.[4] That they were
conceived as a set is shown by some meaningful

elements: their matching size (54.2 × 38.5 cm each);
the uniformly written text, in a very large Gothic
minuscule with the music supplied in the form of
large square notes on red four-line staves, five text
lines and five staves per page. The same black and
dark brown ink has been employed for the text and
the music, while the chapter headings, the antiphons,
the responses and the versicles are provided in red
ink. The whole set of manuscripts shows uniformity
in figural and ornamental apparatuses.

At the end of the 1920s, the Very Rev. Bede Jarrett,
Provincial of the Dominicans in England, bought the
five manuscripts from a bookseller in Rome, to whom
the books had been consigned for sale by the Lucchese
nuns 'as they were so poor'. In 1929 the manuscripts
migrated to the Unites States, as a gift from Jarrett to
the Dominican sisters in California, in appreciation
of their 'Dominicanism, its fire and its fidelity'.[5]
Rosenthal approached his study of the five manuscripts
with the attitude of a connoisseur requested to write
an objective analysis as much as with the appreciative
gaze of the dealer: 'We thus have an extraordinary
combination of features, seldom encountered together:
known place of origin and artist, known date,
completeness, unbroken documented provenance and
virtually original condition.'

Eufrasia accomplished the five choir books in a
period of no less than ten years, a justifiable span of

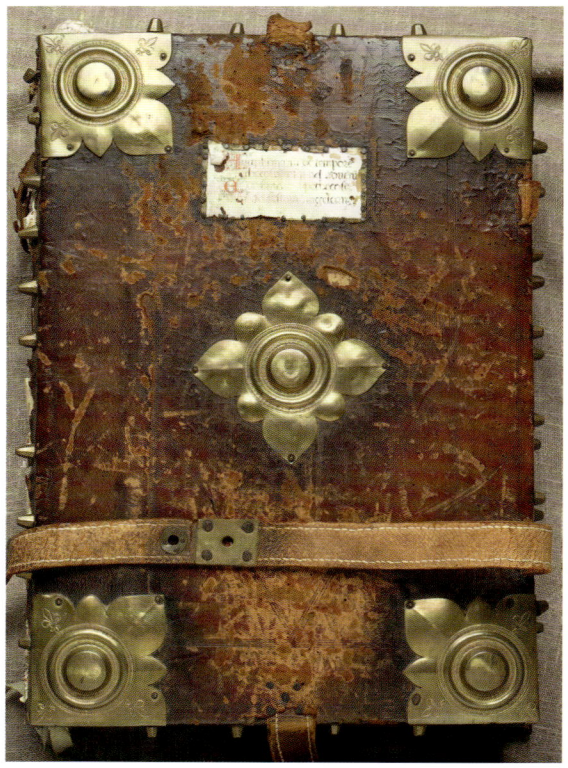

In these five manuscripts, Eufrasia manifested a progressive assurance in handling forms and colours in the representations of Jesus Christ, the Virgin Mary and the saints. While in MS 1 the only decoration consists of six ornamental letters and six penwork initials, MS 2 includes one historiated initial, and subsequent manuscripts reveal a regular increase in sacred stories and portrayals of saints. MSS 3 and 4 show three and four historiated initials respectively, while in MS 5, the Gradual, one witnesses a notable increase in figures, with 12 historiated initials, remarkable for their iconography and variety of colours. As a norm, Eufrasia tended to represent sacred scenes by reducing the elements to the essential, avoiding any reference to arches, ruins and other archaeological features fashionable in Florentine painting and illumination. As to the portrayal of saints, she opted for the half-bust in frontal view, always adding the traditional iconographic attribute that helps to identify the figure.

ANTIPHONARY MS 1, c.1505

Probably the first manuscript written and decorated by Eufrasia, MS 1, an Antiphonary, comprises a few ornamental initials with flowers, fruits and slender acanthus leaves, while the centre of each letter, uniformly depicted in blue, is decorated with white lines forming arabesques. This manuscript seems the work of an artist cautiously proceeding to find her personal manner of expression. Although lacking the variety of iconographic solutions of MS 5 of the series, MS 1 is important for the precision and elegance of the script, the musical notes and the ornamental letters that were to become a constant in the manuscripts written, notated and decorated by Eufrasia until c.1532. Moreover, MS 1 includes a detail that identifies the miniaturist.

33 Original front cover, Antiphonary MS 3, c.1510, leather-covered wooden boards, brass corner bosses, brass centrepiece, rows of pointed studs along the edges, 56 × 40 cm (22 × 15¾ in), Dominican Convent, California

time considering the number and variety of decorations and the size of each volume. As the chronicler of San Giorgio convent at Lucca wrote in 1527, the nuns worked to earn their living and were specialised in making fabric in silk and flax, embroidering, stitching and writing the choir books using large letters, notes and miniatures.[6] As demonstrated above, these books for the Divine Office and the Mass were described in documents of 1527 and 1548 by the nun-chroniclers of San Domenico.[7]

Eufrasia never signed the manuscripts she decorated nor wrote a colophon proper, apart from the note I will treat in the Epilogue, which was attached to the spine of Gradual MS 5 and is now lost. Even these few lines do not report her name. However, it is likely that she found another way to show her presence. I suggest that we interpret as such her choice to add two cherries hanging from acanthus leaves, an 'emblem' that first appeared in Antiphonary MS 1 (*c.*1505), fol.193ᵛ (fig.34), then in MS 3 (*c.*1510), fol.1ʳ (see fig.38), in Antiphonary MS 14 (*c.*1515–20), fols 51ʳ and 117ʳ (see fig.29) and in Gradual 2649 (*c.*1530), fol.49ᵛ (see fig.71). One may object that this was simply a decorative device akin to the fruit, garlands and festoons that Eufrasia included in the manuscripts she decorated. However, while apples, strawberry tree fruits and grapes are not only pervasive but also integrated into the ornamental system of each letter, the two large-sized cherries, by contrast, stand alone, always hanging from a support, ready to attract our attention with their illusionistic three-dimensionality, thereby inviting us to assign them a meaning.

One might be tempted to interpret the two cherries symbolically. Here, the reference text is by Mirella Levi D'Ancona, entirely devoted to botanical symbolism in the Renaissance. Excluding the meaning connected to eating, as in the scenes of the *Flight into Egypt* and as an attribute of the Blessed Gerard of Villamagna (near Florence), who miraculously received a bunch of cherries in January before dying, three alternative meanings can be considered. The first issues from the appearance and substance of the fruit. On account of its red colour and juice, the cherry symbolised the blood of Christ. For this reason, it was often depicted in scenes of the Last Supper and the Supper at Emmaus. The second meaning refers to the cherry's sweetness. It became the symbol of good works that produce sweetness in the hearts of those who accomplish them. The third alternative relates to

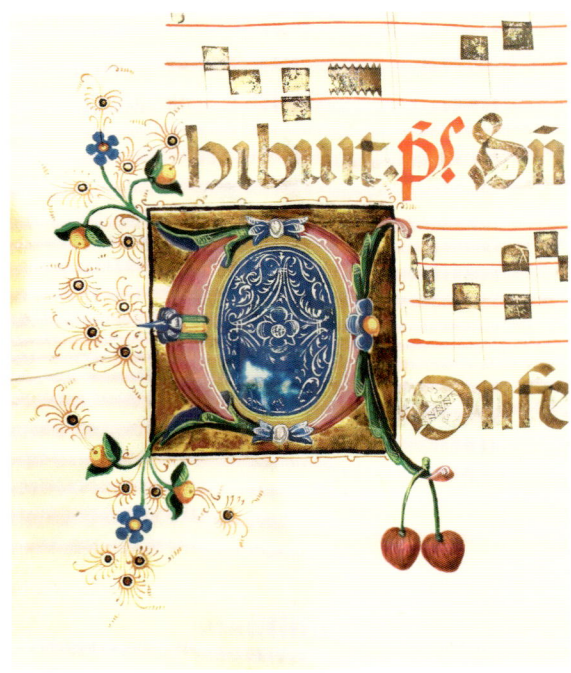

34 Eufrasia Burlamacchi, *Initial C, Confessor Dei – Ornamental Letter with Two Hanging Cherries*, Antiphonary MS 1, fol.193ᵛ, *c.*1505, tempera and gold leaf on parchment, 9.5 × 8 cm (3 ¾ × 3 ⅛ in), Dominican Convent, California

the cherry as the symbol of spring, being the first tree to bear fruit after winter. For this reason, the cherry is often represented in scenes of the Annunciation and Incarnation of Christ.[8]

Would Eufrasia have been aware of these associations? And even if she were, how could we determine which one she was alluding to whenever she reproduced the two juicy cherries? All in all, I would argue for the coexistence of all three meanings, which in no way exclude each other. Rather, they are complementary. But what matters most is that, while Eufrasia's style changed through time, the formal and chromatic rendition of these two fruits never

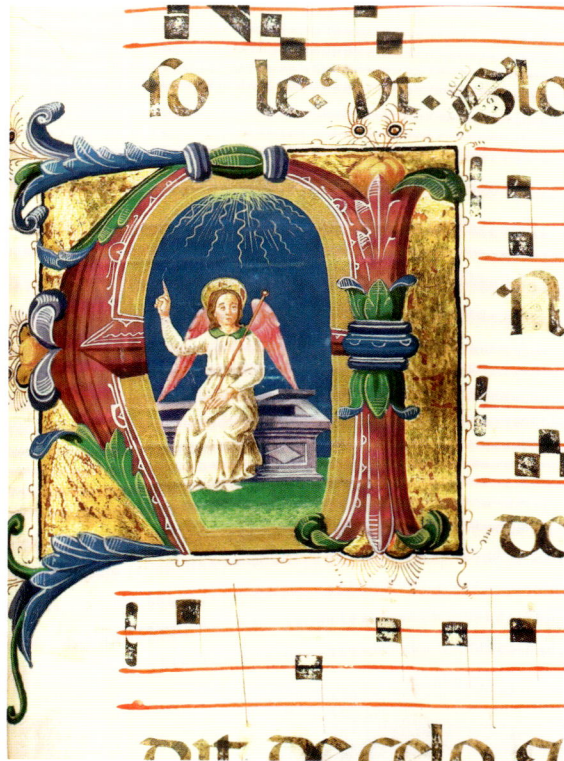

35 Eufrasia Burlamacchi, *Initial A, Angelus autem domini –
Angel Seated on Christ's Empty Tomb*, Antiphonary
MS 2, fol.160ʳ, *c.*1507, tempera and gold leaf on parchment,
14 × 14 cm (5½ × 5½ in), Dominican Convent, California

underwent modifications, a possible indication that she
selected them as her personal emblem.

ANTIPHONARY MS 2, *c.*1507

In the second Antiphonary, ornamental and penwork
initials are the majority, as in MS 1. But this time,
on fol.160ʳ, Eufrasia introduced the first historiated
initial in these volumes, featuring an angel seated
on Christ's empty tomb in an initial A (fig.35). The

initial has acquired the architectural structure that
was to become the norm in many of the initials in
Antiphonary MS 14 and in the two-volume Gradual
MSS 2649–50. The subdued colours of the bars
covered with leaves seem to conform with the general
meaning of the scene. Eufrasia did not represent the
women at the sepulchre; their surprise in finding the
tomb without a lid and in seeing an angel 'clothed in
a long white garment' addressing them is synthesised
in the angel's calm and momentous gesture: the index
finger of his right hand points to Heaven, a clear
declaration that 'Ye seek Jesus of Nazareth, which was
crucified: he is risen; he is not here' (Mark 16:5–6).

Eufrasia depicted the simple and unpretentious
figure of the angel, whose clothes are modelled by
light and shade, as engaged in a gestural dialogue
with the beholder, even more evident thanks to the
compact blue background of the letter. The recourse
to simplicity for a devotional image is not of course
Eufrasia's invention; among religious institutions,
it was at the Florentine monastery of San Marco
that in the first decade of the sixteenth century the
rediscovery of the 'sacred' value of Fra Angelico's
painting occurred, featuring simplified forms, limited
chroma and clear intelligibility of the religious
message. This was the work of a group of artists
– comprising Fra Bartolomeo, Lorenzo di Credi
(1459/60–1537), Giovanni Antonio Sogliani (1492–
1544), Fra Paolino da Pistoia, Antonio del Ceraiolo,
Mariotto Albertinelli (1474–1515) and Cosimo Rosselli
(1439–1507) – that sought to reform religious painting
following Girolamo Savonarola's ideas on art.[9]

Savonarola believed that images assisted the
faithful to remember divine things and could
represent in a synthetic and understandable form
meanings too difficult to be otherwise grasped. Very
much concerned with the correct development of the
Christian community, he saw art as a labour, lest its
practitioners fall prey to the sin of pride. The painter
of religious images should be a good Christian and, at
the same time, a proficient master, prompting people

to devotion. Savonarola was especially against the sin of superfluity (*superfluità*), not only in the arts but also in other relations, as of the individual with God and the Church. All in all, for him the only value of art, intended in both the intellectual and the mechanical sense, lay in its didactic functions and in prompting spiritual and mystical experiences.[10]

For Savonarola, simplicity was to be pursued not only in art but also in the moral sphere, being among the most important Christian virtues. Its personification appears in his 1495 *Compendium of Revelations* (*Compendio di Revelatione*) as Savonarola's companion to his embassy to Paradise, holding in her hands a covered gift for the Virgin Mary. This gift, a three-tiered crown, was anything but simple, but it was Simplicity that, with her attitude, showed how this lavish object was the most suitable gift to honour Mary.[11] Savonarola codified his views in his *On the Simplicity of Christian Life* (*De simplicitate christianae vitae*), published in Florence in 1496, first in Latin, later in the vernacular.[12] Simplicity, however, can appear in various forms and does not derive from mere reduction of elements. In the field of art, simplicity depends on the atmosphere of restraint in form and colour and on an ordered composition. Eufrasia considered these two factors from the outset of her artistic career, bringing them to their perfect manifestation in the two-volume Gradual for the San Romano monastery.

ANTIPHONARY MS 3, *c.*1510

The historiated, ornamental and large penwork initials of MS 3 show that Eufrasia had entered into a new phase of her artistic development. She represented Saint Mary Magdalene, half-length, praying, Saint Dominic and the Virgin Mary, along with ten ornamental initials, some very elaborate, and 30 large penwork initials. In the representation of the Virgin Mary, it becomes manifest how Eufrasia developed

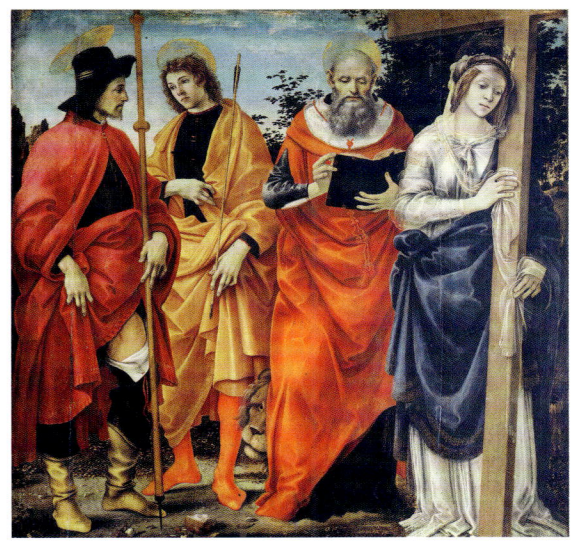

36 Filippino Lippi, *The Saints Roch, Sebastian, Jerome and Helena*, 1481–2, tempera on panel, 157.5 × 147 cm (62 × 57 ⅞ in), Chiesa di San Michele in Foro, Lucca

some features of painting in alignment especially with the work of Filippino Lippi (1457–1504).

A FLEMISH GAZE?

Filippino received two commissions from Lucchese patrons, both in the early 1480s: the Magrini Altarpiece (1481–2), featuring *The Saints Roch, Sebastian, Jerome and Helena*, which is still in the church of San Michele in Foro in Lucca (fig.36), and the Bernardi Altarpiece (1482–3) for the now demolished church of Santa Maria del Corso in Lucca. The latter work comprises two painted panels, titled *Saints Benedict and Apollonia* and *Saints Paul and Frediano*, now in the Norton Simon Museum in Pasadena, and a wooden statue of *Saint Anthony Abbot* by Benedetto da Maiano (1442–97),

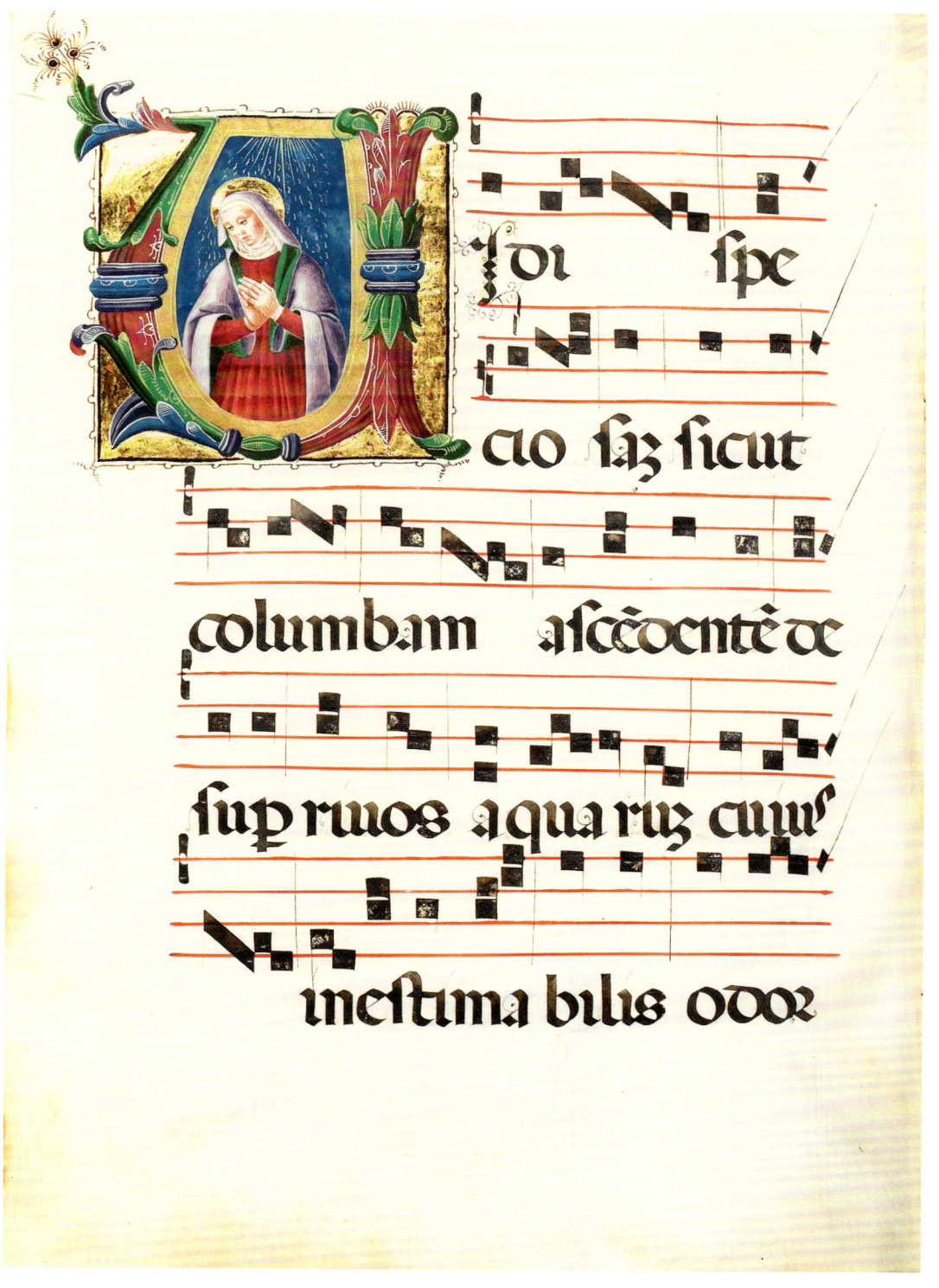

37 Eufrasia Burlamacchi, *Initial V, Vidi speciosam sicut columbam – The Virgin Mary*, Antiphonary MS 3, fol.270^v,
   *c.*1510, tempera and gold leaf on parchment, folium 54.2 × 38.5 cm (21 ⅜ × 15 ⅛ in), initial 14.2 × 14 cm
   (5 ⅝ × 5 ½ in), Dominican Convent, California

polychromed by Filippino, now in the Museo Nazionale di Villa Guinigi in Lucca.[13]

In the Magrini Altarpiece, the rhythmical articulation of the hands and the richness of the folds of the saints' cloaks may have inspired any artist in search of formal novelties to emulate or modify.[14] But for Eufrasia, as a Dominican artist, stylistic inventions came second to the expression of religious content, which, on many occasions, passed through meditation on the mysteries of faith. Perhaps it is this aspect that ideally connects Eufrasia with Filippino: when she depicted Mary and the saints, she always insisted on restrained attitudes, humility and pensive expressions, three ways to manifest devotion in figural representation. The Saint Helena by Filippino and the Virgin Mary depicted by Eufrasia in MS 3, initial V, fol.270ᵛ, remind us that the expression of such sentiments was also believed to be proper to Flemish art (fig.37).

However, a document in the Archivio di Stato at Lucca allows us to put aside the time-honoured explanation that the knowledge of Flemish art first reached Lucca through Filippino in the early 1480s. No doubt, when Filippino's artistic development took place in the last quarter of the fifteenth century, Florentine interest in Flemish painting was widespread, thanks to the agency of merchants and collectors, among whom were some patrons of the painter. His early acquaintance with a work by Jan van Eyck – *Saint Francis Receiving the Stigmata*, 1435–41, Galleria Sabauda, Turin – inspired him at least in the rendition of the landscape when he worked jointly with Sandro Botticelli on the *Adoration of the Magi*, c.1470–72, now in National Gallery, London, no. 592.[15]

But knowledge of Flemish painting had already reached Lucca before Filippino's arrival in the city and was due, to a certain degree, to the trade traffic of the Lucchese merchants headquartered in Bruges since the fourteenth century.[16] The document referred to above alludes to a *Pietà*, painted by Jan Van Eyck (c.1390–1441) on a circular panel (*compasso*), which belonged in

1480 to the Lucchese noblewoman Agata di Poggio. In an agreement with the Lucchese artists Matteo Civitali and Michele di Michele Ciampanti (c.1450–c.1511), subscribed before a notary, Agata declared that she showed the tondo to them both. Her request was to have it perfectly reproduced in the central part of a predella for an altarpiece on the family altar in the church of San Romano; today the whereabouts of both works is unknown.[17] Paula Nuttall connected the widespread tendency to require from Lucchese artists copies of Flemish artworks to the idea that these images best expressed devout sentiments.[18] But even in works made by Italian artists like Fra Angelico, Filippo Lippi and Fra Paolino da Pistoia, such sentiments are easily recognisable.

Without discounting the religious side of the issue, I suspect that what happened in Lucca in the fifteenth century was more a matter of fashion and fame than an expression of intense devoutness. Some painters in Lucca in the second half of the fourteenth century had already depicted a melancholic mood in wall paintings and panels of Mary with the Christ Child.[19] The name of Jan van Eyck may have circulated as a brand denoting quality, a product highly valued in the art market by the same Lucchese merchants who were trading luxury products.

No doubt, Eufrasia's illumination belongs to an art that articulates devout emotions but with subtleties and individualised intensity and precision that can hardly be exclusively associated with Northern European painting. Nor can she have any share in Michelangelo's opinion – as reported by Francisco de Hollanda – that the painting of Flanders appealed 'to women, especially the very old or the very young, and likewise to monks and nuns, and to some noblemen who are tone-deaf to true harmony'.[20] Eufrasia, a woman religious who produced art for both nuns and monks, never renounced the rules of naturalism, combining artistically effective, harmonious composition and devout sentiments to encourage devotion. Here, some more specific words about her sources of inspiration are in order.

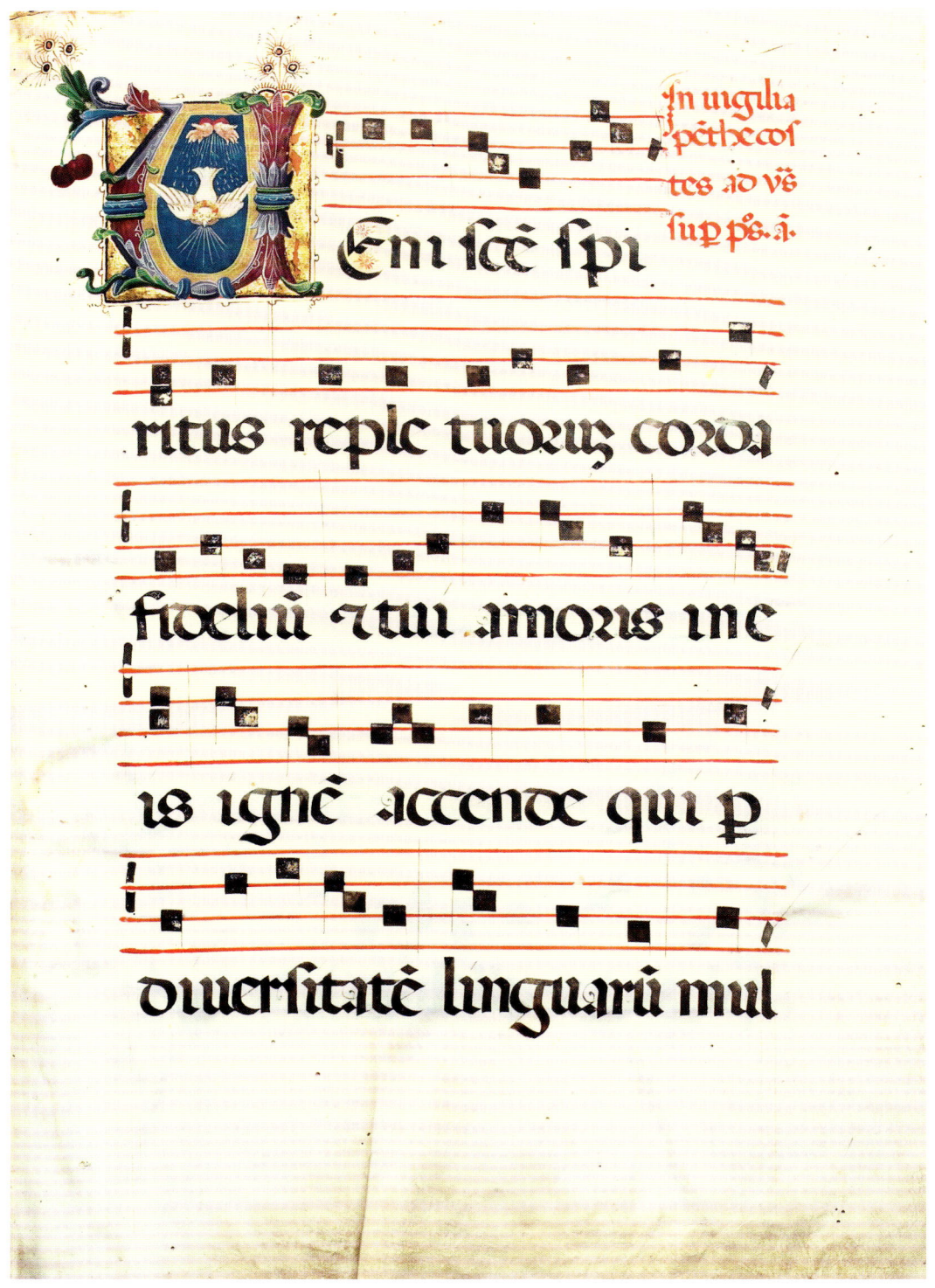

38 Eufrasia Burlamacchi, *Initial V, Veni sancte spiritus – The Holy Ghost*, Antiphonary MS 3, fol.1ʳ, *c.*1510, tempera
    and gold leaf on parchment, folium 54.2 × 38.5 cm (21⅜ × 15⅛ in), initial 8.5 × 8 cm (3⅜ × 3⅛ in),
    Dominican Convent, California

SOURCES OF INSPIRATION: FROM HEAVEN TO EARTH AND BACK

In a recent contribution, Fredrika H. Jacobs raised the question of the sources of inspiration for nun-artists. She stated that conventual communities were sympathetic to mystical visions, claiming that recording them kept many a blessed hand (*benedetta mano*) busy. The Poor Clare Caterina Vigri's (1413–63) visions in the convent of the Corpus Domini in Bologna might have inspired her to write poems and prayers and, also, offered material for her paintings.[21] When these visions occurred in the convent of San Domenico in Lucca, the nun-chroniclers were particularly careful to provide the reader with plenty of details for spiritual edification and, also, to elevate their convent's standing. Heavenly manifestations were seen as the proof of God's preference bestowed upon the convent, showed to the nuns by means of his angels and saints. These extraordinary happenings also helped the nun-chroniclers to substantially differentiate the necrologies of the community, which were otherwise monotonously similar. Visionary experiences elevated the sisters who had them: they were the holy recipients of God's messages.

Eufrasia never experienced mystical visions, but she gave visual form to texts that resonated with them, as in the descent of the Holy Spirit depicted as a dove in MS 3, fol.1ʳ (fig.38): 'Come Holy Ghost to fill the hearts of your faithful and kindle in them the fire of your love who through the variety of tongues [...].'[22] The image presents the Holy Ghost in terms emphasised by the text: the small flames proceed from God's hands to the faithful. Eufrasia thus alludes to what lies beyond the image, that is, the hearts of those who will receive the flames. The vision is given concrete form through an interplay between God's offering hands and the Holy Ghost, who seems to depart from the blue sky to enter the space of the chants and prayers of the nuns.

Eufrasia's illumination of this vision expresses visually the mystical potential of the cloister, as

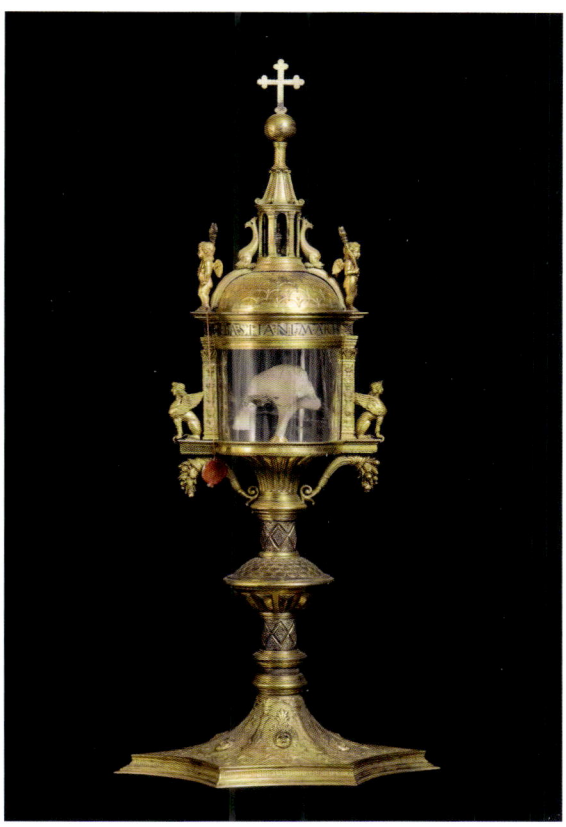

39 Francesco Marti, *Saint Sebastian Reliquary*, before 1491, silver gilt, rock crystal, height 45 cm (17¾ in), Cattedrale di San Martino, Lucca

evidenced by a written description of the later vision of another nun, Sister Perpetua (1497–1534), included in a 1534 necrology in the Chronica of San Domenico. The daughter of the Lucchese goldsmith Francesco di Leonardo Pagni da Marti (1458–1542), Sister Perpetua entered the convent in 1515 at 18 years of age, having already trained in her father's workshop.[23] In fact, she became renowned among the nuns for her proficiency in embroidering with gold and silver threads. Growing older, her sight diminished but 'the

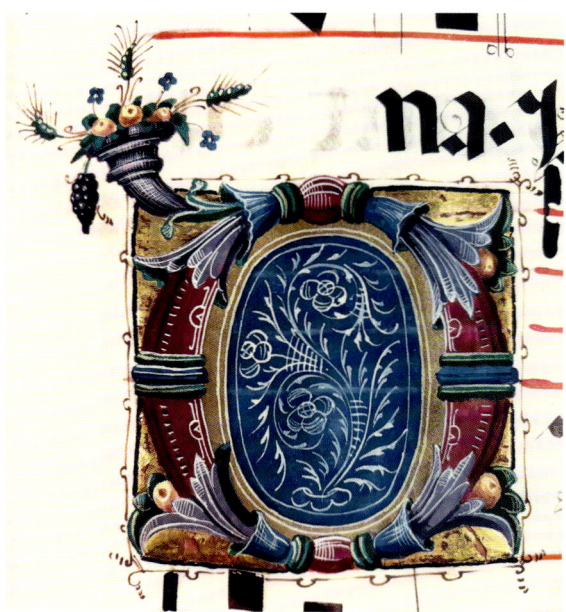

40 Eufrasia Burlamacchi, *Initial D, Dum – Cornucopia
with Spikes, Apples, Bunch of Grapes, Acanthus Leaves
and Flowers*, Antiphonary MS 3, fol.8ʳ, *c.*1510, tempera
and gold leaf on parchment, 8.5 × 8 cm (3⅜ × 3⅛ in),
Dominican Convent, California

intellectual eyes were extremely well endowed with
light'. She often detached herself from the physical
world through prayer, and it was at those moments
that 'God manifested himself by revealing to her the
mysteries of the Incarnation and Passion of Jesus [. . .]'.
The nun-chronicler ends Sister Perpetua's necrology
with a note suspended between the human and the
divine: 'She foresaw many future things, but it is not so
clear whether it depended on her natural instinct or on
angelic revelation.'[24]

Sister Perpetua's mystical visions, so evocative in
terms of visual representations, occurred after 1515.
By that year, Eufrasia had already accomplished the
first set of choir books for her convent. She may
have remembered Sister Perpetua's mystical visions

in the illumination of the manuscripts that followed,
all completed by *c.*1532; at the same time, one
should not dismiss the possibility that the tangible
representations of visions in the liturgical books made
by Eufrasia helped stimulate nuns' visions.

Eufrasia may have had access to designs for
artworks at San Domenico through Sister Perpetua
and her sibling, Sister Felicita (1495–1534). Felicita
entered the convent when she was 17 years old. Like
Perpetua, she was trained in metalwork by their father
Francesco Marti. He had produced a reliquary of
Saint Sebastian for San Martino Cathedral in Lucca
(fig.39), among other works, which was recorded
in the cathedral's inventory of 1492.[25] Aspects of
its design derived from drawings Marti kept in his
workshop, which he used also for other productions.
Documents record that Marti's drawings were
extremely accurate, presenting the designs for projects
in their minutest detail. It seems more than likely
that both Felicita and Perpetua, after using drawings
in their father's workshop, brought some of them to
the San Domenico convent, where they continued
and presumably perfected the artistic activity they
had started in the family context. They may have
shared these drawings with Eufrasia, especially for
the composition of cornucopias, fruit and chalices,
as we will see shortly. These two instances of family
training document that not all artistic proficiency was
acquired within the convent out of natural ability.

Nevertheless, the necrologies of the San Domenico
Chronica describe innate artistic tendencies with
notes bordering on the miraculous. This was the
case of Sister Hilaria Samminiati (1548–78). Her
'noteworthy inclination to art' led her to paint several
panels featuring the Christ Child, Mary and Jesus
and the face of the suffering Saviour.[26] This reference
to natural artistic ability might be seen as a device to
highlight a sister's life as much as the convent's unique
atmosphere, were it not that the nun-chroniclers knew
well the difference between a trained and an untrained
artist. The 1534 necrology of Sister Felicita illustrates

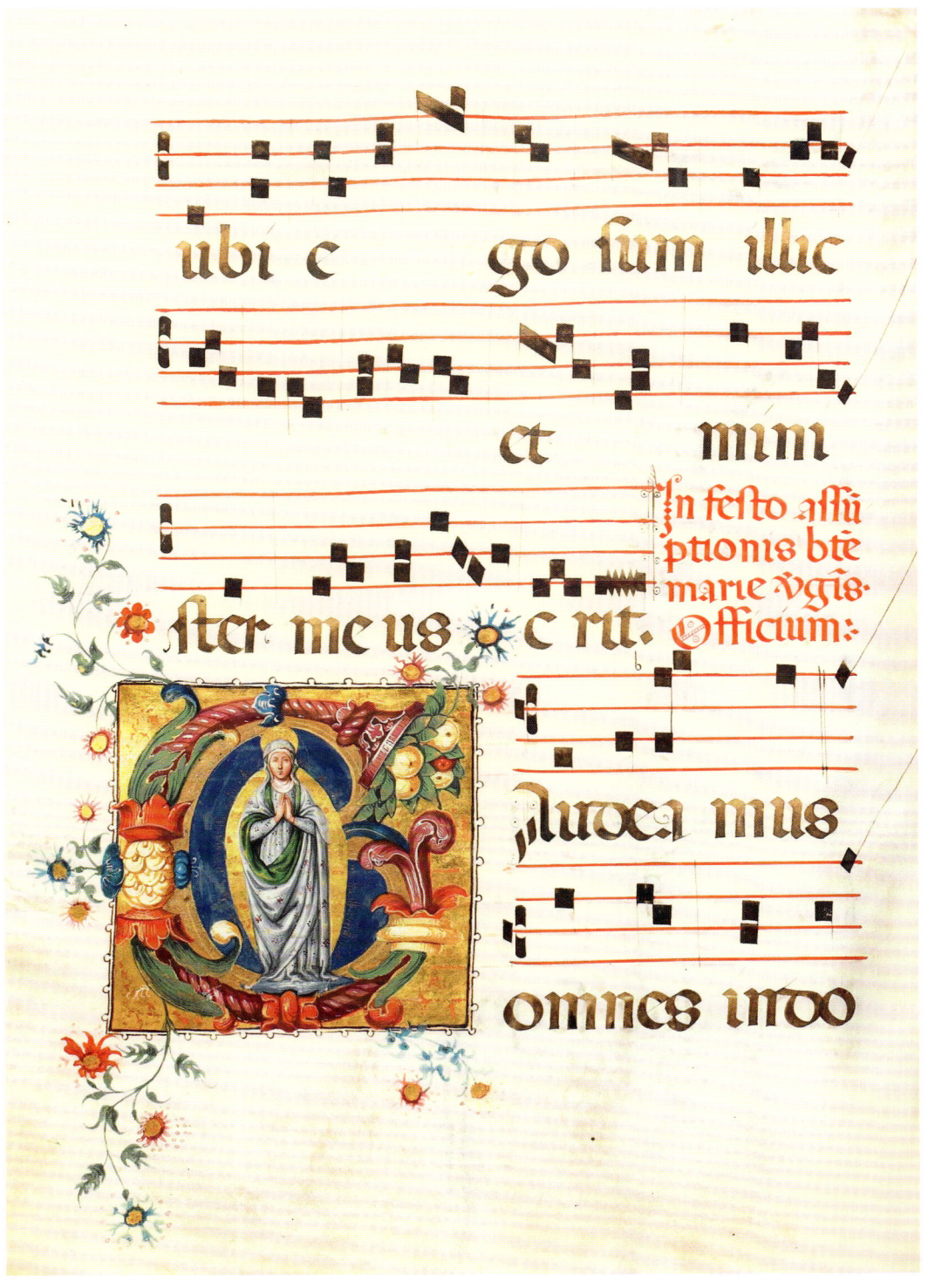

41 Eufrasia Burlamacchi, *Initial G, Gaudeamus omnes – The Assumption of Mary*, Gradual MS 5, fol.168ᵛ, *c*.1515, tempera and gold leaf on parchment, folium 54.2 × 38.5 cm (21⅜ × 15⅛ in), initial 14 × 14 cm (5½ × 5½ in), Dominican Convent, California

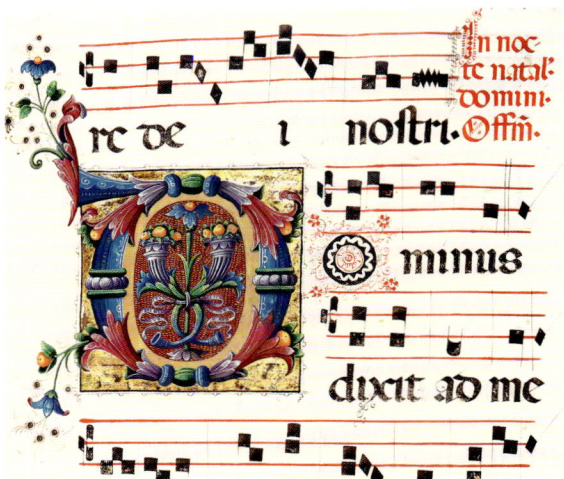

42 Eufrasia Burlamacchi, *Initial D, Dominus dixit – Cornucopias, Fruit, Flowers, Acanthus Leaves and Ribbons*, Gradual MS 2649, fol.41ʳ, *c.*1530, tempera and gold leaf on parchment, 14 × 13.7 cm (5½ × 5⅜ in), Biblioteca Statale, Lucca

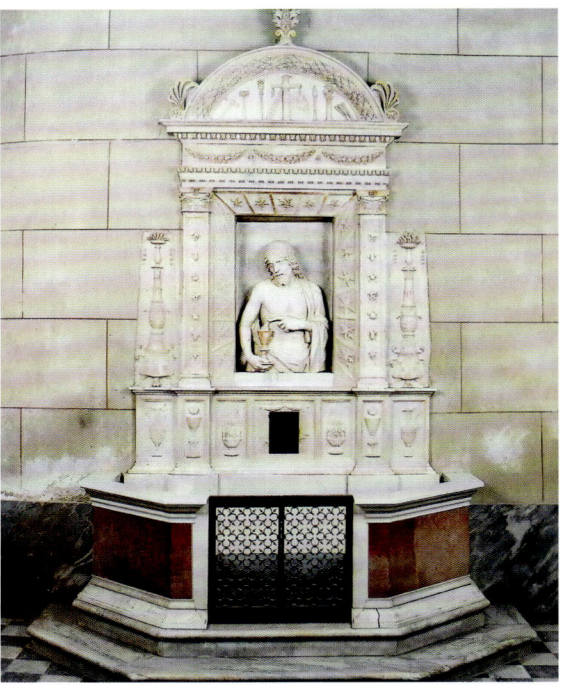

43 Matteo Civitali, *Altar of Christ's Body*, 1496–1501, marble, 450 × 280 cm (177⅛ × 110¼ in), Pieve di Santa Maria e San Jacopo, Lammari (Lucca)

the point. After expressing her own evaluation, the nun-chronicler eagerly reports the judgement of an expert in the goldsmith's art – Sister Felicita's father – on what she had produced:

> [She] worked with her hands in a marvellously accurate manner and was capable of making with them whatever she wished. With golden and silver threads, she made the crown for the Virgin in the inner church; her father, an excellent goldsmith, said that had he received the commission to make such a crown, he would have hardly been able to produce one as beautiful.[27]

If the Marti sisters shared with Eufrasia the drawings used by their father to decorate the Saint Sebastian reliquary, or other similar drawings to which they had access, she would have had at her disposal useful examples of cornucopias filled with

fruits and leaves to be adapted to form the bodies of her initial letters. These *all'antica* containers started to appear in Eufrasia's illumination in Antiphonary MS 3, fol.8ʳ (*c.*1510; fig.40), an initial D with the short ascender featuring a metallic cornucopia filled with apples, ears of corn, leaves and a bunch of grapes.

Eufrasia depicted many cornucopias in the five manuscripts for San Domenico, generally with a smooth surface that best reflected the light, as in the later Gradual MS 5 (*c.*1515), fol.4ʳ, another ornamental D, but also fluted and twisted, as in the last historiated initial of Gradual MS 5, fol.168ᵛ, a G with *The Assumption of Mary* (fig.41), which also shows round 'metallic' motifs on the left similar to those seen in Francesco Marti's Saint Sebastian reliquary. These animated architectural bars, depicted with warm colours, confer movement to the static figure of Mary who, hands joined in prayer, is represented in full frontal view standing on a small cloud, ready to leave for the heavenly sphere.

In the two-volume Gradual for San Romano (1527–*c*.1532), cornucopias appear only once, in MS 2649, fol.41ʳ (fig.42), as the inner decoration of the initial D of *Dominus*, with flutes and a ring forming the brim decorated with half circles, as in Marti's reliquary. On this occasion, Eufrasia dismissed the role of cornucopias as constitutive elements of the letter's frame, prevalent in the California series. By enhancing a decorative pattern as if it were a protagonist of a letter, Eufrasia showed her closeness to Giuliano Amadei's decorative solutions in MS 16 for San Martino Cathedral (see figs 28 and 30 above). At the same time, she departed from him by emphasising the interplay between cornucopias, both empty and filled with fruit, and ribbons that grant stability to the fanciful composition.

Eufrasia also represented another kind of container – a chalice – that had a symbolic value for her community. She certainly knew by direct visual experience the form of this liturgical object, but a drawing would have eased its transposition into illumination. I think here of the drawings of Francesco Marti, but also of some sketches by Matteo Civitali for sculptural monuments. By the end of the 1490s Civitali had already sculpted in San Martino Cathedral some funerary monuments and altars ornamented with antiquarian motifs, such as palmettes, garlands of fruit and laurel, lion masks, shields and medallions. Examples are the 1472 tomb of the humanist and papal secretary Pietro da Noceto (1397–1467) and that of the Cathedral's *Operario* Domenico Bertini (1479), the *Altar of San Regolo* (1484) and the *Tempietto del Volto Santo* (1484).[28] Civitali sculpted the *Altar of the Sacrament* (1488)) for the Church of San Frediano, and the funerary monument

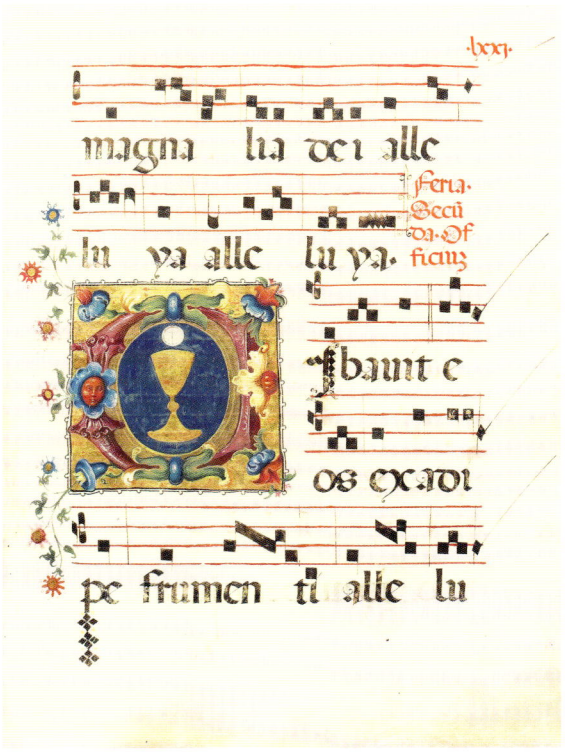

44 Eufrasia Burlamacchi, *Initial C, Cibavit eos – Chalice and Host*, Gradual MS 5, fol.71ʳ, *c*.1515, tempera and gold leaf on parchment, folium 54.2 × 38.5 cm (21⅜ × 15⅛ in), initial 14 × 14 cm (5½ × 5½ in), Dominican Convent, California

dedicated to the patron saint in the church of San Romano (1490).[29] He sculpted a beautiful chalice for the altar in San Frediano that he replicated in the *Altar of Christ's Body* in the church of Santa Maria e San Jacopo at Lammari, close to Lucca (fig.43).

Three chalices depicted by Eufrasia stand out as remarkably sculptural and likely inspired by Civitali's examples: Antiphonary MS 3, fol.46ᵛ; Gradual MS 5, fol.71ʳ (fig.44); and Gradual MS 2650, fol.103ʳ. Nuns considered chalices important not only for the celebration of the Mass but also in the rituals

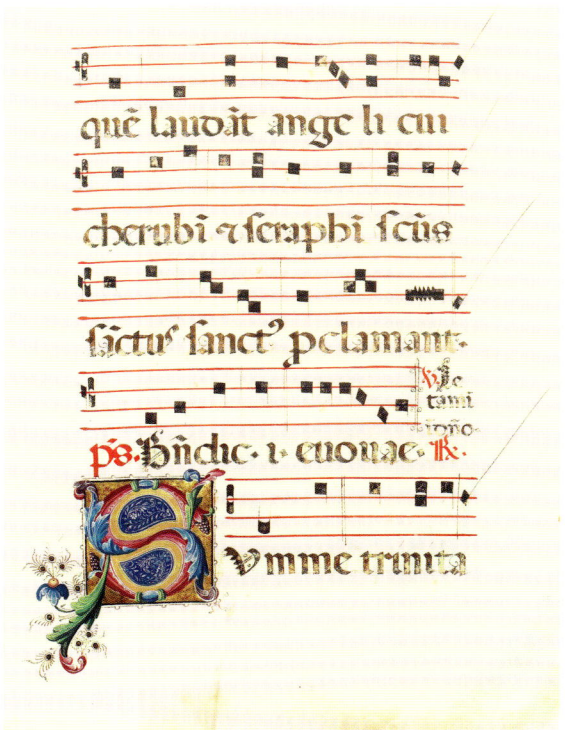

45 Eufrasia Burlamacchi, *Initial S, Summe trinitati –
Acanthus Leaves, Fruit and Flowers*, Antiphonary MS
4, fol.25ʳ, *c*.1513, tempera and gold leaf on parchment,
folium 54.2 × 38.5 cm (21⅜ × 15⅛ in), initial 8 × 8 cm
(3⅛ × 3⅛ in), Dominican Convent, California

associated with death. In the necrologies of San
Domenico, the nun-chroniclers always specified
whether the nuns who passed away were able to
receive communion for the last time, in preparation
for uniting with God in Heaven, while reflecting
on their eagerness to receive it during their lives. A
chalice therefore possessed an important symbolic and
emotional value – the direct connection with the blood
of Christ – that Eufrasia conveyed by suspending it
on a blue background in the body of the letter, with a
white host bearing the sign of the cross.

For Antiphonary MS 4, Eufrasia created four
historiated initials, representing the Three Archangels,
Saint Cecilia, Saint Catherine of Alexandria and Saints
Peter and Paul, along with two ornamental initials, as
on fol.25ʳ (fig.45), and 31 large penwork letters. Since
the manuscript opens with the celebration of the feast
of the Archangels, fol.1ʳ features a miniature with
Gabriel, Michael and Raphael (fig.46). The Archangel
Gabriel was especially dear to Eufrasia, as we will see
in the Epilogue. He was mainly known in her time as
an important figure in two annunciations concerning
future births: the first to Zacharias (Luke 1:11–19) and
the second to the Virgin Mary (Luke 1:26–30). Eufrasia
entrusted to him through prayer the completion of her
first series of manuscripts for her convent.

For depicting this miniature, one of the few where
the characters are represented full-length, Eufrasia
might have had at her disposal two portable models
that served as initial points of reference. The first
was a bronze plaquette made by Francesco Marti,
the important Lucchese goldsmith and the father
of Sister Perpetua and Sister Felicita discussed
above.[30] Marti interpreted in his own way the
novel designs originating in Florence. He became
renowned for making crosses, liturgical objects and
bronze plaquettes which, apart from being kept as
small devotional objects, circulated as models in
artists' workshops.[31] It is highly probable that some
of Marti's plaquettes were in the hands of Eufrasia.
Many figures of saints may have derived from specific
plaquettes: with their linear treatment of the figures,
they were ready to be directly transposed within the
body of the initial letters.

The bronze plaquette I refer to features *Saint
George Killing the Dragon* (Museo Nazionale del
Bargello, Florence; fig.47). True, the Archangel
Michael in the initial D of Antiphonary MS 4, fol.1ʳ,
seems to have little in common with the dynamic
attitude of Saint George's body.[32] But one should

consider the various fashions the process of copying could take. More than a copy, Eufrasia's miniature is a transposition and adaptation of the figure in movement to the motionless inner space of the letter, with modifications that suit the context of an Antiphonary by more clearly invoking the quietude of spiritual engagement despite the raised sword, thereby uniting this figure with others in the volume.

The second model may have been a drawing made by another artist, Antonio del Ceraiolo, for his *Archangel Michael* for the church of the Santissima Annunziata in Florence, now in the Cenacolo di Andrea del Sarto at San Salvi (fig.48).[33] While the cuirass in Eufrasia's miniature is much like the one made by Marti, the shoes and the sword are more like those of Ceraiolo. The son of a wax modeller and later a pupil of Lorenzo di Credi and of Ridolfo del Ghirlandaio (1483–1561), Ceraiolo was active in Florence in the first quarter of the sixteenth century, when Eufrasia was illuminating the five choir books for the San Domenico convent. Although Eufrasia's rendition of Mary, Christ, saints and angels is the closest to Ceraiolo's style, she was never exposed directly to the artist's work since none of his images were in Lucca. For this reason, the striking similarities between works by the two artists should be explained through the circulation of drawings or prints from Ceraiolo to Eufrasia.

Eufrasia's miniature also allows us to consider the patronage of this series of manuscripts. Eufrasia represented Saint Michael with a shield bearing a coat of arms, a red cross on a white field: was it perhaps a clue to the patronage of a Lucchese nobleman, Michele Guinigi, for one of the manuscripts now in California? Two of Guinigi's daughters entered the San Domenico convent: Sister Giovanna (1505–80), a 12-year-old novice in San Nicolao Novello in 1517 who moved to San Domenico in 1518, where she was renamed Sister Angeletta, and her sister Domitilla (1508–32), renamed Sister Brigida in 1520, who became mentally ill before receiving

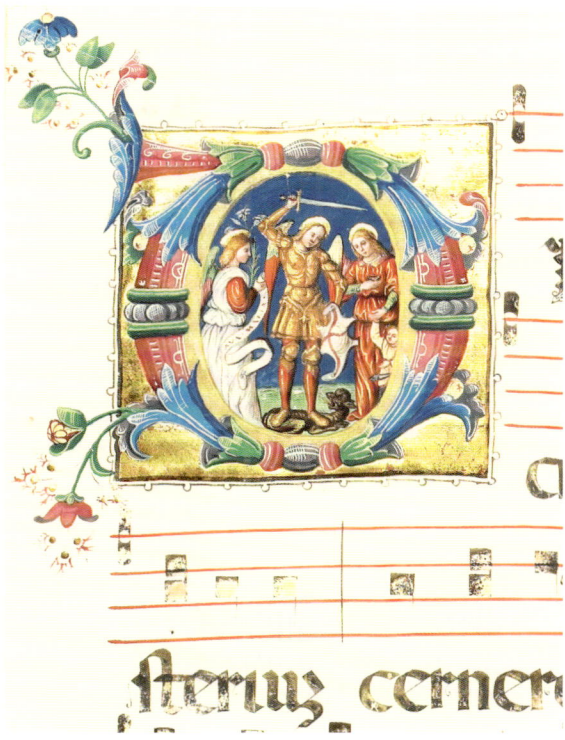

46 Eufrasia Burlamacchi, *Initial D, Dum sacrum misterium cerneret – The Three Archangels*, Antiphonary MS 4, fol.1ʳ, *c*.1513, tempera and gold leaf on parchment, 13 × 13 cm (5 ⅛ × 5 ⅛ in), Dominican Convent, California

the sacred veil.[34] Although the dates 1518 and 1520 show an early and direct connection between the Guinigi family and the San Domenico convent, they seem too late in relation to the completion in *c*.1513 of the California Antiphonary MS 4. However, even before the enrolment in the convent of the Guinigi sisters, the family already had connections with San Domenico through Ser Roberto di Piero Guinigi. Ser Roberto was secretary to Pope Pius III Todeschini Piccolomini (1439–1503) and patron of four altars in Lucca, one of which was in San Martino Cathedral.[35]

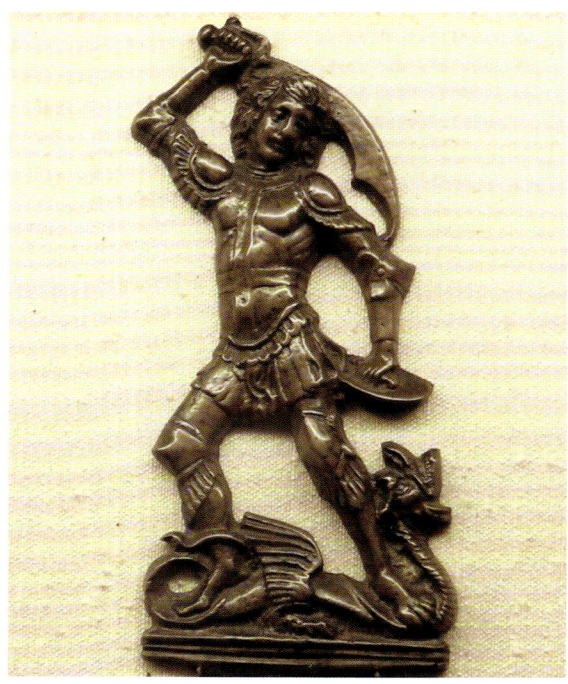

47 Francesco Marti, *Saint George Killing the Dragon*, 1480s, bronze plaquette, 12.5 × 5.5 cm (4 ⅞ × 2 ⅛ in), Museo Nazionale del Bargello, Florence

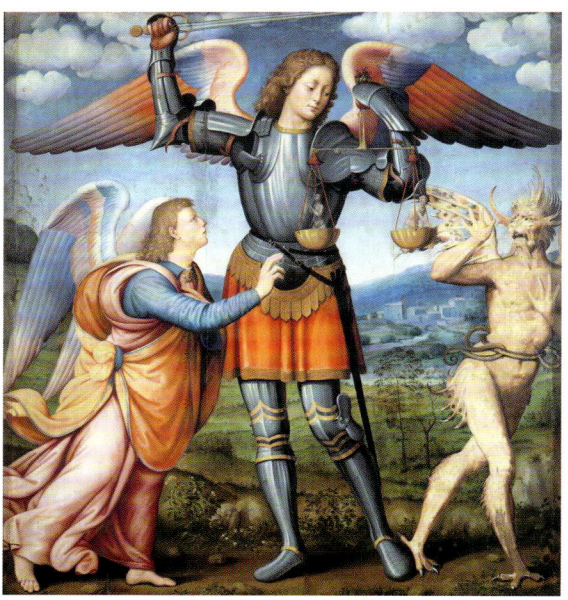

48 Antonio del Ceraiolo, *The Archangel Michael Weighs the Souls with an Angel and a Devil*, 1515–20, oil on panel, 175 × 165 cm (68 ⅞ × 65 in), Cenacolo di Andrea del Sarto in San Salvi, Florence

When the construction of the new building for the San Domenico convent was underway, from 1508 to 1513 according to the plans of Simone del Pollaiolo, Ser Roberto contributed a sum of 250 ducats.[36]

THE SOBER DELICACY OF SAINTHOOD

A drawing with the Archangel Michael may not have been the only iconographic resource from Ceraiolo's works that Eufrasia considered for her miniatures. The sober delicacy of both male and female saints is the main feature of Ceraiolo's altarpieces, detectable in the central panels and in the predellas, like the one of the *Nine Martyr Saints*, now in the Museo dell'Accademia

Etrusca in Cortona (fig.49).[37] This feature may have struck Eufrasia's imagination, leading her not to a simple and passive borrowing from the other artist, nor to a straightforward reduction in size of an iconographic subject. Rather, she always meditated on how to adapt the forms and colours of another medium to large initials that introduced through chant the celebration of important feasts. The process of adaptation presupposes the conception of art not as a value on its own, but as a means for further aims, a process that Eufrasia clarified in her 'lost' colophon, as we will see in the Epilogue.

Federico Zeri was the first to argue that Ceraiolo's predella was once part of an altarpiece featuring an episode narrated in the Gospel (Luke 10:38–42) and seldom represented, that is, *Christ in the House of Martha and Mary*, dated 1524, now in Berlin.[38]

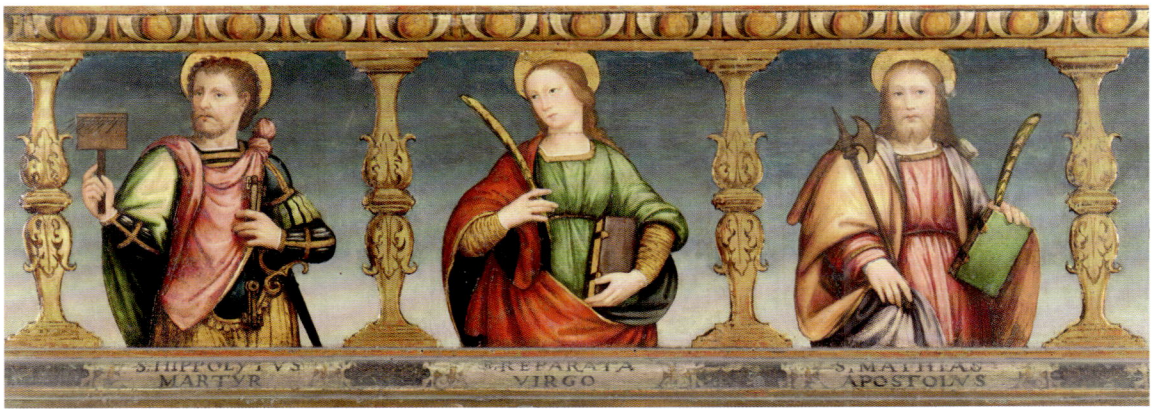

49 Antonio del Ceraiolo, *The Saints Hippolytus Martyr, Reparata Virgo and Mathias Apostolus*, from *Nine Martyr Saints*, Predella, *c.*1512, tempera on panel, each panel 35 × 35 cm (13 ¾ × 13 ¾ in), inv.1890, no.8680, Museo dell'Accademia Etrusca, Cortona

If Eufrasia had at her disposal drawings from this predella, predating 1524, she would have been able to rely on a well of suggestions for the rendition of Mary, Christ, saints and angels, close to her preferred style of devout images as calm, simple and humble, as in Saint Cecilia's portrayal in MS 4, fol.91ᵛ (fig.50).

Some historical circumstances support a likely circulation of Ceraiolo's drawings in San Domenico in Lucca. He was a painter committed to images grounded in simplicity and restrained expressions in the wake of Savonarola's ideas about religious art. Although a lay artist, his stylistic choices made him one of the favourite painters of Dominican religious houses. He worked in Florence for the convents of Santa Caterina da Siena (also known as Santa Caterina in Cafaggio) and Santa Lucia, two of five Dominican convents controlled by the followers of Savonarola.[39] Elisabetta, the artist's sister, took the veil at Santa Lucia in 1518, the same year he worked for the Savonarolan convent of Santa Croce (called La Crocetta), where in 1517–21 documents confirm the presence of his niece.[40] In 1520 he produced an altarpiece for the new choir of Santa Lucia.[41]

The early modern Dominican convents that kept alive Savonarola's heritage were also exchanging works of art, drawings included. In 1515–20 Ceraiolo depicted *The Mystic Marriage of Christ and Saint Catherine* for the convent of Santa Caterina da Siena, now in the Bombeni Chapel in Santa Trinita, Florence. A copy of this painting was acquired by the convent of San Vincenzo at Prato, which had a close relationship with San Domenico at Lucca. It is likely that the drawings for the predella of the *Nine Martyr Saints* referred to above migrated to Lucca, brought there by some Florentine friars upon the request of the sisters of the San Domenico convent, becoming part of the patrimony of its scriptorium and a direct source of inspiration for Eufrasia.

THE SIMPLICITY OF DEVOTION

While we have no direct testimonies of the presence of Ceraiolo's works in Lucca, two altarpieces testify to the relationship of Fra Paolino da Pistoia (*c.*1488–1547) with the convent of San Domenico. Son of

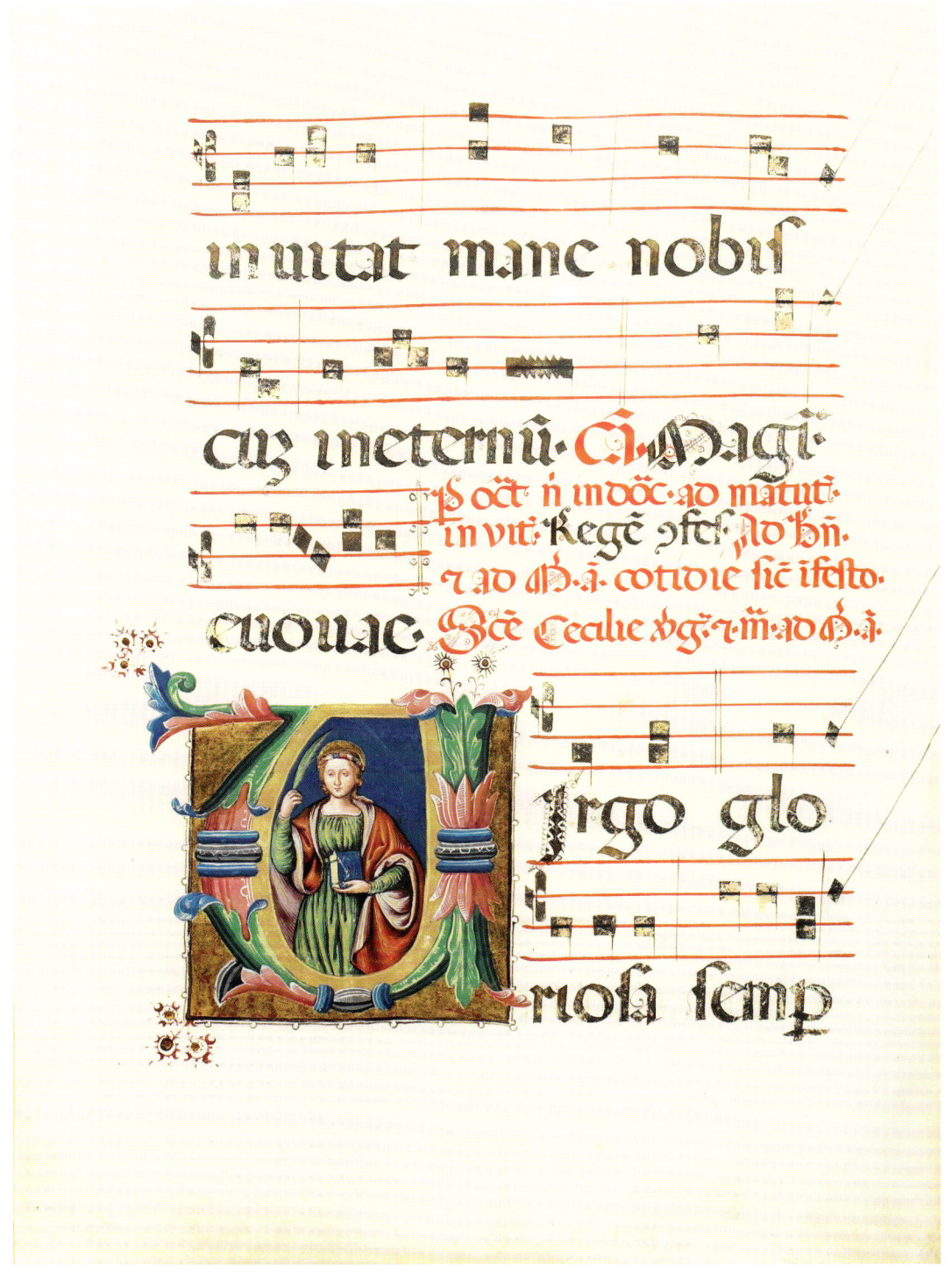

50 Eufrasia Burlamacchi, *Initial V, Virgo gloriosa semper – Saint Cecilia with Book and Palm Frond*, Antiphonary MS 4, fol.91^v, *c.*1513, tempera and gold leaf on parchment, folium 54.2 × 38.5 cm (21⅜ × 15⅛ in), initial 13 × 13 cm (5⅛ × 5⅛ in), Dominican Convent, California

the painter Bernardino del Signoraccio, he entered the Dominican monastery of San Marco in 1503. In 1513 he was modelling statues of terracotta while, in 1515, he restored the frescoes of Fra Angelico in the Chapter Hall of the San Marco monastery. When Fra Bartolomeo died in 1517, Fra Paolino inherited his drawings. These became the basis of the artworks he depicted for the convent of Santa Caterina da Siena in Florence and, also, for the San Domenico convent in Lucca.[42]

Fra Paolino belonged to the second generation of Savonarolan artists who had their headquarters in the monastery of San Marco in Florence, all following a devotional trend in iconography and style. For the convent of San Domenico in Lucca, Fra Paolino twice depicted the *Sacra conversazione*, first in *c*.1534–6 for the exterior church, and again in *c*.1538–40 for the choir chapel (fig.51). When he received the commission for the two panels, the prioresses were Lucia Cenami (1534–6) and Angelica Calandrini (1538–40). Sister Lucia belonged to one of the most powerful families of Lucca which leaned towards the teachings of Erasmus of Rotterdam; Sister Angelica's relatives had connections with the reformist Aonio Paleario.[43]

Both panels were accomplished in the period after Eufrasia illuminated MSS 1, 2, 3, 4 and 5, MS 14, and MSS 2649 and 2650. However, as I suggested regarding Ceraiolo, one may imagine that drawings were sent to Lucca from Florence by Fra Paolino before 1515. True, Eufrasia's illumination is grounded in simplicity, but her figures and ornament, always expressing a refined plasticity, do not present the extreme simplification that is the main feature of Fra Paolino's painting in the 1530s.

ILLUMINATION AND PRINTS

Although living in a convent of strict enclosure, Eufrasia was no exception in searching for models in drawing, painting and sculpture for her illumination.

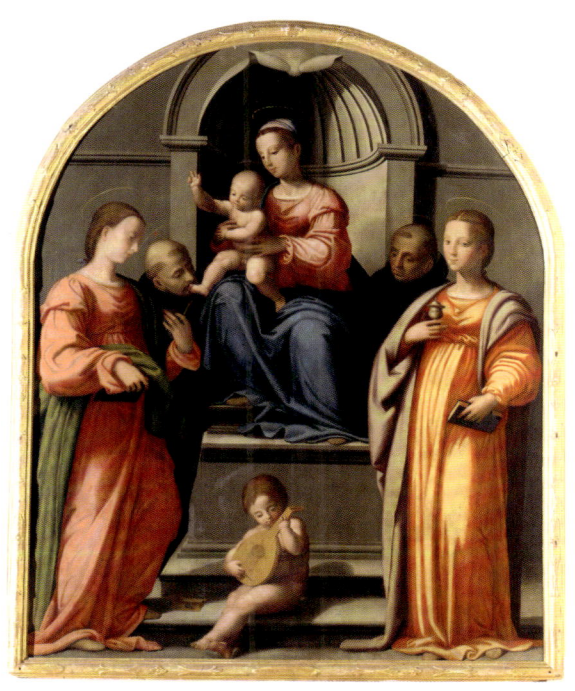

51 Fra Paolino da Pistoia, *Sacra conversazione*, *c*.1534–6, oil on panel, 320 × 212 cm (126 × 83½ in), Museo Nazionale di Villa Guinigi, Lucca

In the sixteenth century and especially within female religious houses, illumination flourished vis-à-vis the diffusion of illustrated printed books. Prints, metal-cuts and woodcuts were often at the nuns' disposal: inexpensive and transportable, they were important sources for miniatures and liturgical implements. This practice was not new, however.

In a seminal co-authored article, Anne van Buren and Sheila Edmunds showed that in the second half of the fifteenth century, at the very moment in which illuminators rendered space and ornament in ways seldom tried before, close exchanges between printed images and illumination were taking place.[44] Even more intriguing is the widespread occurrence of some

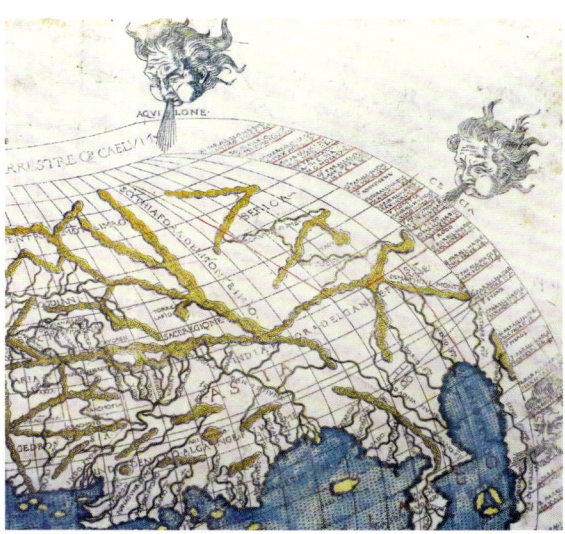

52 Francesco Rosselli, 'Headwinds', metal-cut, in Francesco
   Berlinghieri, *Geographia*, Inc. Magl. N 20, fol.38ʳ, 1482,
   paper sheet, 43.4 × 28.5 cm (17⅛ × 11¼ in), detail,
   Biblioteca Nazionale Centrale, Florence

of the prints, such that, re-elaborated by illuminators,
they themselves became the sources for new prints.[45]
But how did prints reach the convents? It was not
unusual that they arrived through either testaments
or bequests. Alessandro Rosselli (*c.*1475–1526), the
son of the Florentine cartographer and illuminator
Francesco (*c.*1447–before 1513), bequeathed all the
materials of his workshop to one of his sisters, Maria
Rosselli, who lived in the convent of Santa Caterina
da Siena in Florence.[46]

Among the wealth of materials left by Alessandro,
there were many notebooks, engravings after Raphael
(1483–1520) and Baccio Bandinelli (1488–1560), *mappa
mundi* (medieval maps of the world) and plans of
many cities.[47] Plautilla Nelli lived in that convent
and had access to Fra Bartolomeo's notebooks of
drawings, which were probably transferred from
the San Marco monastery to the convent of Santa

Caterina da Siena after the death in 1547 of their
last owner, Fra Paolino. She also had access to prints
made by Marcantonio Raimondi (*c.*1480–1534),
probably including the *Lamentation* and the
engraving after Raphael's *Last Supper*. Sheila Barker
has argued that Sister Plautilla not only worked with
Raimondi's engravings but also used topographic
iconography. This is the case of Jerusalem possibly
coming from the map of Hartmann Schedel (1440–
1514) entitled *Hierosolima* from fol.27 of his 1493 *Liber
chronicarum*, the *Nuremburg Chronicle*, a geographical
history of the world.[48]

I suggest that Eufrasia referred to a world map
printed by Francesco Rosselli in 1482 (fig.52) for
certain ornamental designs that appear in the
manuscripts she created. Specifically, the headwinds
represented in the map may have inspired Eufrasia's
designs for the bars of some of her initials.[49] With
pertinent transformations, these heads were not
far from becoming decorative masks. In Eufrasia's
rendition, the lines that in the map indicate the
direction of the winds took the shape of flowery
stems. Instead of being turned towards the image,
however, they fill the marginal empty spaces of the
borders, as in the miniature of *Saint John the Baptist*
in Gradual MS 5, fol.135ᵛ (see fig.54). Perhaps one
cannot exclude another derivation or conflation
between two arts for this motif in Eufrasia's work.
As in other convents, in San Domenico the art of
modelling the Virgin Mary, the Christ Child or
saints with terracotta and stucco was well known,
seemingly offering some iconographic suggestions.[50]
The possibility of a more direct source, such as
another illumination, can also be considered.
Especially for the masks Eufrasia portrayed frontally,
as in Gradual MS 5, fol.71ʳ (see fig.44), for instance,
she may have reproduced, with some modifications,
the examples offered by Giuliano Amadei, such as
the one within stems, flowers and fruit in the right
margin of MS Landau Finaly 21, fol.1ʳ, depicted in
the 1480s (fig.53).[51]

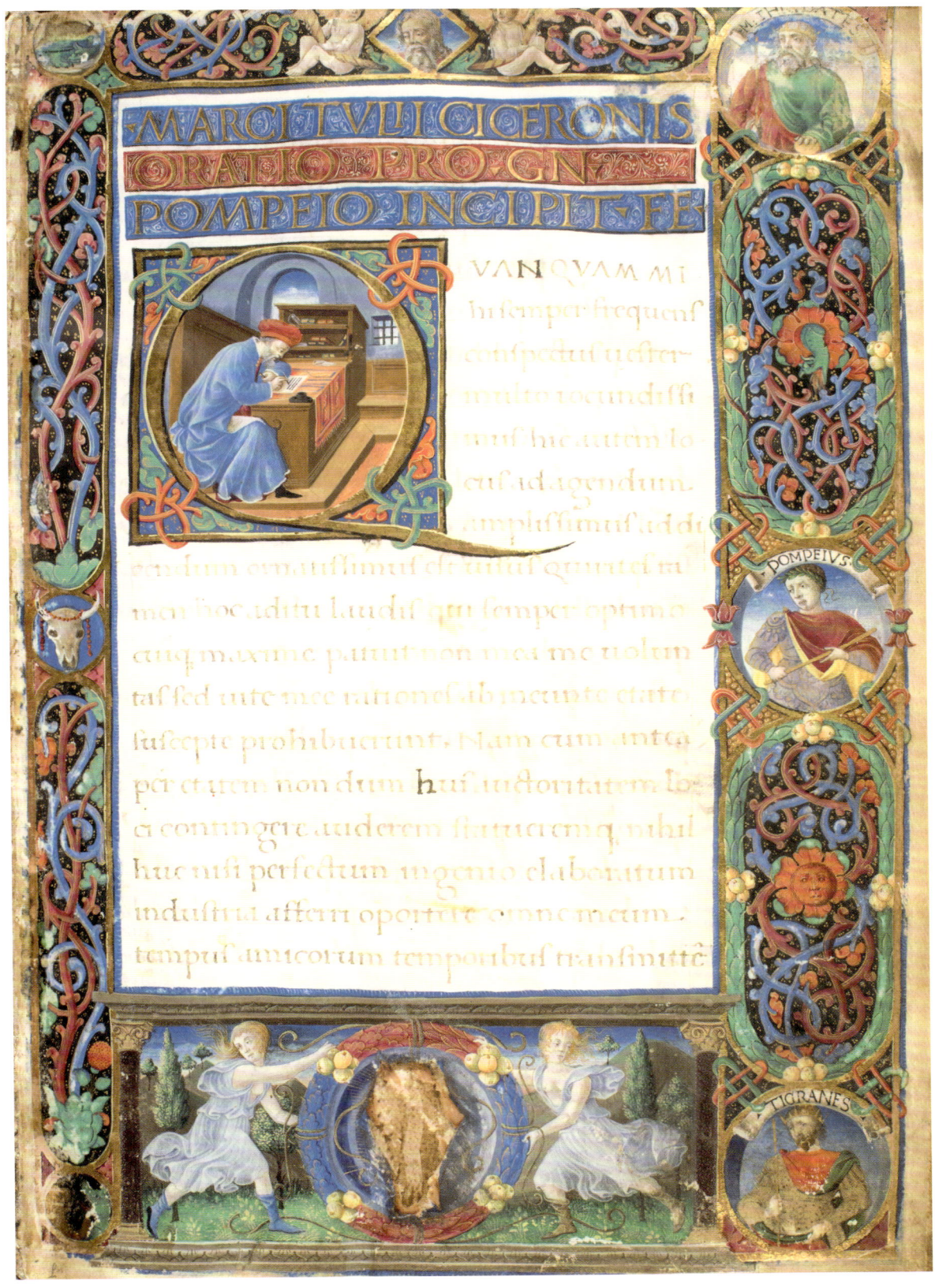

53 Giuliano Amadei, Frontispiece, in M.T. Cicero, *Orationes*, MS Landau Finaly 21, fol.1r, 1480s, tempera and gold leaf on parchment, folium 25 × 13.5 cm (9 ⅞ × 5 ⅜ in), Biblioteca Nazionale Centrale, Florence

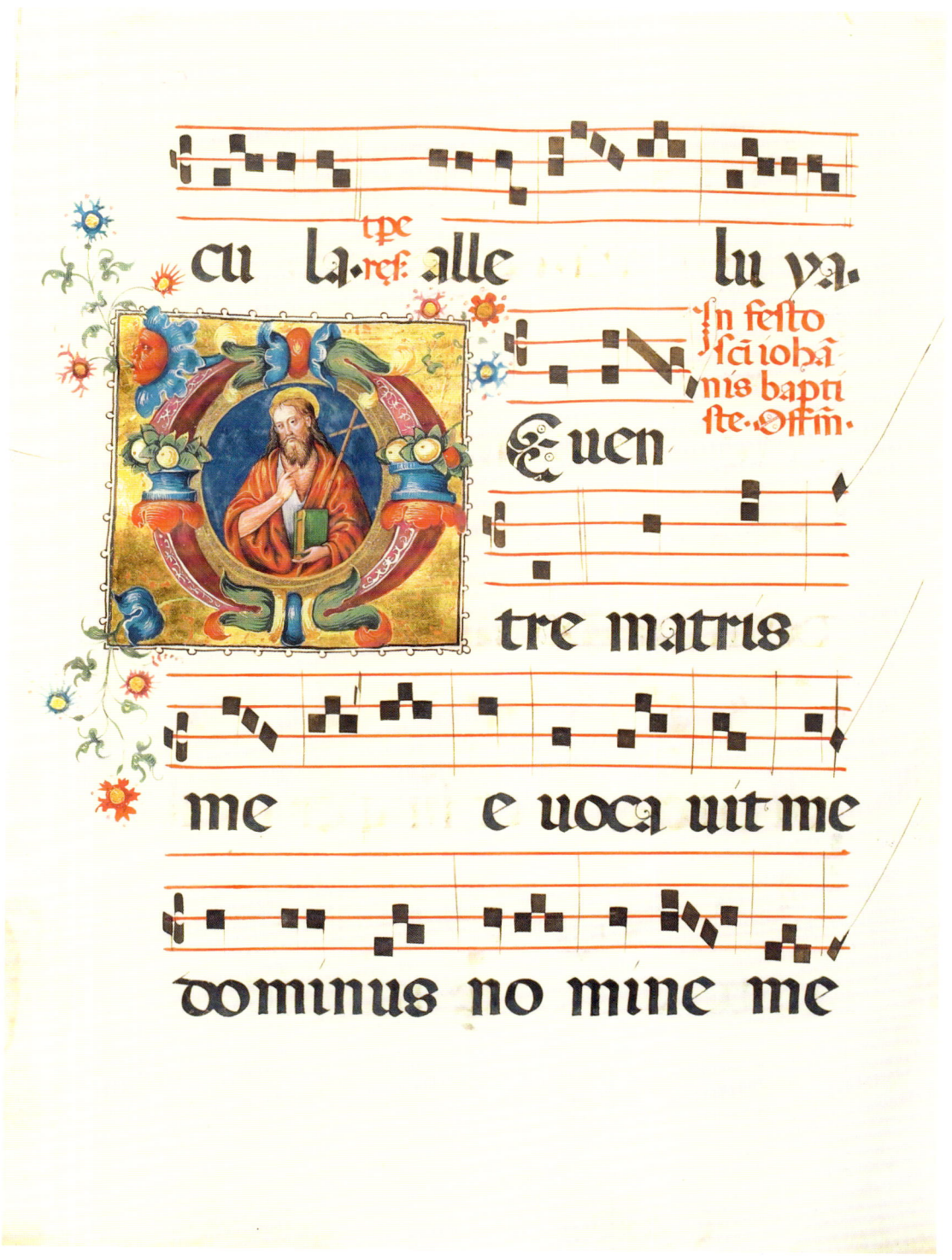

54 Eufrasia Burlamacchi, *Initial D, De ventre matris – Saint John the Baptist*, Gradual MS 5, fol.135ᵛ, *c.*1515, tempera and gold leaf on parchment, folium 54.2 × 38.5 cm (21⅜ × 15⅛ in), initial 14 × 13 cm (5½ × 5⅛ in), Dominican Convent, California.

6

When Means and Ends Meet

GRADUAL MS 5 FOR SAN DOMENICO, *c.*1515

MS 5 is a Gradual *de tempore et de sanctis*, containing the Temporal cycle of the earthly life of Jesus Christ and the Sanctoral cycle with the annual feasts of the saints. This is the last and richest manuscript of the series Eufrasia produced for her convent. It includes 12 historiated, 8 ornamental and 48 penwork initials. Some historiated initials of MS 5 testify to the creative adaptation by Eufrasia of Antonio del Ceraiolo's iconographic solutions, which must have reached her in some form. The Saint Bartholomew with the knife of his martyrdom, depicted in *c.*1510 by the Florentine artist in the altarpiece of the *Virgin Enthroned, the Christ Child, and Four Saints* in the church of Santo Spirito in Florence (fig.55), can be instructively compared with Eufrasia's *Saint John the Baptist* in Gradual MS 5, fol.135ᵛ (fig.54).[1]

Eufrasia depicted the fur covering the saint's body, made his head bend slightly and added a white robe under the red mantle whose folds are highlighted by yellow lines. By isolating the Baptist on a blue background within the letter D, defined by hues of red for the leaves, fruit, roundels and a mask, Eufrasia enhanced his figure and attributes – a book and a simple cross made of reeds – and, also, his melancholy air so delicately expressed in the saint's gaze and posture.

SCULPTURAL DRAPERIES AND SUBTLETIES OF TONAL CHANGES

Apart from these melancholy gazes and humble attitudes, Eufrasia also tended to produce statuary forms draped with monumental cloaks. In this regard, one should consider the influence of another artist who had been living and working in Lucca. Domenico Bigordi, called del Ghirlandaio (*c.*1448–94), contributed significantly to the renewal of art in the city. Some documentary discoveries show that Ghirlandaio, after the completion of works in Pisa in 1478, the following year painted the altarpiece of the *Sacra conversazione* for San Martino Cathedral (fig.56).[2] The panel, in tempera and gold, featuring the Virgin Mary and Child with the Saints Clement, Peter, Sebastian and Paul, for a new altar dedicated to Saint Peter in Chains and the Conversion of Saint Paul, shows elements from Andrea del Verrocchio (*c.*1435–88) in the floor, throne, carpet and curtains, and in the spatial organisation.

The fact that the Christ Child turns his head towards Pope Clement and Peter suggests the names of the patrons, Clemente di Antonio Andrucci and Pietro del fu Lorenzo Spada, who also paid, on 2 December 1478, Jacopo da Villa Basilica, a woodworker, expert in tables and frames, to prepare

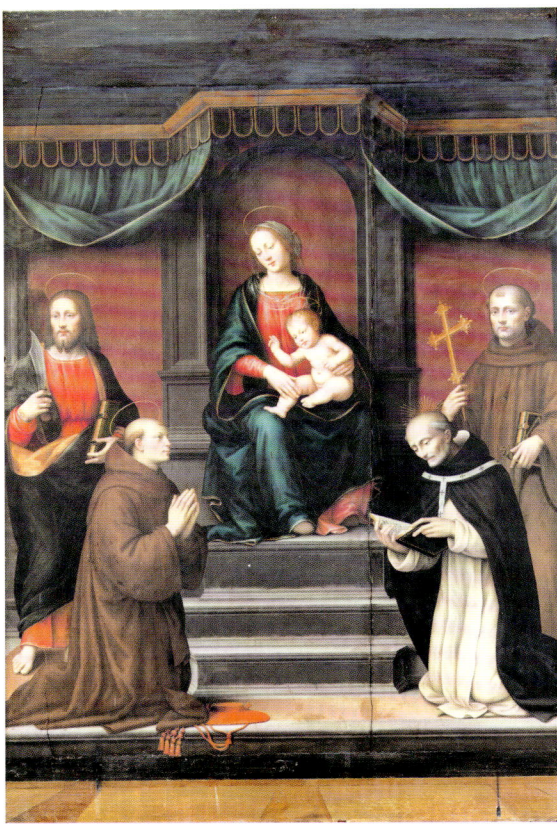

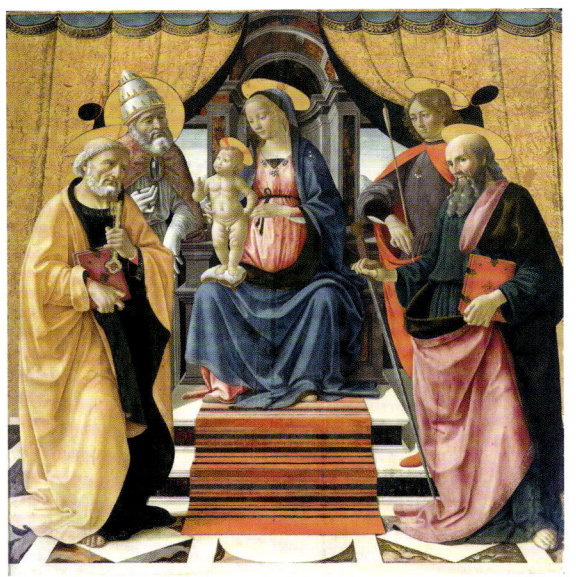

56 Domenico del Ghirlandaio, *Sacra conversazione*, 1479,
    tempera and gold on panel, 170 × 160 cm (66 ⅞ × 63 in),
    Cattedrale di San Martino, Lucca

55 Antonio del Ceraiolo, *Virgin Enthroned, the Christ Child,
    and the Saints Bartholomew, Bonaventura, Giovanni
    Gualberto and Antonino*, *c*.1510, oil on panel, 290 × 140 cm
    (114 ⅛ × 55 ⅛ in), Basilica di Santo Spirito, Florence

the panel 'for the image to be painted for the altar'
('*pro tabernaculo ymaginis pingende*').³ Its emphatic
monumentality and the frame '*all'antica*' (that is,
a square) would be echoed in the works of the
Lucchese artist Vincenzo di Antonio Frediani (*c*.1458–
1505) but, on the whole, many *Sacre conversazioni* in
Lucca continued to reproduce the late Gothic multi-
panel scheme.⁴

Eufrasia may have known the figure of Saint
Peter depicted by Ghirlandaio, most likely through
the filter of Vincenzo Frediani, who was the
protagonist of an episode concerning a work for the

altar of Saint Vincenzo in the Dominican church
of the San Romano monastery. The long contract
for this altarpiece, dated 14 August 1483, specifies
its production in both colour and drawing, as in
Ghirlandaio's *Sacra conversazione* in San Martino
Cathedral. A drawing that reproduced Ghirlandaio's
altarpiece was in the hands of the patron, who
passed it on to the Lucchese painter.⁵ I suspect that
this drawing, now lost, may have circulated outside
Frediani's workshop, arriving at Eufrasia's convent
and inspiring her not only in *c*.1515 for *Saint Peter* in
Gradual MS 5, fol.139ʳ (fig.57), but also some years
later in the rendition of the draperies according to
gradations of tone in two of the most accomplished
miniatures of her career. These are the *Nativity* on
fol.49ᵛ of Gradual 2649 and the *Pentecost* on fol.99ʳ
of Gradual 2650 for the monastery of San Romano
(Biblioteca Statale, Lucca), to which we will return.

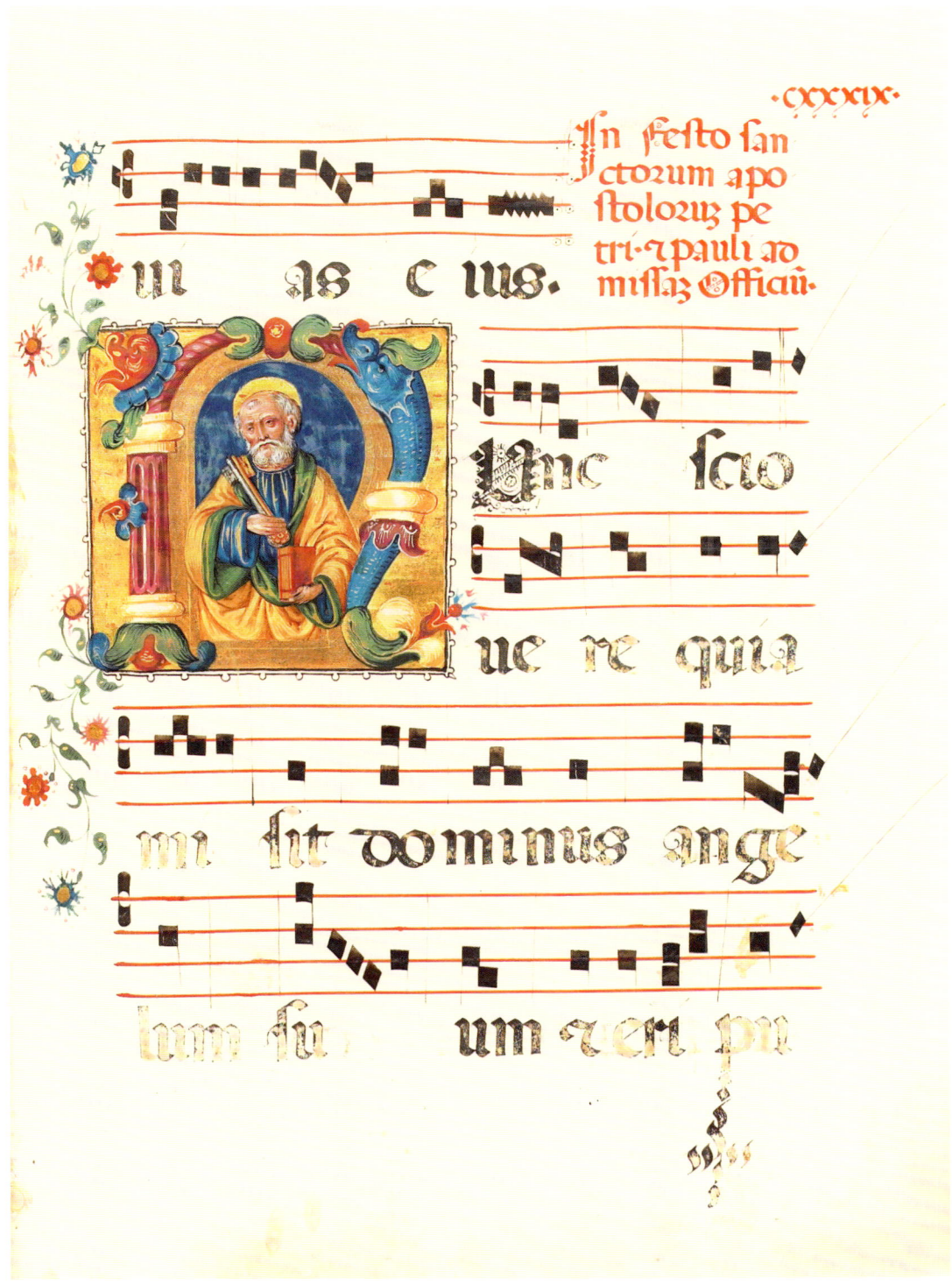

In festo san
ctozum apo
stolozuz pe
tri 2 pauli ad
missaz Officiu

ui is c us.

Nunc scio

ue re quia

m sit dominus ange

lum su um 2 eri pu

57 Eufrasia Burlamacchi, *Initial N, Nunc scio – Saint Peter*, Gradual MS 5, fol.139ʳ, *c.*1515, tempera and gold leaf on parchment, folium 54.2 × 38.5 cm (21⅜ × 15⅛ in), initial 14 × 13 cm (5½ × 5⅛ in), Dominican Convent, California

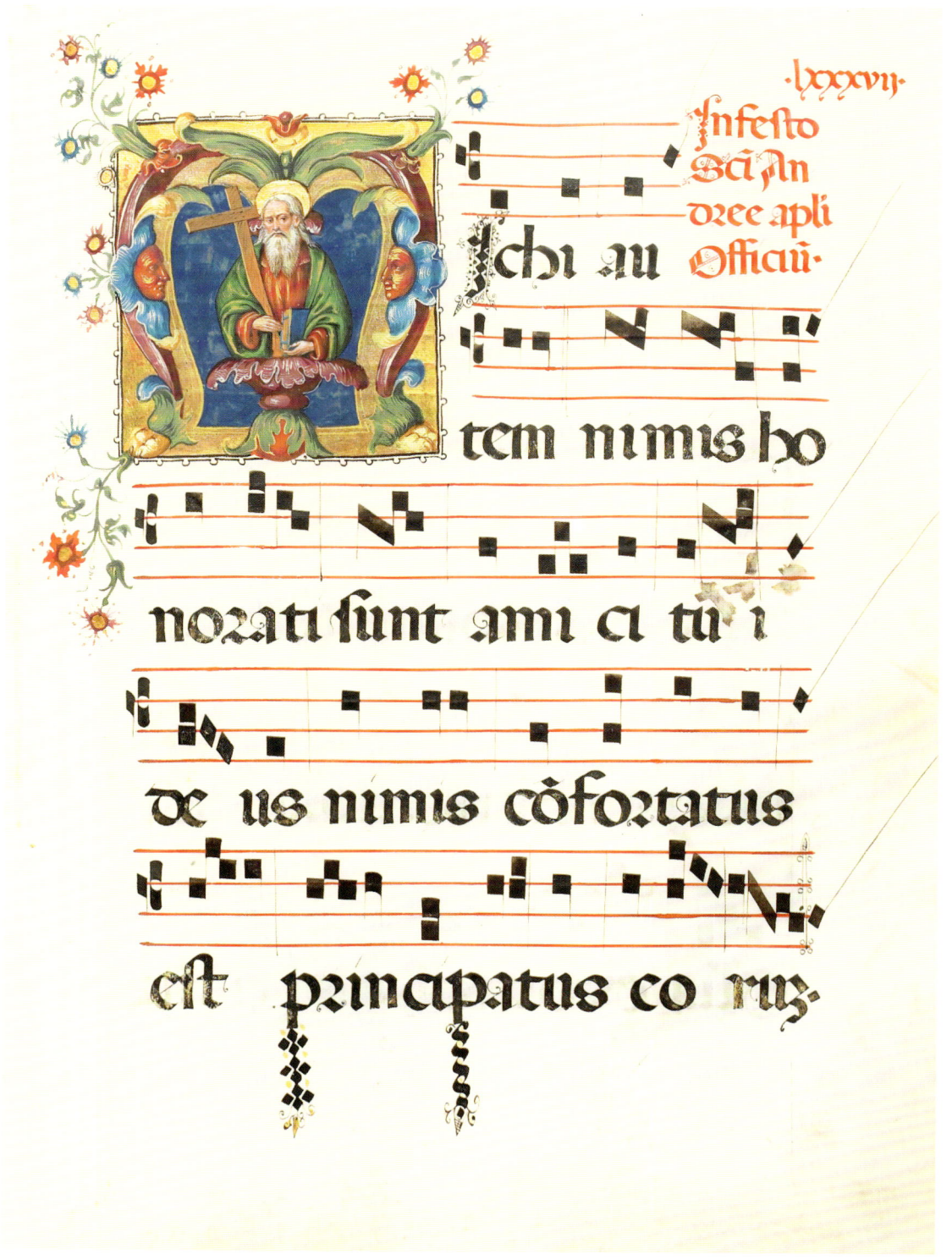

58 Eufrasia Burlamacchi, *Initial M, Michi autem – Saint Andrew*, Gradual MS 5, fol.87ʳ, *c*.1515, tempera and gold leaf on parchment, folium 54.2 × 38.5 cm (21⅜ × 15⅛ in), initial 14 × 13.5 cm (5½ × 5⅜ in), Dominican Convent, California

MS 5 is remarkable not only for the rendition of draperies and subtle tonal changes but also for its ornament, namely the grotesques, which Eufrasia depicted until *c.*1520.[6] She used them in a way that distinguishes her from other early modern artists, especially the Florentine illuminators Gherardo (*c.*1446–97) and Monte (1448–*c.*1533) di Giovanni del Fora, Attavante di Gabriello Attavanti (1452–1520/25), and Francesco Rosselli.[7] These illuminators employed a profusion of grotesques, intermingled with a variety of floral motifs, bunches of fruit, pearls, precious stones, cameos and coins, often arranging them symmetrically to form the frame of the first folium of the manuscript. Eufrasia, by contrast, chose motifs selectively to form the body of the initial letters and never employed them within a frame.[8]

The inherent complexity of Eufrasia's grotesques seems counter to the sacred content of her manuscripts. How does one justify the presence of grotesque ornament in Eufrasia's work, with her blend of artificial and natural elements such as masks framed by petals, flowers rooted in metallic bars, paws and acanthus leaves, side by side with saints, as *Saint Andrew* in Gradual MS 5, fol.87[r], stemming from a vegetable chalice placed on a red sphere covered with acanthus leaves (fig.58)? We might surmise that Eufrasia wished to arouse visual interest and delight in the beholder through their unexpected variety of forms, ideas that were raised by the first commentators on grotesques.[9] Writing of sixteenth-century poetry, James V. Mirollo identified in the concept of 'marvel' (*maraviglia*) a capacity to evoke 'wonder, surprise, the unexpected, the extraordinary, the monstrous and the supernatural', leading to responses that ranged 'from mild surprise to total astonishment'.[10] If we apply this definition to Eufrasia's grotesques, we will see that, after an immediate reaction to the unusual combination, the viewer quickly moves from an emotional surprise to a search for coherence and then to a logical orientation.

The propriety of iconographic themes had been a subject of debate in the Middle Ages, but it was only in the fifteenth century, when the art market expanded, that it became an issue that concerned writers beyond the monastic walls.[11] Almost 50 years before Eufrasia started to illuminate her first set of manuscripts, the Archbishop of Florence, Antonino Pierozzi (1389–1459), devoted a chapter of his *Summa theologica* (*c.*1444–59) to the condition of merchants and craftsmen, with the aim of prescribing ethical behaviour in work. For painters, he advised that they establish fair prices and keep propriety in representing religious themes. He also defined the situation of the lay miniaturists in Florence, stating that they offended

either with pen or brush [...] if they do their work on feast days, or when they demand an excessive price, and especially when they do not put good mixture in their colours, on account of which they fade quickly in the books, or when, to finish quickly, they do not do it diligently, when there has been no contract signed for such a price.[12]

Archbishop Antonino remarked that painters were to avoid 'the vain adornment of clothing' ('*vanos ornatus vestimentorum*'), yet he did not expand his criticism to the fanciful ornament displayed in contemporary illumination. While acknowledging that Archbishop Antonino favoured the simple, the plain and the orderly in pictures, it is likely that he considered the book arts as belonging to a different sphere entirely, unless he wished implicitly to expand also to illumination all the strictures he addressed to painting.

From the thirteenth through the fifteenth centuries, especially in French and English manuscripts, fanciful marginalia filled the empty space of the parchment sheet.[13] In the second half of the fifteenth century, this fanciful repertory became the main subject within the initial letters, treated with the same care and attention reserved to the sacred subjects. As we saw with Giuliano Amadei, in the choir books for San Martino

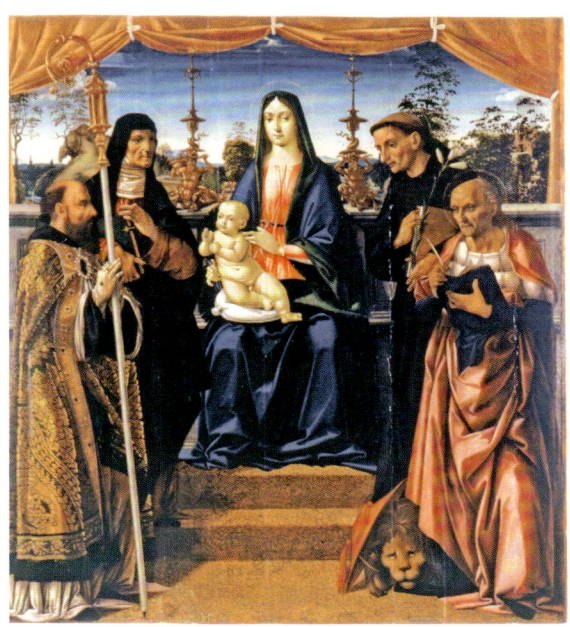

59 Michele Angelo di Pietro Membrini, *Sacra conversazione*, *c.*1492, tempera on panel, 172 × 159 cm (67¾ × 62⅝ in), from the Chiesa di Sant'Agostino, Lucca; Museo Nazionale di Villa Guinigi, Lucca

(MSS 14 and 16), instead of details of sacred scenes or vegetal ornament, he made use of grotesque figures.

In the first decade of the sixteenth century in Lucca, grotesques were not only known but also expressly requested to be portrayed in churches. In a contract of 23 January 1509, the Lucchese canon and rector of the church of San Paolino in Lucca, Guglielmo di Poggio, required the Lucchese painter Agostino Marti to depict a chapel and 'its ceiling with golden stars on a blue background, and its lateral piers with golden leaves and grotesques'.[14]

Apart from Amadei, was it also Marti, whose two sisters were in the convent of San Domenico, who passed the Roman novelties on to Eufrasia, or did they issue from her acquaintance with the work of the Lucchese artist Michele Angelo di Pietro Membrini

(*c.*1465–1525)? In the 1480s the latter probably had been in Rome, if the graffito in the crypto-porch, room 70, of the Domus Aurea with the signature 'MIC.ELANGOLO da LUCA' belongs to him.[15] However, even if Eufrasia knew the works in which Membrini more clearly manifested his enthusiasm for the fashionable Roman ornament, such as the painting of the *Sacra conversazione* (*c.*1492; fig.59), once in the church of Sant'Agostino at Lucca, she would hardly share his archaeological rendition of the ancient motifs in the two elaborate candlesticks with tritons placed on the enclosure balustrade behind Mary, the Christ Child, and the Saints Augustine, Monica, Nicola da Tolentino and Jerome.[16]

No document has remained testifying to the reasons why Eufrasia employed so many grotesques. Rather than trying to explain her preference as one of novel forms, I turn to a more promising interpretation: her interest in the perceptual effects that grotesques elicited. Since it is likely that Eufrasia created neither frescoes nor easel paintings but only illuminations, perhaps she was engaged in finding a solution to a long-standing problem that illuminators faced in the Middle Ages and the Renaissance, namely, how to reconcile in one space figures and ornament that demanded two different ways of looking: the close focus on sacred subjects on the one hand, and the less constrained attention on ornamental patterns on the other.[17] Grotesques could elicit visual interest and delight, but could introduce potential imbalance if opposed to the central theme within the initial letter. The solution that prevailed in medieval and Renaissance manuscripts was to maintain a clear divide between the two.

Eufrasia's illuminations added something very significant to this art form, for she provided ornament with its own autonomy while maintaining the legibility of the figural subject. Her move was to connect sacred figures and grotesque ornament while preserving their distinctive features. Instead of diminishing the size of the grotesques, she enlarged their constitutive elements

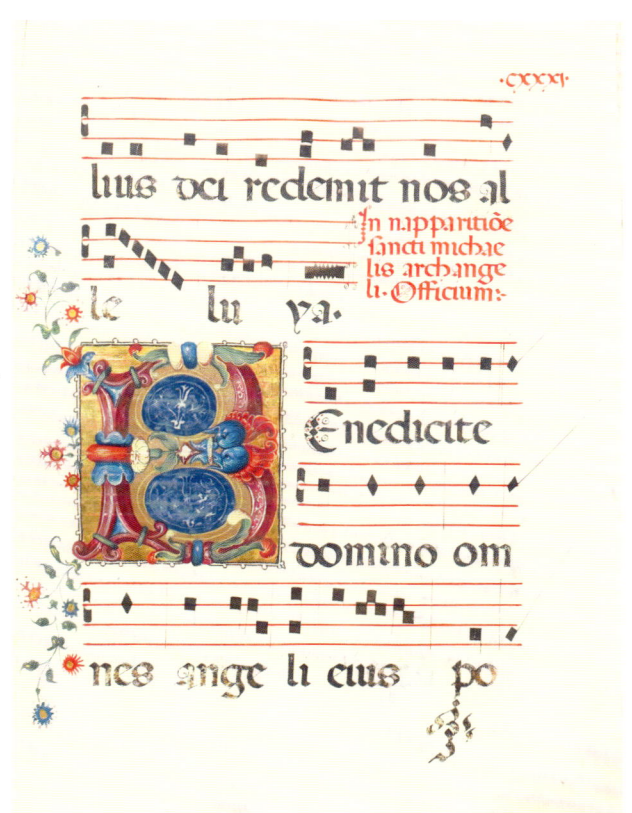

60 Eufrasia Burlamacchi, *Initial B, Benedicite domino – Birds, Flowers, Fruit and Roundels*, Gradual MS 5, fol.131ʳ, *c*.1515, tempera and gold leaf on parchment, folium 54.2 × 38.5 cm (21⅜ × 15⅛ in), initial 14 × 13 cm (5½ × 5⅛ in), Dominican Convent, California

61 Eufrasia Burlamacchi, *Initial P, Protexisti me deus – Saint Peter Martyr*, Gradual MS 5, fol.122ʳ, *c*.1515, tempera and gold leaf on parchment, folium 54.2 × 38.5 cm (21⅜ × 15⅛ in), initial 14 × 13 cm (5½ × 5⅛ in), Dominican Convent, California

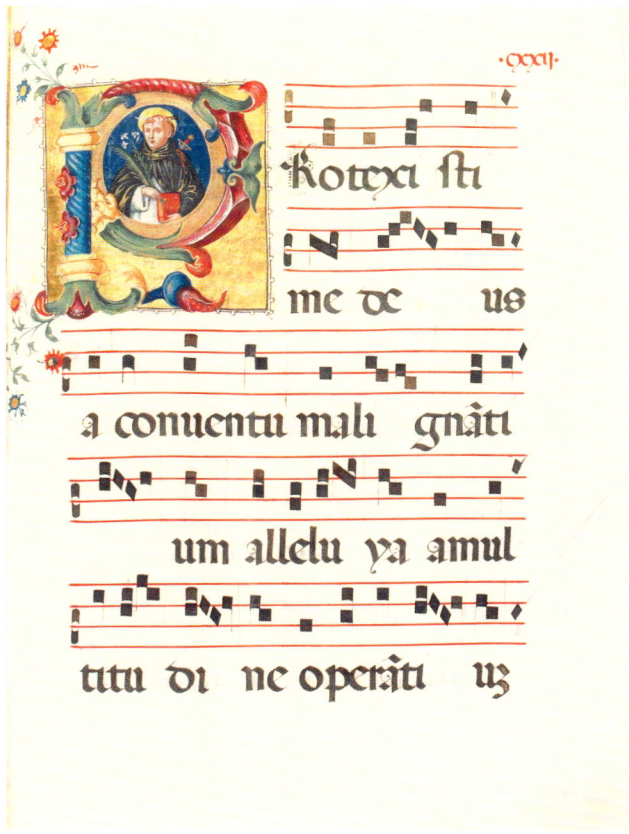

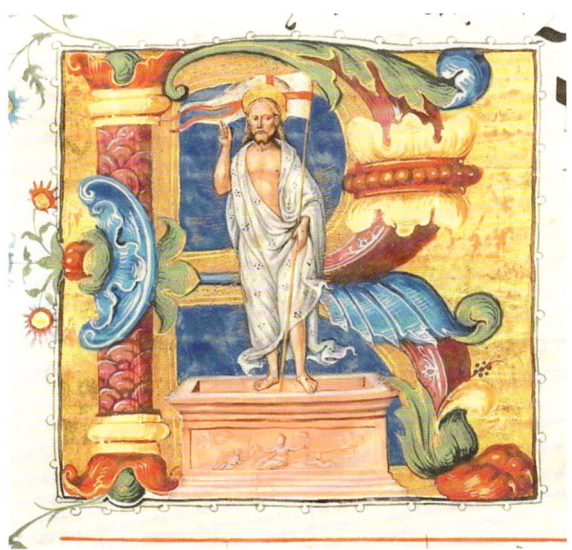

62 Eufrasia Burlamacchi, *Initial R, Resurrection –
Architectural Grotesque Elements*, Gradual MS 5, fol.48ᵛ,
c.1515, tempera and gold leaf on parchment, initial
14 × 14 cm (5½ × 5½ in), Dominican Convent, California

so that they became equal in size with the figural
subjects. In this way she achieved a better control over
grotesques' potential visual anarchism and at the same
time enhanced their decorative qualities. Through this
approach, the long-standing problems of coherence
and emphasis were successfully solved. In practice,
the beholder of many miniatures of Gradual MS 5
is led no longer from the centre to the margins but
comprehends at once the two different components.
By employing just a few figural motifs, such as
birds, flowers, fruits and roundels (fig.60), Eufrasia
concentrated on the architectural elements forming the
frame of the letters as if they were grotesque motifs.
She resorted to distortion by shortening, doubling,
twisting (fig.61), stretching and magnifying column
shafts, capitals and cornices as if they possessed the
potential ambiguity of hybrids.

In the initial R introducing *Resurrection* in
Gradual MS 5, fol.48ᵛ (fig.62), Eufrasia depicted
a strange column with two capitals at each side,
also re-elaborated in other miniatures in the same
manuscript (see figs 57 and 61) and covered with
patterns of small, red, shield-like shapes. Another
shield marks the middle zone of the column. The
ornamental exuberance is always controlled; note how
the yellow leaves on the large, dark red lobe of the
letter are somehow tamed by a sort of bracelet with
red roundels. By such a move, Eufrasia demonstrated
that even structural elements could undergo a visual
metamorphosis not only as an actualisation of
ornament's potentialities but also as the most proper
manner to enhance either the sacred scene or the
saint represented. These decorative solutions can be
considered Eufrasia's most original contribution to
Renaissance ornament.

If Eufrasia's preference for grotesques was indeed
so pervasive in MS 5, the last manuscript made for
her convent in *c*.1515, why did she avoid using them
to frame sacred scenes and portrayals of saints in
the two-volume Gradual for the monastery of San
Romano, illuminated from 1527 to *c*.1532? As an artist
who had come to terms with a difficult issue, one
would have expected her to improve on her discovery,
applying the new ornamental solutions to ever more
demanding tasks, vying with other artists to achieve
the best results, and even seeking to demonstrate her
virtuosity.[18] Perhaps the expectation for modesty and
humility at San Romano led to this restraint.

Be that as it may, to frame the images in the two-
volume Gradual MSS 2649–50 discussed in the next
chapter, Eufrasia resorted to the most widespread
decorative patterns of 50 years earlier: candelabra and
acanthus leaves. These ornamental motifs, long and
regular, were rendered with cool hues and with no
trace of the exuberance which was one of the most
remarkable features in the five choir books for San
Domenico.

7

Naturalism in Supernatural Spaces

THE TWO-VOLUME GRADUAL FOR THE SAN ROMANO MONASTERY: MSS 2649–50, 1527–*c*.1532

The large two-volume Gradual MSS 2649–50, likely the last of Sister Eufrasia's enterprises, can be considered the work of her maturity – in 1527 she was 49 years of age – in which she depicted six sacred scenes, nine large ornamental initials and 103 penwork letters.[1] These volumes testify to Eufrasia's ability to change her repertory according to the demands of the patron, who, on this occasion, was Fra Lorenzo Orsucci. He had been confessor to the sisters of San Domenico for four years – 1522 to 1526 – and prior of the San Romano monastery, a capacity he held in 1526 for one year only since his health failed quickly, leading him to blindness by 1527.[2]

Fra Lorenzo, as confessor to the nuns in San Domenico when Eufrasia had already completed the five choir books for her convent and MS 14 for San Martino Cathedral, knew personally her proficiency in writing, notating and illuminating manuscripts. Thus, it should come as no surprise that he engaged her in such an important enterprise. Beside Fra Lorenzo, the Lucchese merchant Stefano Spada made Eufrasia's artistic enterprise possible, granting money

to purchase the large quantity of parchment sheets needed to produce such an important book.[3] Spada was a wealthy merchant, elected Elder many times in Lucca's oligarchic government, and a member of the General Council.[4] His coat of arms – two argent swords on an azure field – is represented, though inverted, in the lower margin of MS 2650, fol.1ʳ (fig.63), surrounded by a garland of laurel leaves.[5]

Spada had a close relationship with the convent of San Domenico. His two daughters, Faustina and Stephana, were choir nuns there, and an enslaved person of his household, bought in 1501 and christened Zita, was a servant nun (*conversa*) in the same convent with the name of Sister Antonina. They entered the San Domenico convent in 1514, 1521 and 1524 respectively,[6] just a few years before Eufrasia started to write, notate and illuminate the two-volume Gradual.

The miniatures of this Gradual testify to the further change Eufrasia's art underwent. In the five choir books for her convent, she updated the solutions of fifteenth-century illumination in both figures and ornament, without changing the readability of the initials. Ornament always expressed a sense of dynamism, interacting with the staves, notes and words. Representations of fruit, instead of simply filling a chalice forming a vertical or horizontal bar,

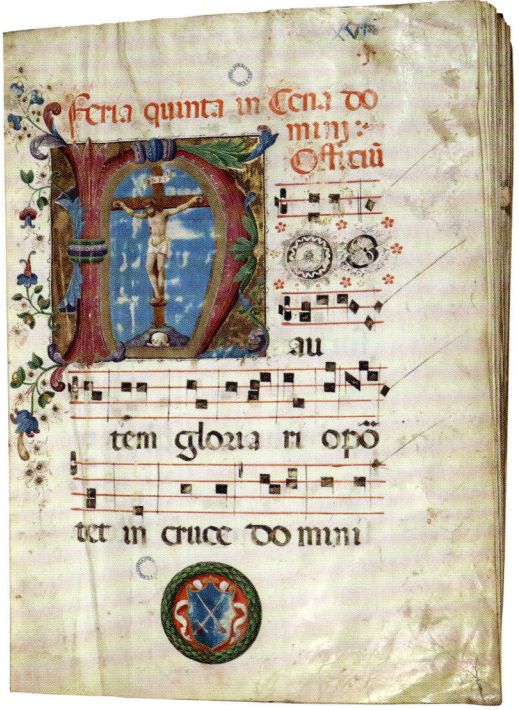

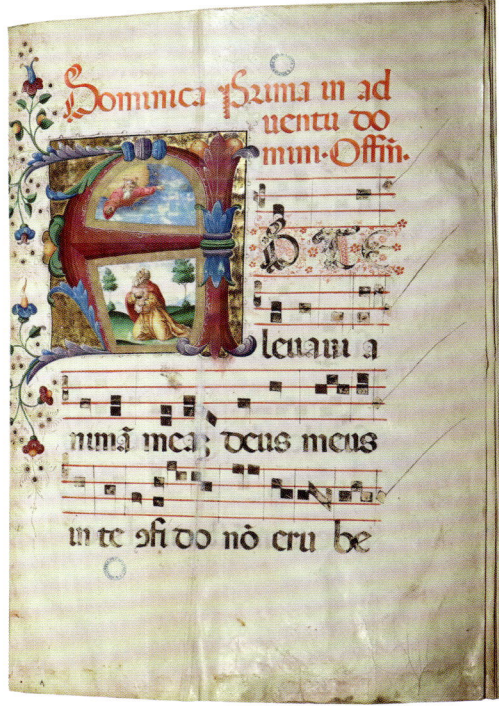

63 Eufrasia Burlamacchi, *Initial N, Nos autem – Crucifixion and Coat of Arms of Stefano Spada*, Gradual MS 2650, fol.1ʳ, *c.*1532, tempera and gold leaf on parchment, folium 60.5 × 43.3 cm (23 ⅞ × 17 in), Biblioteca Statale, Lucca

64 Eufrasia Burlamacchi, *Initial A, Ad te levavi animam meam – God the Father and David Playing the Psaltery*, Gradual MS 2649, fol.1ʳ, *c.*1530, tempera and gold leaf on parchment, folium 59.3 × 43.2 cm (23 ⅜ × 17 in), initial 19 × 17 cm (7 ½ × 6 ¾ in), Biblioteca Statale, Lucca

rather functioned as markers of space in relation to the notes; they were, in this way, markers of time. Also, Eufrasia insisted on subtleties produced by ink lines. They appear around the gold leaf glued on the parchment and constitute the penwork finials in the large and empty lower margin of the folium, especially with the descenders of the initials P and Q, but also with M.

In the two-volume Gradual for San Romano, by contrast, she did not abandon her experiments with the initials, but this time she substituted naturalism, reinterpreted in supernatural spaces, for the flat blue background within the letters and the grotesques forming the bars of the initials. To attain this effect, Eufrasia always introduced the sky in the background of the initials, either in a landscape or as an independent and limitless azure field to show the close connection between the human and the divine worlds.

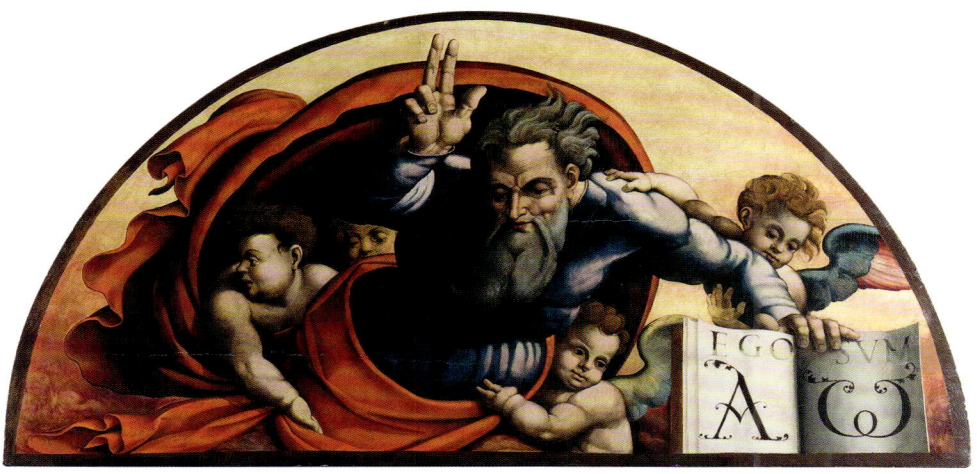

65 Agostino di Francesco Marti, *God the Father with Angels*, *c.*1520, oil on panel, 100 × 230 cm (39 ⅜ × 90 ½ in), Sacristy, Cattedrale di San Martino, Lucca

LUCCA MEETS ROME

The Gradual MS 2649 opens with one of the most powerful among Eufrasia's miniatures and one of the more inspiring for both her community and her own proficiency in chant. On fol.1ʳ, the A of *Ad te levavi animam meam* ('I lifted up my soul unto thee'; Psalm 143:8) is filled with the representation of God in Heaven and David kneeling in an undulating field, playing the psaltery and invoking God (fig.64). Notwithstanding its relatively small size (19 × 17 cm), the initial possesses the amplitude of a wall painting, conferred to the two personages and the landscape by the meaning of the episode. The horizontal bar of the initial A creates two sections, as if to distinguish Heaven from earth, in which the infinity of the sky with the golden cloud behind God compares with the terrestrial atmosphere with blue mountains, soft green hills and trees. Eufrasia gave her image a naturalness by means of her technique: the use of *sprezzatura* in

the rendition of the leaves and the grass harmonises with the movement of the sounds produced by David's psaltery.

The bodily and spiritual energy characterising both God the Father, with the triangular halo symbolising the Trinity,[7] and David, sharing some similarities with biblical figures depicted by Attavante Attavanti,[8] are unusual in Eufrasia's illumination. However, as we will see in the colophon discussed in the Epilogue, she had a strong and lively character, partially manifested, where the images allowed more scope for artistic freedom, in ornament, comprising, as we saw, grotesques, masks, monsters, animated leaves and architectural elements.

The energy of Eufrasia's representations of David and God the Father could be explained by her contact with a new approach to the figural arts that she did not know before 1526 or, had she known it, had no occasion or desire to express it. Her belief that an energetic depiction of the human body reflected the inner movements of the soul was no doubt in

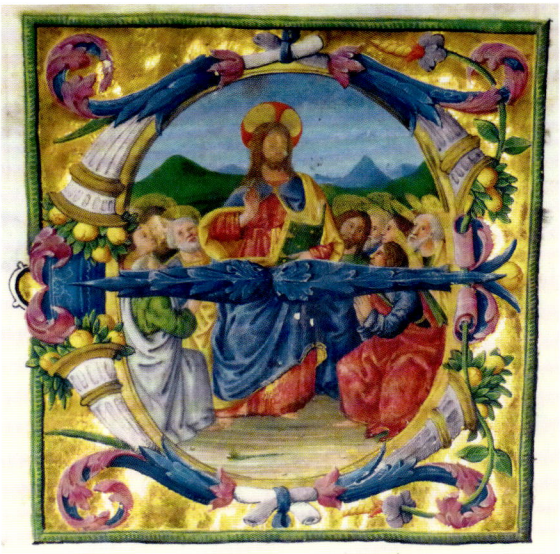
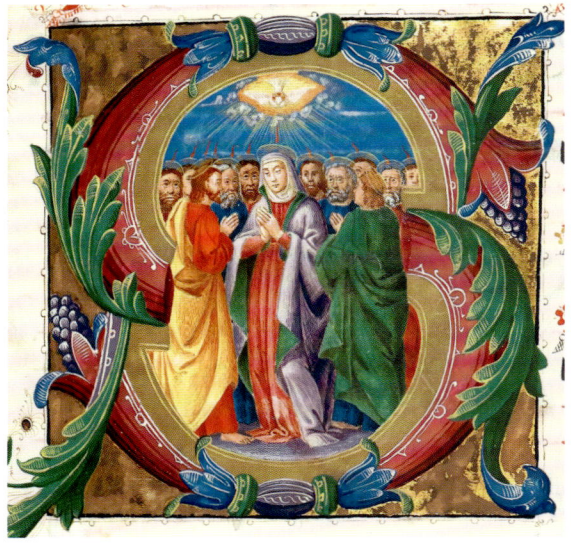

66 Giuliano Amadei, *Initial E, Christ Speaking to the Apostles*, cutting Bargello 2067C, *c.*1496, tempera and gold leaf on parchment, 13.8 × 12.5 (5⅜ × 4⅞ in), Museo Nazionale del Bargello, Florence

67 Eufrasia Burlamacchi, *Initial S, Pentecost*, Gradual MS 2650, fol.99ʳ, *c.*1532, tempera and gold leaf on parchment, 18.6 × 18.6 cm (7⅜ × 7⅜ in), detail, Biblioteca Statale, Lucca

line with what Michelangelo conceived as an aim of painting. However, instead of pointing to Ezechia da Vezzano, called Zacchia il Vecchio (*c.*1490–*c.*1561), as the painter who introduced Michelangelo's stylistic novelties to Lucca, as some art historians have claimed, it seems to me more likely that Eufrasia came to know Michelangelo's artistic solutions from another Lucchese painter.[9]

This painter is Agostino Marti, son of the goldsmith Francesco and Eufrasia's contemporary. He first trained in his father's workshop and later studied painting with Michele Angelo di Pietro Membrini: his father and Membrini had their workshops in the same building. In 1509 he was a 'maestro', and in 1523 he depicted the *Wedding of the Virgin* for the church of San Michele in Foro at Lucca. Like Michelangelo,

he depicted a series of images of God the Father energetically moving in Heaven surrounded by angels, as in the painting in the sacristy of San Martino Cathedral (*c.*1520; fig.65). This work reproduces some figures from the vault of the Sistine Chapel depicted by Michelangelo in 1508–12, especially those in the *Creation of the Sun and the Moon*.[10] Most likely, a drawing that could have inspired Eufrasia's approach to the figure of God the Father arrived in her hands after 1518, when Agostino returned from a journey to Rome. At any rate, he was used to drawing illustrations for books, as the documents testify. Some of these illustrations may have been passed on to his sisters, Felicita and Perpetua, in the San Domenico convent, and thence to Eufrasia.[11]

In this two-volume Gradual, Eufrasia meditated

more on painting than on miniature, confining the heritage of Giuliano Amadei to the ornamental initials, with just one exception. If the cutting 2067C in the Museo Nazionale del Bargello by Amadei, representing *Christ Speaking to the Apostles* (fig.66), belonged to a manuscript coming from San Frediano or San Martino in Lucca, it may have been of some importance for the scene of the *Pentecost* in Gradual 2650, fol.99ʳ (fig.67).¹² A marked similarity is detectable in the apostles' faces, showing surprise, attention, concern and love. Yet, it is in these two manuscripts for San Romano that Eufrasia not only re-elaborated the formal solutions for bodies, drapery folds, space and light of the works by Domenico Bigordi (del Ghirlandaio), Filippino Lippi and Antonio del Ceraiolo, but also seemingly interpreted some aspects of the art of another Florentine painter, Fra Bartolomeo, in the cross-hatching for deepening shades and for increasing the subtlety of tonal changes in small and large areas.¹³

THE LIGHT OF THE SFUMATO

The Florentine artist Baccio della Porta became Fra Bartolomeo in the monastery of San Marco in Florence in 1500. In 1509 he depicted the oil-on-canvas altarpiece *God the Father, Saint Mary Magdalene and Saint Catherine of Siena*, initially commissioned by the prior of the Reformed Dominicans of San Pietro Martire in Murano, but in 1512 presented to Fra Sante Pagnini (1470–1541) of the San Romano monastery in Lucca (fig.68).¹⁴

Fra Bartolomeo never had direct contact with the convent of San Domenico at Lucca but had a close relationship with the monastery of San Romano, especially with Fra Pagnini, who was prior there from 1507 to 1509 and from 1513 to 1515. The presence of Fra Pagnini at San Romano might also account for the depiction by Fra Bartolomeo of two large altarpieces in Lucca, the *Madonna with Saint Stephen*

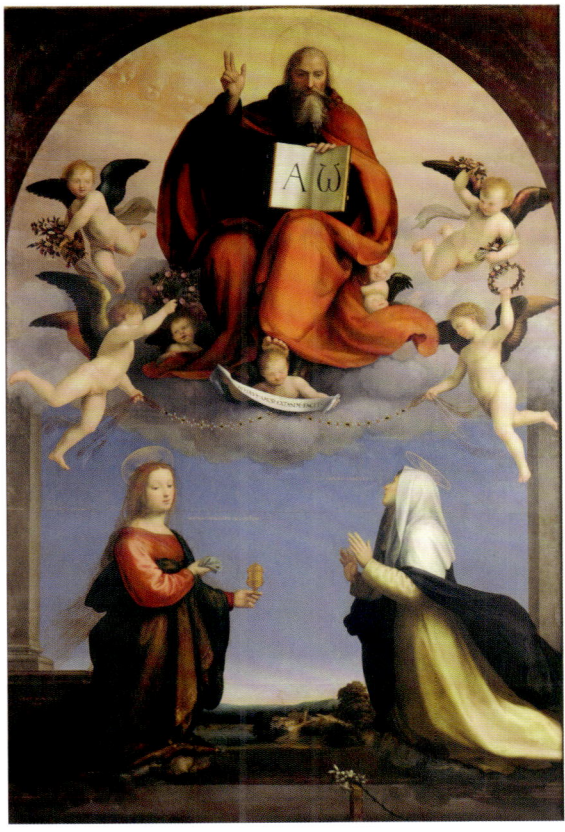

68 Fra Bartolomeo, *God the Father, Saint Mary Magdalene and Saint Catherine of Siena*, 1509, oil on canvas, 365 × 238 cm (143¾ × 93¾ in), Museo Nazionale di Villa Guinigi, Lucca

and Saint John the Baptist (1509) and the *Madonna della Misericordia* (1515). The former, for San Martino Cathedral, is still in situ; the latter was commissioned by Sebastiano Lambardi da Montecatini for a chapel he had built in the church of San Romano, and is now in the Museo Nazionale di Villa Guinigi in Lucca.¹⁵ In 1509 Eufrasia was in the new convent and likely in 1505 had already begun to illuminate the first of the five choir books now in California, completing the set in *c.*1515. But, whereas a miniature like the *Nativity* in

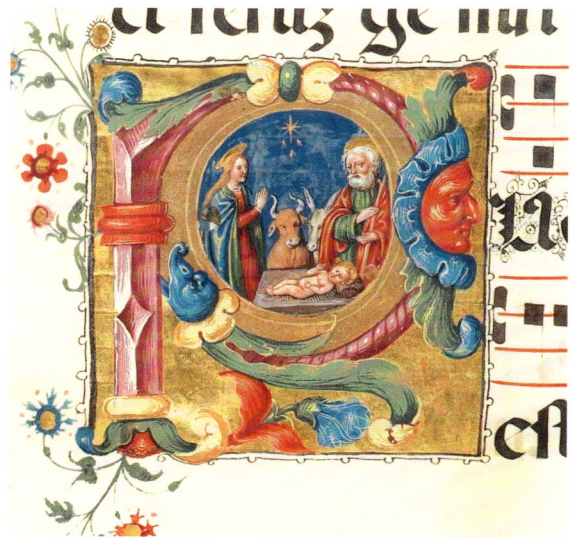

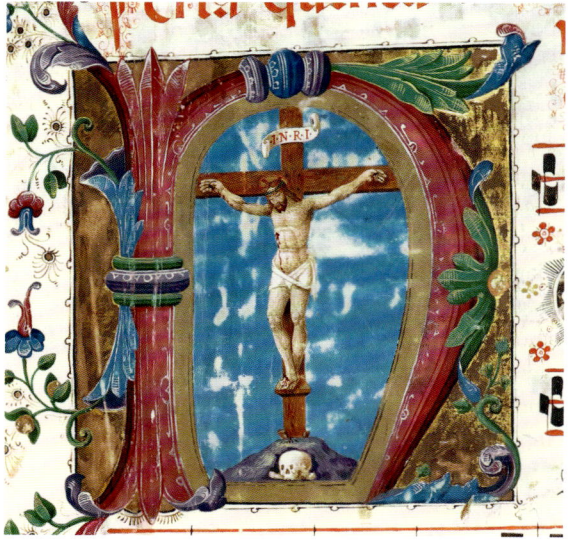

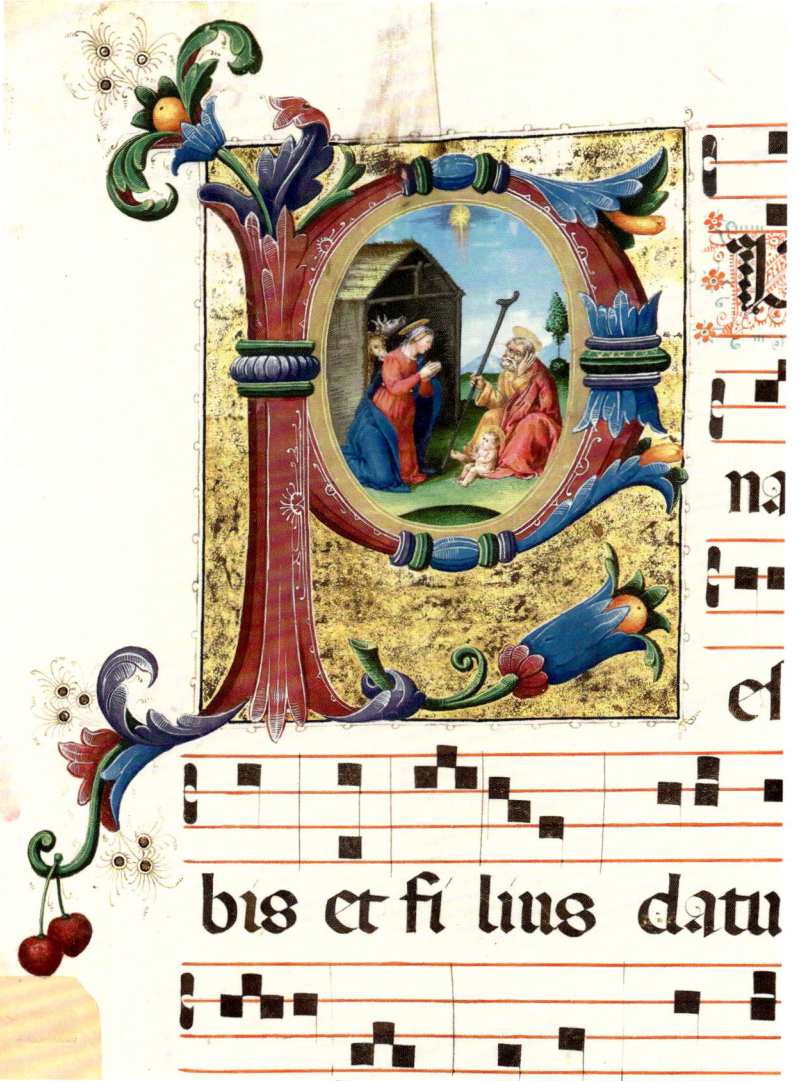

69 (above left) Eufrasia Burlamacchi, *Initial P, Nativity*, Gradual MS 5, fol.7ᵛ, *c.*1515, tempera and gold leaf on parchment, 14 × 14 cm (5 ½ × 5 ½ in), Dominican Convent, California

70 (above right) Eufrasia Burlamacchi, *Initial N, Crucifixion*, Gradual MS 2650, fol.1ʳ, *c.*1532, tempera and gold leaf on parchment, 19.7 × 19.3 cm (7 ¾ × 7 ⅝ in), Biblioteca Statale, Lucca

71 Eufrasia Burlamacchi, *Initial P, Puer natus est – Nativity*, Gradual MS 2649, fol.49ᵛ, *c.*1530, tempera and gold leaf on parchment, folium 59.3 × 43.2 cm (23 ⅜ × 17 in), initial 22.7 × 18.2 cm (8 ⅞ × 7 ⅛ in), Biblioteca Statale, Lucca

Gradual MS 5, fol.7ᵛ, does not betray any contact with Fra Bartolomeo's conception of forms, colours and light (fig.69), this influence is clearly detectable in the *Nativity* in Gradual MS 2649, fol.49ᵛ, *c.*1530 (fig.71). This miniature seems to be Eufrasia's response to Fra Bartolomeo's work, but it is unlikely that she could have seen directly how the friar depicted the dress and the veil of Saint Catherine of Siena, remarkable for the delicacy and attention to the play of light and shade. As elsewhere, Eufrasia came to know inspirational artworks through other sources.

As we saw above, when Fra Bartolomeo died in 1517, Fra Paolino inherited his drawings, which he used to depict altarpieces for the convent of Santa Caterina da Siena in Florence and for the San Domenico convent in Lucca. Some of these drawings may have already circulated before his arrival in Lucca. Even if delicacy and play of light and shade can be best conveyed through colours, a drawing with an abundance of sfumato was surely useful in the rendition of a mantle imbued with light, as in the figure of the kneeling Mary in the *Nativity* in MS 2649, fol.49ᵛ (fig.71). This miniature is particularly interesting since it expresses the importance of Mary in the scene. Joseph, depicted in meditation, supports the Christ Child, seated on his cloak, intently looking at His mother. In the simplicity of the environment, Mary praying shows the profound engagement of a woman with the mystery of the Incarnation.

As required for a Gradual, Eufrasia interpreted religious history – which, as a nun, she considered the 'True History' – in her illuminations, representing other episodes of Christ's life such as the *Crucifixion* (fig.70) and the *Resurrection*.[16] The models for the former must have been many, but it is likely that her direct source was a painting by the Lucchese artist Ansano di Michele Ciampanti (1474–1535; fig.72), with substantial transformation in the suppleness of the body, thanks to her technique of spreading colours in parallel lines to confer plasticity and luminosity to the skin. For this technique, she may have considered both

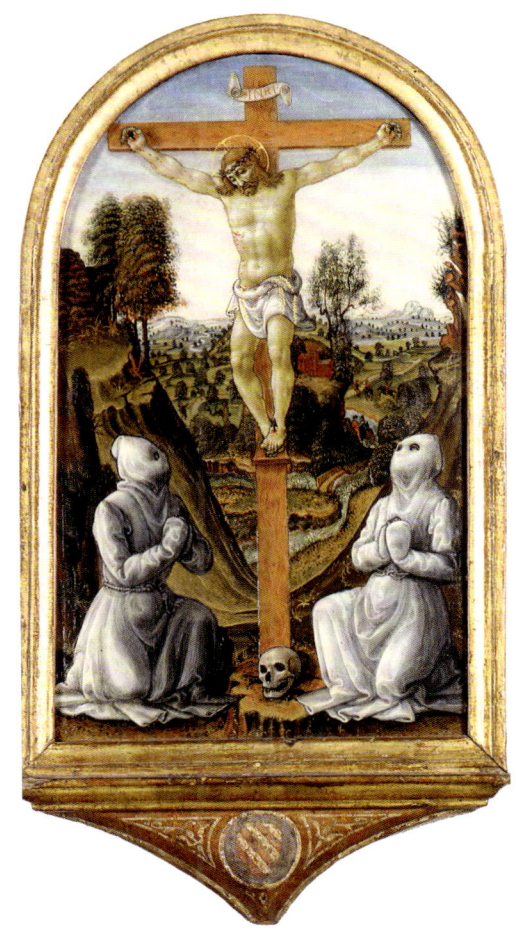

72 Ansano di Michele Ciampanti, *The Crucifix Worshipped by two White Penitents*, early sixteenth century, tempera on panel, 73 × 38 cm (28 ¾ × 15 in), Museo Nazionale di Villa Guinigi, Lucca

painting and prints, demonstrating that the sources of her inspiration belonged to a wide sphere of art.

Eufrasia depicted the *Resurrection* once in *c.*1515 and a second time in *c.*1532. In Gradual MS 5 in California, fol.48ᵛ (fig.73), Christ resurrected is vaguely reminiscent of Piero della Francesca's

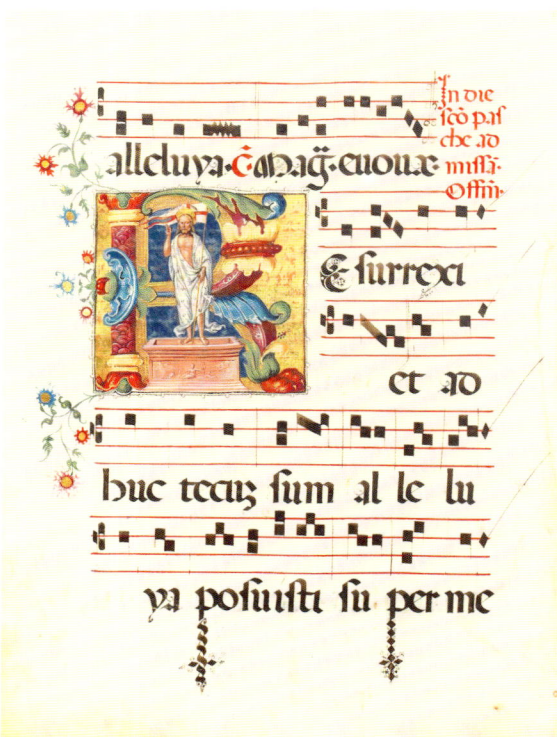

73 Eufrasia Burlamacchi, *Initial R, Resurrexi et adhuc
tecum sum – Resurrection*, Gradual MS 5, fol.48ᵛ, *c.*1515,
tempera and gold leaf on parchment, folium 54.2 × 38.5
cm (21⅜ × 15⅛ in), initial 14 × 14 cm (5½ × 5½ in),
Dominican Convent, California

Resurrection at Sansepolcro, most likely through
the rendition of Giuliano Amadei. Eufrasia
offers a personal interpretation of antiquity in the
reproduction of a bas-relief in the sarcophagus of rose
marble, featuring a female figure with a torch, a vessel
and two putti in a landscape.[17]

THE SPREZZATURA

In Gradual MS 2650, fol.31ᵛ (fig.74), the resurrected
Christ belongs stylistically to the High Renaissance,
comparable with the Capponi Altarpiece (*c.*1497–
1509) depicting the same subject, now in the Galleria
dell'Accademia in Florence, by Raffaellino del Garbo
(*c.*1470–*c.*1528).[18] The miniature of Eufrasia's shows
a true triumph over death – but also a triumph of
colours and delicacy of shape – for the splendid
ascensional energy which carries the supple body of
Christ towards Heaven. To arrive at these effects,
Eufrasia again chose the *sprezzatura* technique,
rather different from the homogeneous fields of
colours (*campiture*) or the gradation of shades
usually employed in fifteenth- to sixteenth-century
illumination.

When Eufrasia was working on her first set of
manuscripts for her own convent, the choir books
now in California, the author Baldesar Castiglione
(1478–1529) theorised about art in his treatise *The Book
of the Courtier*, first published in 1528. Castiglione
considered art to be based in skill, as a process of
manipulation in which artists consciously arranged,
contrasted and harmonised their figures. He
identified two distinct aspects of this process. The first
attends to light and shade:

> Good painters, by their use of shadow, manage to
> throw the light of objects into relief, and, likewise, by
> their use of light, to deepen the shadows of planes
> and bring different colours together so that all are
> made more apparent through the contrast of one with

another; and the placing of figures in opposition one to another helps them achieve their aim.[19]

The second aspect is the manner of applying paint to the surfaces:

> Often too in painting, a single line which is not laboured, a single brush stroke made with ease and in such a manner that the hand seems of itself to complete the line desired by the painter, without being directed by care or skill of any kind, clearly reveals [...] excellency of craftmanship.[20]

This is Castiglione's definition of *sprezzatura*. The verb *sprezzare* means to scorn or despise, so that the usual translation of the term as 'nonchalance' is too cool, perhaps too neutral to suggest that meaning.[21] However, if a painter shows an easy handling of the pictorial matter, it should imply scorn for the potential difficulty or restriction involved. *Sprezzatura* therefore goes beyond human limitations in the sense that, in addition to this manifestation of skill and the response it should cause, for Castiglione it was also the very source from which grace sprung.[22] By means of *sprezzatura*, Eufrasia expressed grace in her works. From Leon Battista Alberti to Giorgio Vasari, grace describes the achievements of art, a harmonious elegance in which rules were followed but at the same time overcome. Simplicity, purity and naturalness are the other concepts springing from grace. Contrary to expectations, Eufrasia conceived of grace as a quality encompassing not only gestures of sacred figures and delicacy of colours but also aspects of the settings, including landscape, trees, hills, clouds and Heaven.

Outstanding examples of the application of *sprezzatura* in Eufrasia's miniatures are found in Gradual MS 5 in California and in the two-volume Gradual for San Romano. In Gradual MS 5, fol.146ᵛ, featuring *Saint Mary Magdalene* (fig.75), Eufrasia employed four colours only: yellow, blue, red and green. She applied them according to the diverse

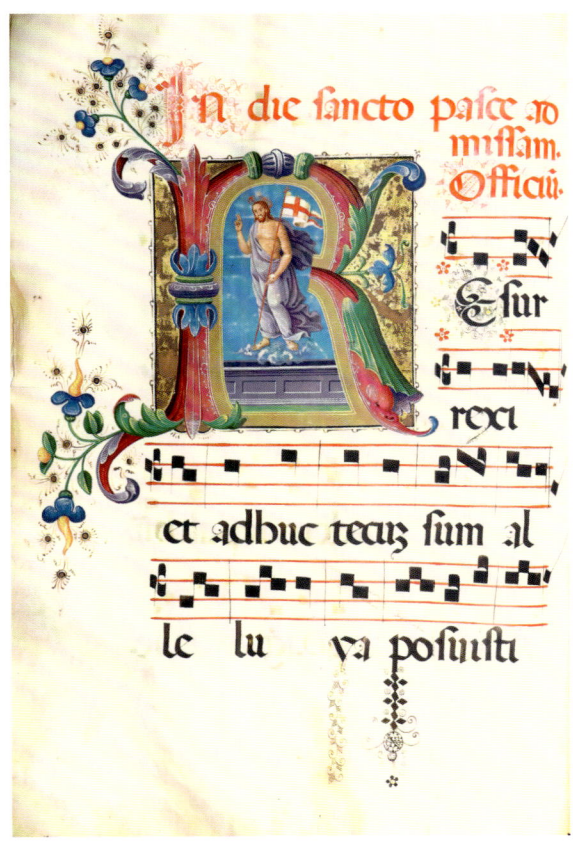

74 Eufrasia Burlamacchi, *Initial R, Resurrexi et adhuc tecum sum – Resurrection*, Gradual MS 2650, fol.31ᵛ, *c*.1532, tempera and gold leaf on parchment, folium 60.5 × 43.3 cm (23⅞ × 17 in), initial 19 × 17.5 cm (7½ × 6⅞ in), Biblioteca Statale, Lucca

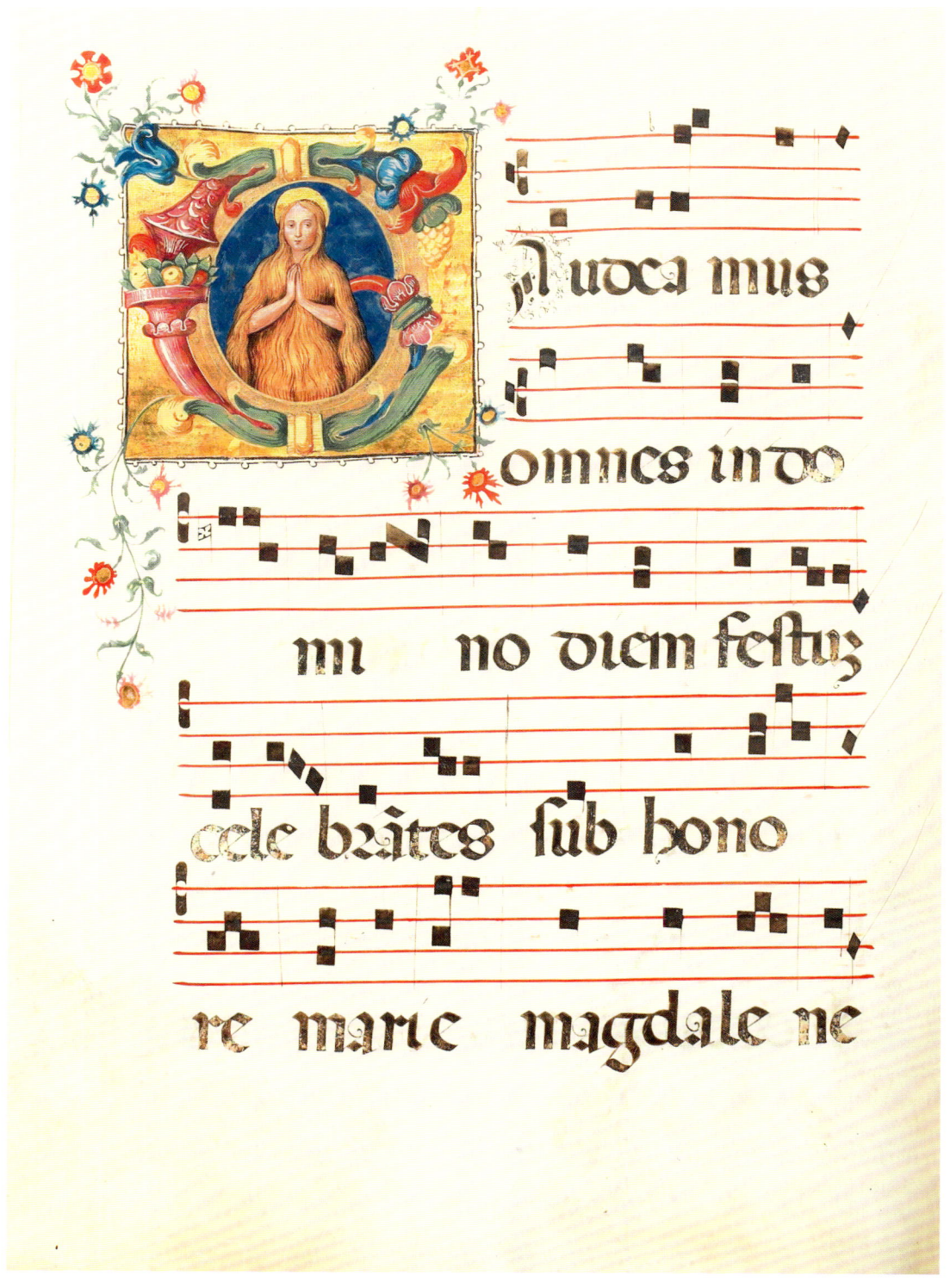

75 Eufrasia Burlamacchi, *Initial G, Gaudeamus omnes in domino – Saint Mary Magdalene*, Gradual MS 5, fol.146[v], *c.*1515, tempera and gold leaf on parchment, folium 54.2 × 38.5 cm (21⅜ × 15⅛ in), initial 14 × 14 cm (5½ × 5½ in), Dominican Convent, California

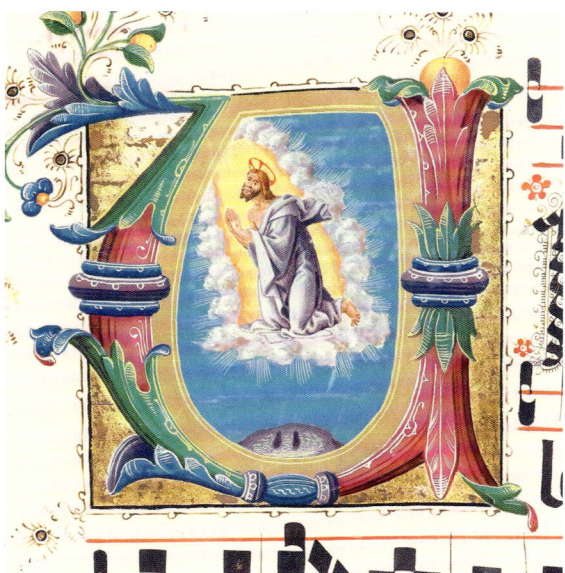

76 Eufrasia Burlamacchi, *Initial V, Ascension of Christ*,
Gradual MS 2650, fol.87ᵛ, *c.*1532, tempera and gold leaf
on parchment, 15.3 × 14.8 cm (6 × 5 ⅞ in), Biblioteca
Statale, Lucca

initials. In order to render the source of light,
coming always from the left, as an integral part of
the illustration, Eufrasia varied the intensity of the
colours, applied with thin and irregular brushstrokes,
as if a part of a mantle or the plumage of a bird were
partially bathed in light and partially in shade. But
the most outstanding *sprezzatura* effect of them
all is to be seen in the miniature of the *Ascension
of Christ* in Gradual MS 2650, fol.87ᵛ, where a
supernatural atmosphere is suggested by the wide
use of azure and white (fig.76).

As I have argued above regarding sources of
inspiration, Eufrasia never experienced mystical
visions, but she could imagine them. The *Ascension
of Christ* is the only instance in which Eufrasia tried
to render one of the most important moments in
Christ's life without having the support of the Sacred
Scripture: the Ascension is not described there, even
as it is predicted (John 6:62). As usual, Eufrasia
chose a simple and effective solution for making
manifest the momentous event of Christ's passage
from earth to Heaven. She depicted the imprints
of his feet left at the top of a hill as last signs of
impalpable materiality over which she represented a
frame of luminous and soft clouds, rendered by rapid
and vibrant brushstrokes of grey and white tempera,
surrounding the kneeling, humble Saviour in the
attitude of praying. Her approach suggests a visionary
quality that she learned through her knowledge of
visions experienced by other sisters at San Domenico,
as discussed in Chapter 5.

materials she wished to render. For example, with
no fear of contrasting yellow with yellow, in this
miniature she used both gold leaf and yellow paint.
She glued the most shining yellow – the gold leaf –
onto the parchment, which forms the background.
In the acanthus leaves that frame the letters, yellow
colour comes out of the inner parts of the long
chalice-like green containers; at the joining points of
these chalice-like vegetable containers she depicted
roundels that look like heavy golden rings. In the
rendition of the grapes and apples, she used quick
brushstrokes to arrive at sculptural effects.

In the two-volume Gradual MSS 2649–50, the
naturalistic effects that illustrate Eufrasia's concern
with plasticity and three-dimensionality are attained
not only in historiated but also in ornamental

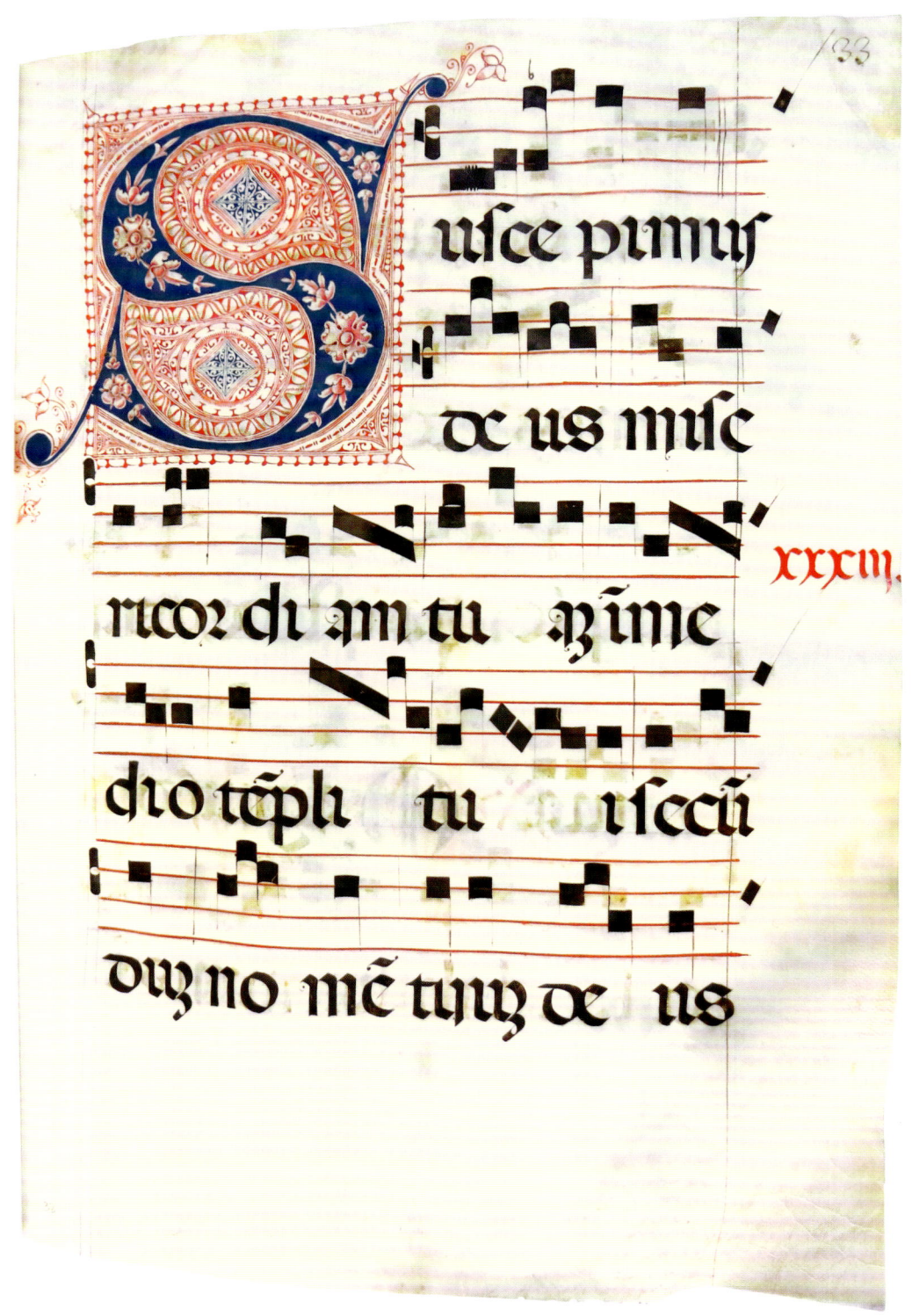

77 Anonymous calligrapher, *Initial S, Suscepimus deus*, Gradual Sanctoral MS 2645, fol.33ʳ, *c.*1515, tempera and ink on parchment, folium 56.1 × 40.2 cm (22 ⅛ × 15 ⅞ in), initial 13.9 × 13.8 cm (5 ½ × 5 ⅜ in), Biblioteca Statale, Lucca

8

The Logic of Detail

In her study on the Renaissance *virtuosa*, Fredrika H. Jacobs theorised that early modern artists and viewers believed that female artists paid close attention to detail, had a preference for geometric pattern, and a predilection for ornament and over-refinement. Together these interests revealed a *donnesca mano* or 'feminine hand'.[1] However, in medieval and early modern illumination, close attention to detail is the norm for both female and male artists. In what does the difference consist, if any? Unless one wishes to state that penwork initials do not strictly belong to illumination, the logic of detail must be applied to all illuminators. Furthermore, it is rather difficult to distinguish a male from a female hand in initials consisting of lines, points and geometrical figures. Therefore, in an art form in which an artist's gender cannot be distinguished visually, what should be judged is always the degree of inventiveness and the accuracy in the rendition of the motifs. For this reason, a comparison between the penwork initials made by Eufrasia and contemporary work by a male calligrapher in the monastery of San Romano in Lucca will be very instructive.

GRADUAL MS 2645 FOR SAN ROMANO

The monastery of San Romano, from its foundation in 1236, was an intellectual centre with its own scriptorium for book production. The community was closely tied to Florence and especially to the monastery of San Marco.[2] The long administrative, economic and cultural process in which San Romano was drawn towards San Marco culminated in 1498, with the inclusion of the Lucchese monastery in the jurisdiction of the San Marco Congregation.[3]

In *c.*1515 a Gradual Sanctoral (a book for the Mass with the annual cycle of the feast days devoted to the saints) was written and illuminated for the monastery of San Romano, now MS 2645 in the Biblioteca Statale, Lucca. It presents many calligraphic letters, ornamented with a variety of geometrical and naturalistic motifs and rich with colour: apart from the canonical red and blue, the initials are also decorated with yellow, orange, rose and green.[4] Sfumato effects diminish the contrast of the pure chromatic hues. The bars of the letters, of a uniform basic colour, are decorated with flowers and leaves forming volutes, framed with extreme precision, producing contrasts that create an illusion of intarsia in the body of the letter. It is possible that the illuminator of the choir book had access to something from the field of wooden intarsia. In 1452 the artist Leonardo di Francesco Marti (*c.*1407–61) had used this technique to produce intricately detailed choir stalls for San Martino Cathedral, now preserved in the Cathedral and in the Museo Nazionale di Villa Guinigi in Lucca.[5]

The style of the artist who produced the penwork initials of MS 2645 is rather close to the work of Fra Benedetto del Mugello (*c.*1390–1448), Fra Angelico's brother, who was active in the San Marco monastery as scribe and calligrapher.[6] The only initial which features the image of a saint, namely Saint Andrew Apostle, can be compared to the miniatures of the Psalter MS 529 (Biblioteca di San Marco, Florence), illuminated in *c.*1505 by Fra Eustachio (Tommaso di Baldassarre; 1473–1555).[7]

However, the penwork initials made by Eufrasia belong to another artistic sphere. In all the manuscripts she illuminated, ornament takes either naturalistic or geometrical forms, constituting the frame or filling the spaces of large penwork letters. But the important point here is that Eufrasia was both illuminator and *cantrix*. Even if the anonymous calligrapher at San Romano were also a *cantor*, his approach to decorating the letters is static: the abstract motifs are applied to entirely fill the spaces, and the naturalistic five-petal flowers in the S of MS 2645, fol.33ʳ (fig.77), are simply placed on the blue background. If one searches for rhythm, it is expanding neither in space nor in time. By contrast, Eufrasia, being a *cantrix*, knew how to manage the relationship between the complexity of a penwork initial that expanded its elements in space and the movement of the notes in time. The abstract motifs she drew within the letters are organised in such a manner as to seem in constant visual movement, as discussed below. Eufrasia understood that from the encounter between the visual and the aural issued the beauty of abstraction connected to immaterial substance, with no reference to the material world.

Although it is generally acknowledged that the creation of inner ties within conventual communities was orchestrated by just a few people (among them the bishop, the confessor and the prioress, who directed the convent's spirituality), Eufrasia, in her capacity as *cantrix*, also contributed to strengthening them by determining the musical life of the convent.

She chose the chants for most liturgical occasions, conducted the musical performance, led chants and antiphons and established appropriate pitch, tone, tempo and cadence.[8] This acquaintance with chant was imbued in Eufrasia's mind and soul and, consequently, in her artistic practice.

ORNAMENT AND CHANT

After the completion in *c.*1515 of the five manuscripts for her convent, in a long note Eufrasia wrote and appended to MS 5, she stated that she hoped to be among the elect chosen to honour the Lord eternally by singing a chant she quoted partially from Saint John (Revelation 7:12): 'Blessing, and glory, and wisdom, and thanksgiving, and honour, and power and might, be unto our God for ever and ever. Amen.' Notwithstanding her desire to honour the Lord in Heaven, Eufrasia had to wait for more than three decades before her wish was fulfilled. In fact, after finishing the five manuscripts for San Domenico, by 1520 she had completed Antiphonary MS 14 for San Martino Cathedral and by *c.*1532, the two-volume Gradual MSS 2649–50 for the Dominican monastery of San Romano.

In this long span of time, Eufrasia perfected not only her miniatures but also her penwork initials. If one compares the calligraphic letters in Gradual MS 5 in California, for example the G on fol.169ʳ (fig.78), with those in the two-volume Gradual MSS 2649–50 (fig.79), in both cases a work of collaboration with other nuns who followed the basic patterns she passed on to them, one can easily detect an increase in complexity and imaginative solutions. On the whole, the penwork initials envisaged by Eufrasia point to the power of abstraction. For us, it is difficult to think of abstract decoration independently, since one needs a reference to some objective reality to make sense of it, which Arthur Danto called 'aboutness'.[9] In the manuscripts under consideration, the abstract

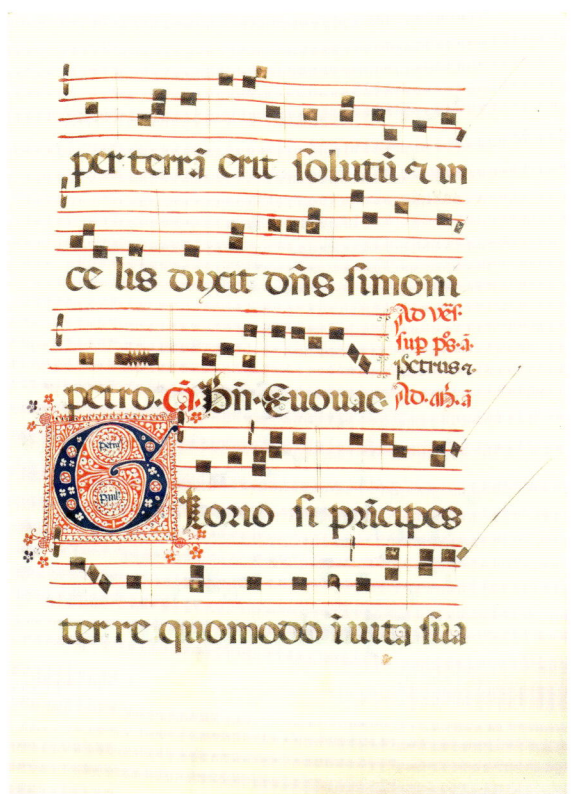

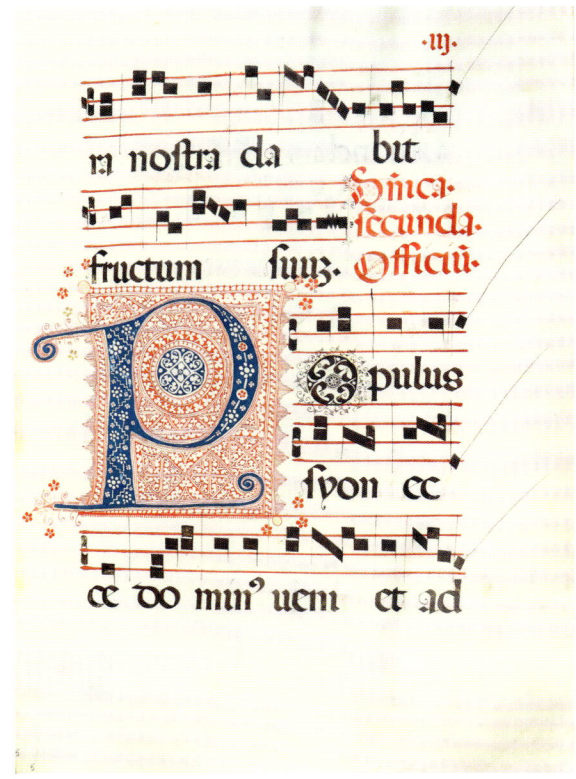

78 Eufrasia Burlamacchi, *Initial G, Gloriosi principes*, Gradual MS 5, fol.169ᵣ, *c*.1515, tempera and ink on parchment, folium 54.2 × 38.5 cm (21⅜ × 15⅛ in), initial 13 × 13 cm (5⅛ × 5⅛ in), Dominican Convent, California

79 Eufrasia Burlamacchi, *Initial P, Populus Syon*, Gradual MS 2649, fol.5ᵣ, *c*.1530, tempera and ink on parchment, folium 59.3 × 43.2 cm (23⅜ × 17 in), initial 18.3 × 14.2 cm (7¼ × 5⅝ in), Biblioteca Statale, Lucca

decoration of the letters refers to a specific 'aboutness', that is, the expressive unfolding of the chant, a process in which the decorative components of music are set in motion in a spatial field.

I do not deny that these decorative works, with their complex variety of patterns, fulfilled the expected function of embellishing the page. But the long acquaintance with both chant and decoration – an acquaintance that only a *cantrix*-illuminator could have – may have inspired one individual 'from within' to overcome the visual limitations of the letter with

the aim of making it compete with the visual-free possibilities of the chant.

The decoration is clear and elegant, showing the draughtsmanship of a gifted artist. Yet, Eufrasia's penwork style may appear somewhat outmoded. The dense two-colour pattern used to embellish letters in chant texts had deep roots in monastic decorative practice and had become widespread in the thirteenth century, with an increase in virtuosity during the fifteenth century.[10] A case in point is the book production in the Dominican Observant

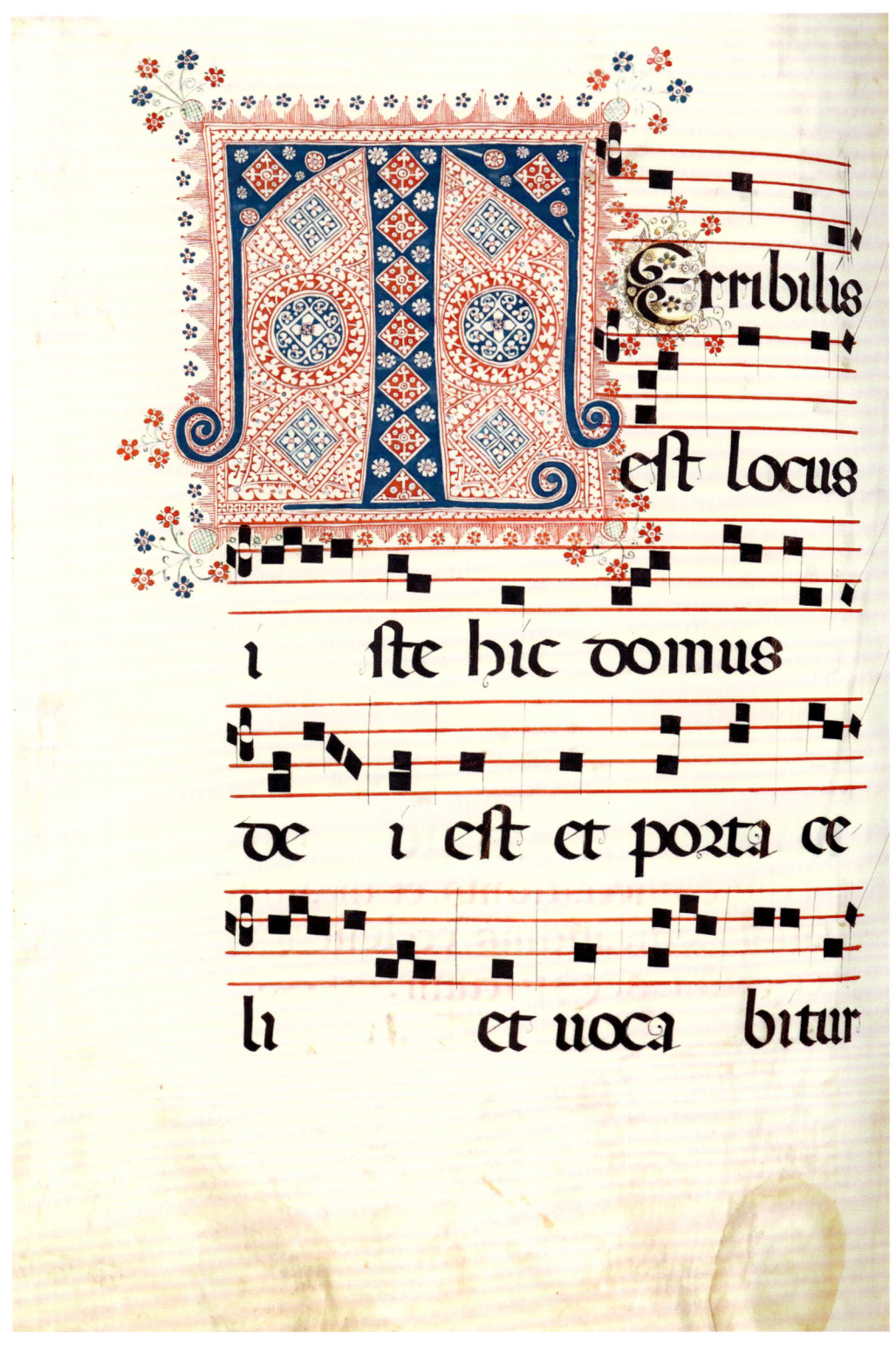

80 Eufrasia Burlamacchi, *Initial T, Terribilis est locus*, Gradual MS 2650, fol.249ᵛ, *c.*1532, tempera and ink on parchment, folium 60.5 × 43.3 cm (23 ⅞ × 17 in), initial 17.5 × 16.8 cm (6 ⅞ × 6 ⅝ in), Biblioteca Statale, Lucca

convent of San Pier Martire in Florence, where the nuns copied the so-called 'breviaries' but in fact psalters, decorating them with a profusion of blue and red penwork initials. They also sold their works to other convents, as occurred with San Domenico in Pisa.[11] The frequency with which red and blue appear in penwork surrounds and infills led some scholars to endow both colours with symbolic meaning: red pointing to Christ's sufferings and blue to Heaven.[12] A different – and down to earth – interpretation may best account for the use of these colours, however: their chromatic contrast enhanced the experience of seeing, reading and singing (fig.80).

I have already suggested that both diction and chant with their aural qualities are inspirational for the decoration of a manuscript. The two-volume Gradual MSS 2649–50 comprises a long series of chants that in their nature are not descriptive but performative. They imply iterability, the endless repetition of verbal acts which, in their duplication, bear witness to accepted religious and cultural conventions that made performance and ritual fulfil their expected aims.[13] But even if repetition is not always a voluntary act in speaking, singing or hearing, one of its possible outcomes is the re-signification of concepts. Where liturgical texts are concerned, both read and sung, re-signification could mean recalling an original meaning that over time had become less vivid. Thus, there is a difference between responses to familiar and unfamiliar texts and chants. With the former, re-signification would tend to be a more personal experience, one of spiritual appropriation.[14]

One can understand the connection between aural and visual arts in relation to re-signification, which takes place when an active mind finds visual correlatives to words, whether uttered or sung. Since the convent rules prescribed that chants be performed as plainly as possible and that texts be read in the most restrained manner, the ornamental complexity Eufrasia displayed in the initials she envisaged seems to compensate for the absence of decorative effects in both chant and speech. If this counterbalance holds true, even penwork initials could tell us something

more than figural images normally do about nuns' cognitive and emotional attitudes.

In the long series of penwork initials it is possible to detect the compositional method that Eufrasia taught to other nuns. She first picked up the musical elements that served a decorative function in melody, harmony and rhythm – absent in the prescribed chant – and then translated them into visual forms. Melodic ornamentation includes trills, turns, grace notes and flourishes, augmentation and diminution, and the use of contrary, oblique and parallel motion. Modulation, a decorative device, is often a means of calling attention to harmonic relationships as well as accelerando and ritardando. Failure to appreciate the extent to which music is decorative may be due to undervaluation of its spatial features – especially its 'vertical' harmonic features – just as one may underestimate the temporal features of the 'static' visual arts.[15] In a way, ornament, considered in chant, uttered prayers and visual arts, becomes effective through well-expressed repetition.

Memory of the whole decoration and expectation of the single solution were eased by the visual recognition of structural and decorative elements, like dots, lines, circles, squares, lozenges, crosses, flowers, ribbons and interlaces that changed only slightly from one letter to another. Ornament, unfolding in limited spaces, enhanced the intensity of emotional effects; moreover, penwork initials also elicited an appreciative reaction of an aesthetic kind, the pleasure to recognise the beauty of simple forms organised in dynamic systems becoming more and more compound according to a decorative logic. This can be described as the urge to fill all the letters' empty spaces with a variety of motifs of different size, parallel to the urge to fill the physical empty space of the church with notes of different pitch and colour.

Thus, the initials Eufrasia and her companions decorated so carefully may be interpreted as their attempt to make more graspable a reality – that of chant and, along with it, that of the sacred meaning – that would have faded away with the very unfolding of the chant itself.

Epilogue

The Lost Colophon

In an autograph note in Gradual MS 5, Sister Eufrasia declared that she completed this, the fifth manuscript of the group of liturgically related volumes she made for San Domenico, in *c.*1515, when she would have been 37 years old.[1] Eufrasia's original text no longer exists, having been lost seemingly when the manuscripts were sold on the market in the late 1920s. It was, however, providentially copied by the scholar Innocenzo Taurisano in 1914:

> Let it be known to all those who will come shortly after us, that these songbooks were written around the year of Our Lord 1515 by a most worthless servant of Jesus Christ, whose name pray to the Lord he will be pleased to write in the Book of Life. If any good is found in the books, it is the Lord, giver of all goods, to be thanked; after Him you should thank sweetest Angel Gabriel to whom I recommended this work, which went beyond the strength and ability of the scribe. The aforementioned angel protected the books from many dangers that occur in writing them and I humbly pray you to pardon the defects you will find in them. Please pray the Lord to pardon those and all the other countless defects of mine. Through your blessed prayers, ask the Lord to bring me to that happy fatherland of eternal life to sing for unending centuries that sweet song *Blessing, and glory, and wisdom and thanksgiving. Amen.*[2]

The note is revealing in several ways. One is that, instead of describing a feeling of elation for her accomplishment, Eufrasia referred to the Last Judgement, expressing a desire to be among the elect honouring the Lord eternally by singing a specific chant inspired by Saint John (Revelation 7:12).

Furthermore, Eufrasia entrusted the protection of her work to Gabriel and, perhaps, considered her five manuscripts as a work divinely conceived and inspired, developed under God's protection and delivered through God's assistance. Hers had been a mental and spiritual conception that took the form of words and images. Her preference for Gabriel also shows that, well before post-Tridentine spirituality, angels were considered individual guardians. If in Florence Michael was surpassed by Raphael in his role of guardian angel, in Lucca it was Gabriel who performed this task. Sharon Strocchia found that Eufrasia's contemporaries drew similarities between angels and nuns. Both formed themselves into corporations to protect other faithful, the nuns through their prayers; contemporaries saw both as mediators between the human world and the divine sphere.[3] In the San Domenico convent, angelic names – Angela, Angeletta, Angelica, Archangiola, Cherubina, Gabriella, Michaela, Raffaella and Serafina – appear as a mark of new spirituality in the early sixteenth century, but they never surpassed in importance the names of other saints.[4]

Eufrasia certainly was not alone among Italian nuns of this period in composing a colophon note for a manuscript. There were, in fact, many. An analysis by Melissa Moreton identified two primary themes in these colophons within a varied spectrum of possibilities: the presentation of self as a pious woman in the monastic community and a desire to convey a more individualised identity.[5] What Eufrasia wrote cannot be considered a true colophon since it was not within the manuscript but on a spine and since her name does not appear within it, as was customary. Rather, she recorded how the manuscripts arrived at their completion, qualifying herself neither as 'unworthy' (*indegna*) nor as 'sinner' (*peccatrice*) but as 'most worthless servant' (*vilissima serva*).

Moreton suggested that the choice of terminology used in scribal colophons intentionally connected nuns to their spiritual leaders, as with the Dominican nuns of San Jacopo a Ripoli in Florence and of San Niccolò in Prato. In this light, the phrase '*indegna serva e schiava di Jesu Cristo*' employed by the nun-scribes refers to Saint Catherine of Siena. In Catherine's letters to Raymond of Capua, who was her confessor and biographer, and to fellow spirituals, kings and popes, this phrase was a means of presenting herself.[6] Since Saint Catherine's letters and her writings in general were read in late medieval and Renaissance Italy, particularly by female Dominicans, Eufrasia may have connected herself to the Sienese saint.

Nonetheless, I would suggest an additional connection for Eufrasia, more in line with the religious environment of the San Domenico convent in Lucca. As Sister Hilaria Cenami wrote in the first 31 pages of the San Domenico Chronica, the Lucchese convent was founded in 1502 by a group of nuns seeking to actualise a monastic life of strict observance as preached by Fra Girolamo Savonarola. As discussed in Chapters 1 and 2, Eufrasia participated in the foundation of the San Domenico convent and was deeply familiar with Savonarola's teachings.[7] He often introduced his sermons and letters with the phrase in the vernacular: 'Brother Hieronymo of Ferrara, useless servant of Jesus Christ' ('*Frate Hieronymo da Ferrara servo inutile di Jesu Christo*') or in Latin: '*Frater Hieronymus inutilis servus Iesu Christi*'.[8] The printed texts that report his words were much read within convents and monasteries even after his death in 1498, especially in Florence, Prato and Lucca.[9] Eufrasia's phrase can be placed within this Savonarolan frame. She substituted 'most worthless' (*vilissima*) for 'useless' (*inutile*), keeping unchanged the concept of servility, with all its implications.

Yet, this is not the most important feature of Eufrasia's 'colophon'. Considered as a whole, it is a climactic text indeed, the result of a consummate writer and excellent singer, aware of the principle that desired effects need specific strategies; in her case, humility and fervent devotion contributed to overcoming human limitations. Eufrasia's final aim was to be accepted in Heaven to praise the Lord in the way she knew best on earth. As an expert in chant, she hoped to perform, with the angels and the blessed, 'that sweet song *Blessing, and glory, and wisdom and thanksgiving*'. Thus, it is not by chance that she ends her 'colophon' insisting on chant, the activity she knew by long experience, giving her both an awareness of God's presence and a feeling of complete joyfulness.

For many nuns of the San Domenico convent, the aim of their life was to join themselves with Jesus as their spiritual spouse, a wish inserted as the usual formula by the various nun-chroniclers who composed the convent's necrologies. By contrast, Eufrasia insisted neither on the joys of spiritual marriage nor on being part of supernatural light. Her ultimate desire was to manifest her spiritual state through unending harmonious notes, sometimes reflected in her approach to illumination and resounding in what she called 'that happy fatherland of eternal life'. The arts brought Eufrasia beyond concerns of intellect and emotion, and closer to spiritual fulfilment.

Notes

ABBREVIATIONS

ASDLu = Archivio Storico Diocesano, Lucca
ASF = Archivio di Stato, Florence
ASLu = Archivio di Stato, Lucca
BNCF = Biblioteca Nazionale Centrale, Florence
BSLu = Biblioteca Statale, Lucca
Cinq. = Cinquecentina
CRSGF = Corporazioni Religiose Soppresse dal Governo
    Francese
CSD = Chronica di San Domenico, Lucca [held at
    Bibbiena]
CSG = Chronica di San Giorgio, Lucca
CSR = Chronica di San Romano, Lucca
Inc. = Incunabulum

PREFACE

1   For Eufrasia's dates of birth and death, see 'Chronica di San Domenico di Lucca', Archivio del Monastero di Santa Maria del Sasso, Bibbiena (Arezzo) (hereafter CSD), t.i, fol.3ᵛ; t.ii, fol.35.

2   Caroline Murphy, 'Plautilla Nelli: Between Cloister and Client. A Study in Negotiation', in Jonathan Nelson (ed.), *Suor Plautilla Nelli (1523–1588): The First Woman Painter of Florence*, Edizioni Cadmo, Florence, 2000, pp 57–65. See also Sheila Barker, 'Painting and Humanism in Early Modern Florentine Convents', in Sheila Barker and Luciano Cinelli, OP (eds), *Artiste nel chiostro. Produzione artistica nei monasteri femminili in età moderna*, *Memorie Domenicane* special issue, vol.132, no.46, 2015, pp 105–39.

3   Sheila Barker, *Artemisia Gentileschi*, Lund Humphries, London, 2021.

4   Sheila Barker (ed.), *'La grandezza dell'universo' nell'arte di Giovanna Garzoni*, exh.cat., Galleria degli Uffizi, Florence, 28 May–28 June 2020, Sillabe, Livorno, 2020.

5   Kate J.P. Lowe, *Nuns' Chronicles and Convent Culture in Renaissance and Counter-Reformation Italy*, Cambridge University Press, Cambridge, 2003, esp. ch.8; Ann Roberts, *Dominican Women and Renaissance Art: The Convent of San Domenico of Pisa*, Ashgate, Aldershot, 2008; Marilyn Dunn, 'Convent Creativity', in Allyson M. Poska, Jane Couchman and Katherine A. McIver (eds), *The Ashgate Research Companion to Gender and Women in Early Modern Europe*, Ashgate, Farnham, 2013, pp 53–73, pp 67–8.

6   Catherine Turrill Lupi, '*Parenti, clienti e cognoscenti*: The Nun-Artisans of Santa Caterina da Siena and Their Clients', in Marcello Fantoni, Louisa C. Matthew and Sara F. Matthews-Grieco (eds), *The Art Market in Italy (15th–17th Centuries)*, Franco Panini Editore, Modena, 2003, pp 95–103, pp 95–6.

7   Mary D. Garrard, 'The Cloister and the Square: Gender Dynamics in Renaissance Florence', *Early Modern Women: An Interdisciplinary Journal*, vol.11, no.1, 2016, pp 5–44, p.11.

8   Vincenzo Marchese, *Memorie dei più insigni pittori, scultori e architetti domenicani*, Giusti, Lucca, 1845–6, 2nd edn, 1869, p.345; Innocenzo Taurisano, OP, *I Domenicani in Lucca*, Baroni, Lucca, 1914, pp 11, 160–61, 225.

9   Marco Paoli, *I corali della Biblioteca Statale di Lucca*, Leo S. Olschki, Florence, 1977, pp 37–43, 58–64.

10 Gerardo Mansi, *I patrizi di Lucca. Le antiche famiglie lucchesi ed i loro stemmi*, Titania, Lucca, 1996, p.140.

11 Mark Gregory D'Apuzzo, 'Le monache di Savonarola tra arte e committenza', in Vera Fortunati (ed.), *Vita artistica nel monastero femminile. Exempla*, Editrice Compositori, Bologna, 2002, pp 131–45, p.144; Mark Gregory D'Apuzzo, 'Eufrasia Burlamacchi (?–1548)', in Vera Fortunati (ed.), *Italian Women Artists from Renaissance to Baroque*, exh.cat., National Museum of Women in the Arts, Washington, DC, 16 March–15 July 2007, Skira, New York, 2007, pp 96–101.

12 Ileana Tozzi, 'I corali miniati di Suor Eufrasia Burlamacchi, fondatrice del monastero di san Domenico a Lucca', *Arte cristiana*, vol.829, no.4, 2005, pp 217–22; Ileana Tozzi, 'Suor Eufrasia Burlamacchi. I corali del monastero di San Domenico a Lucca', *Alumina*, vol.3, no.11, 2005, pp 20–25.

13 Roberts, *Dominican Women and Renaissance Art*, p.28.

14 Dunn, 'Convent Creativity', p.59.

15 Alexa Greist, 'Manuscript Illumination', in Andaleeb Badiee Banta and Alexa Greist (eds), *Making Her Mark: A History of Women Artists in Europe, 1400–1800*, exh.cat., Baltimore Museum of Art, Baltimore, MD, 1 October 2023–7 January 2024, and Art Gallery of Ontario, Toronto, 30 March–1 July 2024, Fredericton, New Brunswick, Goose Lane Editions, 2023, pp 194–6. In Greist's entry there are some errors (p.195): Eufrasia was born in 1478 (not in 1482); she was a Dominican nun in Lucca (not in Prato); she heard Savonarola speak in 1492 (not in 1596 – the friar died in 1498, Eufrasia in 1548).

16 Loretta Vandi, 'The Eternal Flame. Eufrasia Burlamacchi and Savonarolan Art in the Lucchese Convent of San Domenico', in Loretta Vandi, *Four Essays*, Umeå University Press, Umeå, 2007, pp 19–53.

17 Svetlana Alpers, 'Art History and its Exclusions: The Example of Dutch Art', in Norma Broude and Mary D. Garrard (eds), *Feminism and Art History: Questioning the Litany*, Westview Press, Boulder, CO, 1982, pp 183–99, p.198.

18 Linda Nochlin, 'Why Have There Been No Great Women Artists?', in *Women, Art and Power*, Harper & Row, New York, 1988, pp 145–78, p.149.

INTRODUCTION: A MULTIFACETED ARTIST

1   Sharon T. Strocchia, *Nuns and Nunneries in Renaissance Florence*, Johns Hopkins University Press, Baltimore, MD, 2009, pp 21–3.

2   Sylvie Duval, 'Chiara Gambacorta e le prime monache del monastero di san Domenico di Pisa: l'Osservanza domenicana al femminile', in Gianni Festa and Gabriella Zarri (eds), *Il velo, la penna e la parola. Le domenicane: storia, istituzioni, scritture*, Nerbini, Florence, 2009, pp 93–112.

3   Carolyn Muessig, George Ferzoco and Beverly Mayne Kienzle (eds), *A Companion to Catherine of Siena*, Brill, Leiden and Boston, MA, 2012.

4   Girolamo Savonarola, *Prediche sopra i salmi*, ed. Vincenzo Romano, A. Belardetti, Rome, 1969–74, vol.i, p.182.

5   Loretta Vandi (ed.), *Suor Eufrasia Burlamacchi (1478–1548). Scrivere, miniare, cantare nella Lucca del Cinquecento*, exh.cat., Biblioteca Statale, Lucca, 23 September–15 December 2023, Maria Pacini Fazzi, Lucca, 2023.

6   Claudio Leonardi (ed.), *Caterina Vigri: la santa e la città*, Sismel-Edizioni del Galluzzo, Florence, 2004; Ilaria Bianchi, 'La gloria della serafica Chiara e del suo ordine: suor Dorotea Broccardi copista e miniatrice nel convento di San Lino a Volterra', in Vera Fortunati (ed.), *Vita artistica nel monastero femminile. Exempla*, Editrice Compositori, Bologna, 2002, pp 106–13; Mirella Levi D'Ancona, *Miniatura e miniatori a Firenze dal xiv al xvi secolo. Documenti per una storia della miniatura*, Leo S. Olschki, Florence, 1962, p.11; Jeffrey F. Hamburger, *Nuns as Artists: The Visual Culture of a Medieval Convent*, University of California Press, Berkeley, CA, 1997.

7   Loretta Vandi, 'Eufrasia Burlamacchi', in Giovanna Murano (ed.), *Autographa ii.1. Donne, sante e madonne (da Matilde di Canossa a Artemisia Gentileschi)*, La Mandragora, Imola, 2018, pp 114–15.

8   CSD, t.i, fol.1^r.

9   Jonathan K. Nelson (ed.), *Plautilla Nelli (1524–1588)*.

The Painter-Prioress of Renaissance Florence, S.E.I., Florence, 2008.

10 Giorgio Vasari, *Le vite de' più eccellenti architetti, pittori et scultori italiani, da Cimabue insino a' tempi nostri*, ed. Luciano Bellosi and Aldo Rossi, Einaudi, Turin, 1986, vol.v, p.80.

11 Maria Teresa Filieri (ed.), *Matteo Civitali e il suo tempo. Pittori, scultori e orafi a Lucca nel tardo Quattrocento*, Silvana Editoriale, Cinisello Balsamo, MI, 2004.

12 Megan Holmes, *Fra Filippo Lippi, the Carmelite Painter*, Yale University Press, New Haven, CT, 1999; Timothy Verdon, *Fra Angelico*, Brepols, Turnhout, 2020.

13 Federico Zeri, 'Antonio del Ceraiolo', *Gazette des Beaux-Arts*, vol.109, no.70, 1967, pp 139–54; Susy Marcon, 'Amadei, Giuliano', in Milvia Bollati (ed.), *Dizionario biografico dei miniatori italiani: secoli ix–xvi*, Bonnard, Milan, 2004, pp 10–13.

14 Maurizia Tazartes, 'Ipotesi di percorso per Agostino Marti', *Ricerche di Storia dell'Arte*, nos 43–4, 1991, pp 149–64.

15 Nicole Dacos, *La découverte de la Domus Aurea et la formation des grotesques à la Renaissance*, The Warburg Institute and Brill, London and Leiden, 1969.

16 Massimiliano Coli, 'Da monastero domenicano a manifattura. Come le monache di S. Domenico di Lucca vissero e raccontarono la perdita del loro monastero finito a pezzi nella Manifattura Tabacchi', *Rivista di archeologia, storia e costume*, vol.33, no.4, 2005, pp 201–33.

I CHILDHOOD AND RELATIVES

1 Girolamo Tommasi, *Sommario della storia di Lucca dall'anno MIV all'anno MDCC*, G.P. Vieusseux, Florence, 1847, ch.iii; Michael E. Bratchel, *Lucca 1434–1494: The Reconstruction of an Italian City-Republic*, Clarendon Press, Oxford, 1995.

2 Silvana Seidel Menchi, *Erasmo in Italia: 1520–1580*, Bollati Boringhieri, Turin, 1987.

3 Simonetta Adorni Braccesi, 'Lando, Ortensio', *Dizionario Biografico degli Italiani*, 63 (2004), Treccani online [accessed 7 January 2022]; Chiara Quaranta, 'Paleario, Aonio', *Dizionario Biografico degli Italiani*, 80 (2014), Treccani online [accessed 7 January 2022].

4 Marino Berengo, *Nobili e mercanti nella Lucca del Cinquecento*, Einaudi, Turin, 1965, p.22.

5 Ortensio Lando, *Forcianes quaestiones, in quibus varia Italorum ingenia explicantur, multaque alia scitu non indigna. Auctore Phylalethe Polytopinsi cive*, Neapoli [but Lyon], 1535, p.15; Aonii Palearii Verulani, *Orationes ad Senatum populumque Lucensem*, Vincenzo Busdraghi, Lucca, 1551.

6 Augusto Mancini, *Storia di Lucca*, Sansoni, Florence, 1950, pp 195–7.

7 Bratchel, *Lucca 1434–1494*, p.295.

8 Mancini, *Storia di Lucca*, pp 114, 174; Renzo Ristori, 'Le origini della Riforma a Lucca', *Rinascimento*, vol.3, 1952, pp 227–92.

9 Tommasi, *Sommario della storia di Lucca*, p.120.

10 Gerardo Marsi, *I patrizi di Lucca. Le antiche famiglie lucchesi ed i loro stemmi*, Titania, Lucca, 1996, pp 9–10, 129–41. The genealogical tree of the Burlamacchi has been preserved in a parchment of 1260 with the names of the family's first generations, comprising Buglione, Baldinotto, Brunetto and Trasmondino (Burlamacchi House, Lucca, private archive).

11 Mancini, *Storia di Lucca*, p.133.

12 Giuseppe Vincenzo Baroni, 'Burlamacchi', in 'Notizie genealogiche delle famiglie lucchesi', eighteenth century, BSLu, MS 1108, fols 223^r–473^v; Michele Luzzati, 'Burlamacchi', *Dizionario Biografico degli Italiani*, Società grafica romana, Rome, 1972, pp 433–6.

13 Romano Silva, *La Basilica di san Frediano in Lucca. Urbanistica, architettura, arredo*, Maria Pacini Fazzi, Lucca, 2010, pp 165–70.

14 CSD, t.i, fol.3^v.

15 CSD, t.i, fol.9^r; t.ii, fol.1.

16 Baroni, 'Burlamacchi', BSLu, MS 1108, fols 258^r–273^v; ASLu, Notari, no.761, Ser Benedetto Franciotti, fol.102^v; Gherardo Burlamacchi, 'Ricordi sulle famiglie nobili lucchesi', sixteenth century, BSLu, MS 1941, fols 4^v–6^r, 39^v.

17 Baroni, 'Burlamacchi', BSLu, MS 1108, fols 251^v, 273^r.

18 Massimiliano Coli, '"La grande et animosa impresa di sancto Georgio." Come e perché il monastero di s. Giorgio di Lucca nacque e crebbe savonaroliano', *Memorie domenicane*, vol.115, no.29, 1998, pp 321–87, p.343, n.16.

19 Berengo, *Nobili e mercanti*, pp 32–5.

20 CSD, t.i, fol.4^v.

21 CSD, t.v, 'Libro della fabbrica', fols 1^v–3^v.

22 CSD, t.i, fols 3^{r-v}, 6^r.

23 Luzzati, 'Burlamacchi', pp 434–5.

24 Burlamacchi, 'Ricordi', BSLu, MS 1941.

25 Marisa Desideri Trigari, 'Burlamacchi, Pacifico', *Dizionario Biografico degli Italiani*, Società grafica romana, Rome, 1972, pp 451–2.

26 Burlamacchi, 'Ricordi', BSLu, MS 1941, fol.45^r.

27 Luzzati, 'Burlamacchi', p.434. Contrary to his usual policy, Andrea Doria of Genoa wrote a letter to the General Council of Lucca to free Ser Giovanni; ASLu, Anziani, Copialettere, no.548, bundle 25, 12 November 1543, fol.21^v.

28 Michele Luzzati, 'Burlamacchi, Francesco', *Dizionario Biografico degli Italiani*, Società grafica romana, Rome, 1972, pp 440–46; Mancini, *Storia di Lucca*, p.243; Berengo, *Nobili e mercanti*, pp 190–218.

29 Girolamo Savonarola, *Epistola a tutti gli eletti di Dio*, Bartolomeo de' Libri, Florence, 1497, BNCF, Magl. Cust. D 1, fols 4^r–6^r.

2 A WALLED ADOLESCENCE AND WOMANHOOD

1 Valdo Vinay, 'Il piccolo catechismo di Lutero come strumento di evangelizzazione fra gli italiani dal xvi al xx secolo', *Protestantesimo*, vol.25, 1970, pp 65–84; Silvana Seidel Menchi, 'Le traduzioni italiane di Lutero nella prima metà del Cinquecento', *Rinascimento*, series ii, vol.28, no.17, 1977, pp 31–108.

2 *Libretto volgare, con la dechiaratione de li dieci commandamenti, del Credo, del Pater noster, con una breve annotatione del vivere christiano*, Nicolò di Aristotile detto Zoppino, Venice, 1525; BNCF, Guicciardini 23, 2, 11.

3 Ludwig von Pastor, *Storia dei papi*, iv, Desclée e compagni editori pontifici, Rome, 1908, p.260.

4 Simonetta Adorni Braccesi, *'Una città infetta.' La Repubblica di Lucca nella crisi religiosa del Cinquecento*, Leo S. Olschki, Florence, 1994.

5 Simonetta Adorni Braccesi, 'Libri e lettori a Lucca tra Riforma e Controriforma: un'indagine in corso', in Albano Biondi and Adriano Prosperi (eds), *Libri, idee e sentimenti religiosi nel Cinquecento italiano*, Panini, Modena, 1987, pp 39–46.

6 Loretta Vandi, 'The Eternal Flame. Eufrasia Burlamacchi and Savonarolan Art in the Lucchese Convent of San Domenico', in Loretta Vandi, *Four Essays*, Umeå University Press, Umeå, 2007, pp 19–53, pp 24–6.

7 Armando Felice Verde, OP, *Il Breviario di frate Girolamo Savonarola. Postille autografe trascritte e commentate*, SISMEL-Edizioni del Galluzzo, Florence, 1999, pp 21–6. Savonarola also delivered a sermon in the San Domenico convent in Pisa, testified by a letter to the prioress. See Roberto Ridolfi (ed.), *Le lettere di Girolamo Savonarola*, Leo S. Olschki, Florence, 1933, liii–lv; p.31, no.xiv.

8 On Eufrasia's presence in San Nicolao Novello and on her attendance at the sermons delivered by Savonarola, see the documents written by the notary Acconcio Nuccorini in ASLu, Notari, no.848, fol.78^r (Lucca, 13 March 1490); Notari, no.850, fol.161^r (Lucca, 18 May 1491); Notari, no.856, fol.186^r (Lucca, 28 November 1492).

9 Girolamo Savonarola, 'Breviarium', BNCF, Banco Rari 310; Verde, *Il Breviario*, p.25.

10 All translations from the Authorized, or King James, Version (KJV).

11 Patrick Macey, 'The Lauda and the Cult of Savonarola', *Renaissance Quarterly*, vol.45, no.3, 1992, pp 439–83, p.460: '*Ecce quam bonum et quam iocundum / habitare fratres in unum. / In quanto è gran dolcezza / a fare a tutti un cuore, / con iubilo e prontezza / donarlo al salvatore, / e con un gran fervore / cantare ecce quam bonum.*'

12 BNCF, Banco Rari 310, fols 215^v–217^r: '*eius predicationes scripte sunt sicut umbra respectu vive vocis*'. Unless otherwise noted, all translations are my own.

13 Loretta Vandi, 'Re-forming Images through Lettering. Savonarola's Heritage in a Corpus of Sixteenth-Century Woodcuts in the Biblioteca Statale, Lucca', in Marianne Grivel and Emmanuel Lurin (eds), *The Lettering of Prints. Forms and Functions of Writing in the Printed Image in Sixteenth-Century Europe*, Peter Lang, Bern, 2021, pp 119–41, pp 125–6.

14 Pseudo-Burlamacchi, *La vita del beato Ieronimo Savonarola, scritta da un anonimo del sec. xvi e già attribuita a Fra Pacifico Burlamacchi, pubblicata*

secondo il codice ginoriano, ed. Principe Piero Ginori Conti, Leo S. Olschki, Florence, 1937, ch.xxxiv, *Delle predicationi del servo di Dio et del gran frutto in tutte le conditioni di ciascuno*, pp 85–6. See also Lorenzo Polizzotto, *The Elect Nation: The Savonarolan Movement in Florence, 1494–1545*, Clarendon Press, Oxford, 1994, pp 8–53.

15 Innocenzo Taurisano believed that the biography was authored by Fra Pacifico: *I Domenicani in Lucca*, Baroni, Lucca, 1914, pp 77–90, an opinion successfully contrasted by Roberto Ridolfi, 'La questione dello "Pseudo-Burlamacchi" e della "Vita Latina"', in *Opuscoli di storia letteraria e di erudizione. Savonarola, Machiavelli, Guicciardini, Giannotti*, Bibliopolis libreria editrice, Florence, 1942, pp 3–27.

16 Pseudo-Burlamacchi, *La vita del beato Ieronimo Savonarola*, p.86.

17 Domenico Di Agresti, *Sviluppi della riforma monastica savonaroliana in Lucca*, Leo S. Olschki, Florence, 1980, pp 122–7; Massimiliano Coli, '"La grande et animosa impresa di sancto Georgio." Come e perché il monastero di s. Giorgio di Lucca nacque e crebbe savonaroliano', *Memorie domenicane*, vol.115, no.29, 1998, pp 321–87, pp 343–4.

18 Marino Berengo, *Nobili e mercanti nella Lucca del Cinquecento*, Einaudi, Turin, 1965, pp 372–3.

19 Di Agresti, *Sviluppi della riforma monastica savonaroliana*, pp 53–116; Sharon T. Strocchia, 'Savonarolan Witnesses: The Nuns of San Jacopo and the Piagnone Movement in Sixteenth-Century Florence', *Sixteenth Century Journal*, vol.38, no.2, 2007, pp 393–418.

20 Di Agresti, *Sviluppi della riforma monastica savonaroliana*, p.131; Lorenzo Polizzotto, 'When the Saints Fall Out: Women and the Savonarolan Reform in Early Sixteenth-Century Florence', *Renaissance Quarterly*, vol.46, no.3, 1993, pp 486–525, p.523.

21 Strocchia, 'Savonarolan Witnesses', p.405.

22 Perugia, Archivio del monastero della Beata Colomba, fol.173^v; Di Agresti, *Sviluppi della riforma monastica savonaroliana*, p.137.

23 CSD, t.i, fol.1^r.

24 ibid.

25 ibid.

26 Sharon T. Strocchia, 'Naming a Nun: Spiritual Exemplars and Corporate Identity in Florentine Convents, 1450–1530', in William J. Connell (ed.), *Society and Individual in Renaissance Florence*, University of California Press, Berkeley, CA, 2002, pp 215–40.

27 CSD, t.ii, fols 12, 19.

28 CSD, t.i, fols 15^v, 17^v.

29 CSD, t.iii, fol.19^r.

30 CSD, t.ii, fols 153–4.

31 CSD, t.i, fols 9^r–15^r.

32 Sharon T. Strocchia, 'Begging for Favours: The "New" Clares of S. Chiara Novella and their Patrons', in Peter Howard and Cecilia Hewlett (eds), *Studies on Florence and the Italian Renaissance in Honour of F.W. Kent*, Brepols, Turnhout, 2016, pp 277–94, p.281.

33 The Rota or Ruota, a wooden container turning on a pivot, allowed objects to be introduced in the convent without opening the door: CSD, t.i, fols 4^v–5^r.

34 CSD, t.ii, fols 34–5; ASLu, Notari, no.1936, notary Giuseppe Piscilla de Luca, fol.379^r–v (23 July 1523): 'AN. D. MDXXIII Ind. xi Die xxiii Julii – Ven. *Dom. Soror Petra de Cenamis de Luca Priora conventus et monasterii sancti Dominici de Luca monialium, faciens instantiam cum consensu presentia et voluntate venerandae sororis Raphaella franchi de Luca suppriore isti conventus et monasterii et Suor Christine et Suor Hilarie de Cenamis et Suor Gabriella et Suor Eufrasie de Burlamachis de Luca consiliares isti conventus et monasterii presentium et consentientium in hoc* [. . .].'

35 CSD, t.i, fol.23^v; Strocchia, 'Savonarolan Witnesses', p.401.

36 CSD, t.i, fol.17^r.

37 Anabel Thomas, *Art and Piety in the Female Religious Communities of Renaissance Italy. Iconography, Space, and the Religious Woman's Perspective*, Cambridge University Press, Cambridge, 2003.

3 MATTERS OF DEPENDENCE AND AUTONOMY

1 Fredrika H. Jacobs, *Defining the Renaissance Virtuosa. Women Artists and the Language of Art History and Criticism*, Cambridge University Press, Cambridge, 1997, p.111.

2 Mary D. Garrard, *Artemisia Gentileschi and Feminism*

in *Early Modern Europe*, Reaktion Books, London, 2020; Fredrika H. Jacobs, 'Woman's Capacity to Create: The Unusual Case of Sofonisba Anguissola', *Renaissance Quarterly*, vol.47, no.1, 1994, pp 74–101.

3   CSD, t.i, fol.51ᵛ.

4   CSD, t.ii, fol.256.

5   CSD, t.ii, fol.257.

6   Kate J.P. Lowe, 'The Progress of Patronage in Renaissance Italy', *Oxford Art Journal*, vol.18, 1995, pp 147–50.

7   Ann Roberts, *Dominican Women and Renaissance Art: The Convent of San Domenico of Pisa*, Ashgate, Aldershot, 2008, pp 237–41.

8   Innocenzo Taurisano, OP, *I Domenicani in Lucca*, Baroni, Lucca, 1914, p.159. Taurisano also spoke of the documented presence of three other miniaturists: Sister Agata, Sister Gabriella and Sister Nicolosa (p.157). On Sister Benedetta Arnolfini, see Massimiliano Coli, 'Le grandi famiglie lucchesi e la loro influenza sui monasteri savonaroliani di S. Giorgio e S. Domenico in Lucca', *Memorie domenicane*, vol.33, no.119, 2002, pp 95–129, p.112.

9   CSD, t.i, fol.5ᵛ; t.iii, fol.4ᵛ; t.ii, fol.2.

10 CSD, t.i, fol.5ʳ.

11 Roberts, *Dominican Women and Renaissance Art*, pp 181, 202.

12 Rome, Archivio dell'Ordine dei Predicatori, *Regesta*, MS iv.15, f.66ʳ.

13 CSD, t.i, fol.5ᵛ.

14 Agnese di Bartholomeo Bechaio and Benedetta Arnolfini are recorded for the first time in San Domenico in Pisa in a list of 1494, while Raphaela di Giovanni Burlamacchi and Christina di Nicolao Burlamacchi are reported from 1436 and 1455 respectively. See Roberts, *Dominican Women and Renaissance Art*, appendix 4, pp 321–6. Roberts suggests that the four nuns were eager to leave Pisa in 1502, since the city was besieged by Florence (p.225).

15 Gigetta Dalli Regoli, 'Le intersezioni tra le arti: le tipologie elaborate nella miniatura dei secoli xi e xii', in Chiara Bozzoli and Maria Teresa Filieri (eds), *Scoperta armonia. Arte medievale a Lucca*, Edizioni Fondazione Ragghianti, Lucca, 2014, pp 133–54.

16 CSD, t.iii, fol.4ʳ.

17 CSD, t.ii, fol.34.

18 CSD, t.ii, fol.12.

19 CSD, t.ii, fol.34.

20 Mark Gregory D'Apuzzo, 'Eufrasia Burlamacchi (?–1548)', in Vera Fortunati (ed.), *Italian Women Artists from Renaissance to Baroque*, exh.cat., National Museum of Women in the Arts, Washington, DC, 16 March–15 July 2007, Skira, New York, 2007, pp 96–101.

21 Roberts, *Dominican Women and Renaissance Art*, p.26.

22 Loretta Vandi, 'The Eternal Flame. Eufrasia Burlamacchi and Savonarolan Art in the Lucchese Convent of San Domenico', in Loretta Vandi, *Four Essays*, Umeå University Press, Umeå, 2007, pp 19–53, pp 35–7.

23 CSD, t.ii, fol.66.

24 ASDLu, CSG, fol.130ʳ–ᵛ.

4 AN ECLECTIC BLEND OF ACANTHUS LEAVES, FLOWERS AND MONSTERS

1   The manuscripts of San Martino Cathedral are recorded in the inventories of its patrimony, written in 1492 and 1540. Pietro Guidi and Ermenegildo Pellegrinetti, *Inventari del Vescovato, della Cattedrale e di altre chiese di Lucca*, Tipografia Poliglotta Vaticana, Vatican City, 1921.

2   Anna Rosa Calderoni Masetti, 'Miniatura a Lucca tra xii e xiii secolo. Prolegomena a un'esposizione', in Chiara Bozzoli and Maria Teresa Filieri (eds), *Scoperta armonia. Arte medievale a Lucca*, Edizioni Fondazione Ragghianti, Lucca, 2014, pp 155–76.

3   Anna Rosa Calderoni Masetti, 'Corali trecenteschi', in Clara Baracchini and Antonio Caleca (eds), *Il Duomo di Lucca*, Cassa di Risparmio, Lucca, 1973, pp 80–85.

4   Ada Labriola, 'Martino di Bartolomeo (Siena, c.1365/1370–1435)', in Maria Teresa Filieri (ed.), *Sumptuosa tabula picta. Pittori a Lucca tra gotico e rinascimento*, Sillabe, Lucca, 1998, pp 202–14; Ada Labriola, 'Martino di Bartolomeo', in Milvia Bollati (ed.), *Dizionario biografico dei miniatori italiani: secoli ix–xvi*, Bonnard, Milan, 2004, pp 742–4.

5   Loretta Vandi, *La trasformazione del motivo dell'acanto dall'antichità al xv secolo. Ricerche di teoria e storia*

dell'ornamento, Peter Lang, Bern, 2002, pp 125–51.

6 Marco Paoli, 'Messale di Lorenzo Trenta', in Filieri (ed.), *Sumptuosa tabula picta*, pp 227–9.

7 Maria Teresa Filieri, 'Matteo Civitali e Baldassarre di Biagio *pictores*', in Maria Teresa Filieri (ed.), *Matteo Civitali e il suo tempo. Pittori, scultori e orafi a Lucca nel tardo Quattrocento*, Silvana Editoriale, Cinisello Balsamo, MI, 2004, pp 79–93.

8 Francesco Caglioti, 'Su Matteo Civitali scultore', in Filieri (ed.), *Matteo Civitali e il suo tempo*, pp 29–77.

9 Gigetta Dalli Regoli, 'Corali quattrocenteschi', in Baracchini and Caleca (eds), *Il Duomo di Lucca*, pp 85–95.

10 Mario Salmi, 'Piero della Francesca e Giuliano Amadei', *Rivista d'Arte*, vol.24, nos 1–2, 1942, pp 26–44.

11 Andrea De Marchi, 'Identità di Giuliano Amadei miniatore', *Bollettino d'arte*, vol.80, nos 93–4, 1995, pp 119–58.

12 Nicole Dacos, *La découverte de la Domus Aurea et la formation des grotesques à la Renaissance*, The Warburg Institute and Brill, London and Leiden, 1969, pp 9–13.

13 Laura Zabeo, 'L'ultimo Amadei a Lucca', *Rivista di storia della miniatura*, no.24, 2020, pp 109–23, colour table.

14 Gaetano Milanesi (ed.), *Le opere di Giorgio Vasari*, Sansoni, Florence, 1878, t.iii, p.229.

15 Jacopo, brother of Fra Pacifico, was Sister Eufrasia's cousin, being the son of Pietro, brother of Eufrasia's father. Maria Teresa Filieri, 'Il rinnovamento delle chiese lucchesi alla fine del Quattrocento', in Filieri (ed.), *Matteo Civitali e il suo tempo*, pp 207–35, pp 219–20.

5 A BLESSED HAND, EXPERT IN COLOUR, ORNAMENT AND CHANT

1 CSD, t.iii, fol.4^v.

2 Massimiliano Coli, 'Da monastero domenicano a manifattura. Come le monache di S. Domenico di Lucca vissero e raccontarono la perdita del loro monastero finito a pezzi nella Manifattura Tabacchi', *Rivista di archeologia, storia e costume*, vol.33, no.4, 2005, pp 201–33, pp 206, 214.

3 Innocenzo Taurisano, OP, *I Domenicani in Lucca*, Baroni, Lucca, 1914, p.11.

4 The courtesy of Jack Doran, the archivist of the library of the Dominican convent in California, made available to me the six pages typewritten by Rosenthal. In 1991 Rosenthal did not notice any 'colophon' written on a piece of parchment and put on the spine of MS 5, the one seen and transcribed by Innocenzo Taurisano in 1914.

5 Simon Tugwell et al. (eds), *Letters of Bede Jarrett*, Downside Abbey & Black Friars Publications, Bath and Oxford, 1989, pp 128–9.

6 ASDLu, CSG, fol.29^r.

7 CSD, t.iii, fol.4^v; t.ii, fol.34.

8 Mirella Levi D'Ancona, *The Garden of the Renaissance. Botanical Symbolism in Italian Painting*, Leo S. Olschki, Florence, 1977, p.90.

9 Federico Zeri, *Pittura e Controriforma. L'arte 'senza tempo' di Scipione da Gaeta*, Neri Pozza Editore, Vicenza, 1997 (1st edn Einaudi, Turin, 1957), pp 22–3.

10 Ronald M. Steinberg, *Fra Girolamo Savonarola, Florentine Art, and Renaissance Historiography*, Ohio University Press, Athens, OH, 1977, pp 47–52.

11 Mark J. Zucker, 'Savonarola Designs a Work of Art. The Crown of the Virgin in the Compendium of Revelations', in Vincenzo De Nardo and Christopher Fulton (eds), *Machiavelli Studies*, vol.5, 1996, pp 119–45, pp 125–32.

12 Girolamo Savonarola, *De simplicitate christianae vitae*, BNCF, Magl. Cust. F 12, Impressum Florentiae Anno Domini m.cccc.lxxxxvi Quinto Kalendas Septembris [28 August 1496]; *Della semplicità della vita cristiana*, BNCF, Magl. Cust. F 13, Impresso in Firenze per Ser Lorenzo Morgiani adi ultimo doctobre m.cccc.xxxxvi [31 October 1496].

13 Patrizia Zambrano and Jonathan K. Nelson, *Filippino Lippi*, Electa, Milan, 2004.

14 Geoffrey Nuttall, 'Filippino Lippi's Lucchese Patrons', in Paula Nuttall, Geoffrey Nuttall and Michael W. Kwakkelstein (eds), *Filippino Lippi. Beauty, Invention and Intelligence*, Brill, Leiden, 2020, pp 85–118, pp 94–103.

15 Paula Nuttall, 'From Reiteration to Dialogue: Filippino's Responses to Netherlandish Painting', in Nuttall et al. (eds), *Filippino Lippi*, pp 187–207, pp 187–90.

16 Claudio Ferri, 'I rapporti tra Lucca, Bruges e le Fiandre dal xv alla metà del xvi secolo, quali

emergono dagli atti notarili esistenti nell'Archivio di Stato di Lucca', *Rivista di archeologia, storia e costume*, vol.30, nos 1–2, 2002, pp 9–52.

17 Claudio Ferri, 'Nuove notizie documentarie su autori e dipinti del '400 lucchese', *Actum Luce*, vol.11, nos 1–2, 1982, pp 53–72, pp 54–6, 61–4; Stefano Martinelli, 'Dalle Fiandre a Lucca: modalità di ricezione e rielaborazione nella pittura lucchese del secondo Quattrocento', in Valentino Anselmi (ed.), *Nuovi studi su Matteo Civitali. Il Salvator coronatus di Santa Maria Corteorlandini e la Madonna col Bambino di Colle di Compito*, Maria Pacini Fazzi, Lucca, 2021, pp 65–87.

18 Paula Nuttall, *From Flanders to Florence*, Yale University Press, New Haven, CT, and London, 2004, pp 231–46.

19 Antonino Caleca, 'Pittura del Duecento e del Trecento a Pisa e a Lucca', in Enrico Castelnuovo (ed.), *La pittura in Italia*, vol.i, Electa, Milan, 1986, pp 233–64.

20 Francisco de Hollanda, *De la pintura antigua por Francisco de Hollanda*, Spanish version, Manuel Denis [1563], ed. E. Tormo, J. Ratés Impresor, Madrid, 1921; Francisco de Hollanda, *On Antique Painting*, trans. Alice Sedgwick Wohl, Pennsylvania State University Press, University Park, PA, 2013, p.179.

21 Fredrika H. Jacobs, *Defining the Renaissance Virtuosa. Women Artists and the Language of Art History and Criticism*, Cambridge University Press, Cambridge, 1997, p.111.

22 MS 3, fol.1ʳ: '*Veni sancte spiritus reple tuorum corda fidelium et tui amoris in eis ignem accende qui per diversitatem linguarum* [. . .].'

23 CSD, t.i, fol.13ᵛ.

24 CSD, t.ii, fols 10–11.

25 CSD, t.i, fol.12ʳ. Anna Rosa Calderoni Masetti, 'Miniatura del Quattrocento a Lucca', in Emanuela Sesti (ed.), *La miniatura italiana tra gotico e rinascimento*, Leo S. Olschki, Florence, 1985, pp 639–54, pp 649–50.

26 CSD, t.ii, fol.62.

27 CSD, t.ii, fols 11–12.

28 Riccardo Parmeggiani, 'Pietro da Noceto', *Dizionario Biografico degli Italiani*, 83 (2015), Treccani online [accessed 23 January 2022].

29 Clara Baracchini and Antonio Caleca (eds), *Il Duomo di Lucca*, Cassa di Risparmio, Lucca, 1973, pp 44–8.

30 Marco Collareta and Clara Baracchini, 'Grandi maestri e tecniche di riproduzione. Lo spazio dell'oreficeria nell'arte a Lucca tra Quattro e Cinquecento', in Maria Teresa Filieri (ed.), *Matteo Civitali e il suo tempo. Pittori, scultori e orafi a Lucca nel tardo Quattrocento*, Silvana Editoriale, Cinisello Balsamo, MI, 2004, pp 191–203; also documentary appendix, pp 569–72.

31 John Pope Hennessy, 'The Study of Italian Plaquettes', in Alison Luchs (ed.), *Italian Plaquettes. Studies in the History of Art*, no.22, 1989, pp 19–32, pp 21, 32.

32 Collareta and Baracchini, 'Grandi maestri', p.197, fig.19, p.203.

33 Serena Padovani and Silvia Meloni Trkulija (eds), *Il cenacolo di Andrea del Sarto a San Salvi: guida al museo*, Libreria editrice Salimbeni, Florence, 1982, pp 25–6, no.6. On a drawing of a man with a cuirass, attributed to Antonio del Ceraiolo (Département des Arts graphiques, Musée du Louvre, Paris, inv.2682), see Matteo Gianeselli, 'De Domenico à Ridolfo del Ghirlandaio. Pratiques et fortune d'un atelier familial à Florence entre les xvᵉ et le xviᵉ siècles', *ArtItalies*, no.19, 2013, pp 39–46, p.42, fig.7.

34 CSD, t.i, fols 14ʳ, 15ʳ; t.ii, fols 9, 66.

35 In 1514 Ranieri di Leonardo da Pisa portrayed Roberto di Piero Guinigi in the altarpiece of *The Virgin and Child with Saints and Donors* (San Colombano, Capannori, near Lucca). See Nuttall, 'Filippino Lippi's Lucchese Patrons', pp 91–2.

36 CSD, t.i, fol.6ʳ.

37 Laura Speranza, 'Antonio del Ceraiolo', in Piera Bocci Pacini and Anna Maria Maetzke (eds), *Il Museo dell'Accademia Etrusca di Cortona*, Giorgi & Gambi, Florence, 1992, pp 155–9.

38 Federico Zeri, 'Antonio del Ceraiolo', *Gazette des Beaux-Arts*, vol.109, no.70, 1967, pp 139–54, pp 141–4.

39 Lorenzo Polizzotto, 'When the Saints Fall Out: Women and the Savonarolan Reform in Early Sixteenth-Century Florence', *Renaissance Quarterly*, vol.46, no.3, 1993, pp 486–525, p.491; Catherine Turrill Lupi, 'Pursuing a Savonarolan Thread: Patrons, Painters, and *Piagnoni* in S. Caterina in Cafaggio', in Marilyn Dunn and Saundra Weddle (eds), *Convent Networks in Early Modern Italy*, Brepols, Turnhout, 2010, pp 85–114.

40 Meghan Callahan, 'Antonio del Ceraiolo at La Crocetta and a Note on Lorenzo di Credi's Niece', *The Burlington Magazine*, vol.152, no.1282, January 2010, pp 7–11, pp 8–9, 11.

41 ASF, CRSGF 111, vol.40, fol.167.

42 Andrea Muzzi, 'Eclettismo e devozione a Pistoia nella prima metà del Cinquecento', in Chiara D'Afflitto, Franca Falletti and Andrea Muzzi (eds), *L'età di Savonarola. Fra Paolino e la pittura a Pistoia nel primo '500*, Marsilio, Venice, 1996, pp 9–35, pp 17, 30.

43 CSD, t.iii, fols 7–8; Simonetta Adorni Braccesi, *'Una città infetta.' La Repubblica di Lucca nella crisi religiosa del Cinquecento*, Leo S. Olschki, Florence, 1994, pp 196–7, 207.

44 Anne H. van Buren and Sheila Edmunds, 'Playing Cards and Manuscripts: Some Widely Disseminated Fifteenth-Century Model Sheets', *The Art Bulletin*, vol.56, no.1, 1974, pp 12–30.

45 Loretta Vandi, 'Carte da gioco e manoscritti. Note sul rapporto tra miniatura quattrocentesca e incisione in area romagnola', *Studi Romagnoli*, vol.49, 1998, pp 123–38. Also, Loretta Vandi, *Il Manoscritto Oliveriano 1. Storia di un codice boemo del xv secolo*, STIBU, Urbania, PU, 2004.

46 Jodoco Del Badia, 'La bottega di Alessandro di Francesco Rosselli merciaio e stampatore, 1525', *Miscellanea fiorentina di erudizione e di storia*, no.2, 1984, pp 24–30; Diego Galizzi, 'Francesco Rosselli', in Milvia Bollati (ed.), *Dizionario biografico dei miniatori italiani: secoli ix–xvi*, Bonnard, Milan, 2004, pp 914–16.

47 ASF, CRSGF 106, vol.80, ins.1, 'Inventario de Roselli per Suor Maria', fol.2ʳ.

48 Sheila Barker, 'Painting and Humanism in Early Modern Florentine Convents', in Sheila Barker and Luciano Cinelli, OP (eds), *Artiste nel chiostro. Produzione artistica nei monasteri femminili in età moderna*, *Memorie domenicane* special issue, vol.132, no.46, 2015, pp 105–39, p.112.

49 Sean Roberts, 'Francesco Rosselli and Berlinghieri's *Geographia* Re-examined', *Print Quarterly*, vol.28, no.1, 2011, pp 4–17.

50 Taurisano, *I Domenicani in Lucca*, pp 170–76.

51 Giovanna Lazzi, 'Il Cicerone Landau Finaly della Biblioteca Nazionale di Firenze', in Sesti (ed.), *La miniatura italiana tra gotico e rinascimento*, pp 309–27.

6 WHEN MEANS AND ENDS MEET

1 Alessandra Tamborino, 'Considerazioni sull'attività di Antonio del Ceraiolo e proposte al suo catalogo', *Proporzioni. Annali della Fondazione Roberto Longhi*, nos 2–3, 2001–2, p.106.

2 Gigetta Dalli Regoli, 'I pittori nella Lucca di Matteo Civitali. Da Michele Ciampanti a Michele Angelo di Pietro', in Maria Teresa Filieri (ed.), *Matteo Civitali e il suo tempo. Pittori, scultori e orafi a Lucca nel tardo Quattrocento*, Silvana Editoriale, Cinisello Balsamo, MI, 2004, pp 95–141, pp 98–101.

3 Massimo Ferretti, 'Domenico Bigordi detto del Ghirlandaio, *Sacra conversazione*', in Filieri (ed.), *Matteo Civitali e il suo tempo*, pp 426–8, p.426.

4 Maurizia Tazartes, *Fucina lucchese. Maestri, botteghe, mercanti in una città del Quattrocento*, Edizioni ETS, Pisa, 2007.

5 For the written agreement, see Filieri (ed.), *Matteo Civitali e il suo tempo*, appendix, p.557.

6 Loretta Vandi, 'Sister Eufrasia Burlamacchi and the Art of the Wayside', *Memorie domenicane*, vol.132, no.46, 2015, pp 87–102.

7 Diego Galizzi, 'Gherardo di Giovanni', 'Monte di Giovanni' and 'Vante di Gabriello di Vante Attavanti', in Milvia Bollati (ed.), *Dizionario biografico dei miniatori italiani: secoli ix–xvi*, Bonnard, Milan, 2004, pp 258–62, 798–801 and 975–9.

8 Anna Rosa Garzelli, *Miniatura Fiorentina del Rinascimento, 1440–1525. Un primo censimento*, 2 vols, La Nuova Italia, Florence, 1985, vol.i, pp 75–82.

9 Vitruvius, *De architectura*, ed. F. Granger, Harvard University Press, Cambridge, MA, 1985, book vii, ch.v.

10 James V. Mirollo, *The Poet of the Marvellous: Giambattista Marino*, Columbia University Press, New York, 1963, pp 117–18, 166.

11 Conrad Rudolph, *'The Things of Greater Importance': Bernard of Clairvaux's Apologia and Medieval Attitude toward Art*, University of Pennsylvania Press, Philadelphia, PA, 1990.

12 *Sancti Antonini Archiepiscopi Florentini Ordinis Praedicatorum Summa Theologica*, Verona, Augustus Caratonius, 1740; repr. Akademische Druck – Universitäts Verlagsanstalt, Graz, 1959, iii, tit.8, sec.4, ch.11; Peter Howard, *Beyond the Written Word:*

Preaching and Theology in the Florence of Archbishop Antoninus 1427–1459, Leo S. Olschki, Florence, 1992.

13 Lucy Freeman Sandler, 'The Study of Marginal Imagery: Past, Present, and Future', in *Studies in Manuscript Illumination 1200–1400*, Pindar Press, London, 2008, pp 76–126.

14 ASLu, Notari, i, 1300, Ser Piero Piscilla, fol.29$^{r–v}$.

15 Nicole Dacos, *La découverte de la Domus Aurea et la formation des grotesques à la Renaissance*, The Warburg Institute and Brill, London and Leiden, 1969, p.147.

16 Dalli Regoli, 'I pittori nella Lucca di Matteo Civitali', pp 126–7; Tazartes, *Fucina lucchese*, pp 78, 83–4.

17 Ernst H. Gombrich, 'Paintings on Walls: Means and Ends in the History of Fresco Painting', in *The Uses of Images. Studies in the Social Function of Art and Visual Communication*, Phaidon Press, London, 1999, pp 14–47.

18 Nicholas Herman, 'Excavating the Page: Virtuosity and Illusionism in Italian Book Illumination, 1460–1520', *Word & Image*, vol.27, no.2, 2011, pp 190–211.

7 NATURALISM IN SUPERNATURAL SPACES

1 Marco Paoli, *I corali della Biblioteca Statale di Lucca*, Leo S. Olschki, Florence, 1977, pp 58–64.

2 CSD, t.ii, fols 3–5; BSLu, CSR, MS 2572, fol.47^{r}.

3 BSLu, CSR, MS 2572, fol.47^{r}.

4 Gerardo Mansi, *I patrizi di Lucca. Le antiche famiglie lucchesi ed i loro stemmi*, Titania, Lucca, 1996, pp 450–51.

5 Bartolomeo Baroni, 'Raccolta universale delle iscrizzioni sepolcrali, armi e altri monumenti si antichi che moderni esistenti nelle chiese e altri luoghi della città di Lucca fino al presente anno MDCCLX', BSLu, MS 1015, fol.154^{v}.

6 CSD, t.i, fols 13^{r}, 15^{r}, 16^{r}.

7 Adolphe Napoléon Didron, *Christian Iconography or The History of Christian Art in the Middle Ages*, 2 vols, Bohn, London, 1851, vol.ii, p.41.

8 Anna Rosa Garzelli, *Miniatura Fiorentina del Rinascimento, 1440–1525. Un primo censimento*, 2 vols, La Nuova Italia, Florence, 1985, vol.ii, p.460, fig.777; also similarities in the *Master of the Book of Hours of Cleveland*, ibid., p.455, fig.770.

9 Ernesto Borelli, *Nel segno di Fra Bartolomeo. Pittori del Cinquecento a Lucca*, Maria Pacini Fazzi, Lucca, 1984, pp 16–27.

10 ibid., pp 11–16.

11 Graziano Concioni, Luigi Ferri and Giuseppe Ghilarducci, *I pittori rinascimentali a Lucca. Vita, opere, committenza*, Rugani Edizioni d'Arte, Lucca, 1988, on Marti's drawings for books, p.223.

12 Laura Zabeo, 'L'ultimo Amadei a Lucca', *Rivista di storia della miniatura*, no.24, 2020, pp 109–23, p.117.

13 Francis Ames-Lewis, 'Drapery "Pattern"-Drawings in Ghirlandaio's Workshop and Ghirlandaio's Early Apprenticeship', *The Art Bulletin*, vol.63, no.1, 1981, pp 49–62.

14 Albert J. Elen and Chris Fischer, *Fra Bartolommeo: The Divine Renaissance*, Museum Boijmans van Beuningen, Rotterdam, 2016, pp 113–21.

15 ibid., pp 123–7, 173–83.

16 Loretta Vandi (ed.), *Suor Eufrasia Burlamacchi (1478–1548). Scrivere, miniare, cantare nella Lucca del Cinquecento*, exh.cat., Biblioteca Statale, Lucca, 23 September–15 December 2023, Maria Pacini Fazzi, Lucca, 2023, pp 51–73.

17 This figure was often sculpted on ancient sarcophagi, such as the one of *Mars and Rea Silvia*, in the Mattei palace in Rome, already studied and reproduced in the fifteenth century; Garzelli, *Miniatura Fiorentina*, vol.i, p.72.

18 Alessandro Cecchi, 'Sfortuna di Raffaellino del Garbo', in Paula Nuttall, Geoffrey Nuttall and Michael W. Kwakkelstein (eds), *Filippino Lippi. Beauty, Invention and Intelligence*, Brill, Leiden, 2020, pp 347–60, p.349, fig.14.2.

19 Baldesar Castiglione, *The Book of the Courtier*, trans. Charles S. Singleton, ed. Edgar Mayhew, Doubleday, Random House, New York, 1959; repr. Baldesar Castiglione, *The Book of the Courtier. The Singleton Translation*, ed. Daniel Javitch, W.W. Norton, New York and London, 2002, ii, 7, p.71.

20 ibid., i, 28, p.35.

21 Wayne A. Rebhorn, *Courtly Performances. Masking and Festivity in Castiglione's Book of the Courtier*, Wayne State University Press, Detroit, MI, 1978, p.31.

22 Castiglione, *The Book of the Courtier*, i, 28, p.34.

8 THE LOGIC OF DETAIL

1 Fredrika H. Jacobs, *Defining the Renaissance Virtuosa. Women Artists and the Language of Art History and Criticism*, Cambridge University Press, Cambridge, 1997, p.89.

2 Domenico Corsi, 'La Biblioteca dei frati domenicani di S. Romano di Lucca nel sec. xv', in *Miscellanea di studi vari in memoria di Alfonso Gallo*, Leo S. Olschki, Florence, 1956, pp 289–302, p.298.

3 Innocenzo Taurisano, OP, *I Domenicani in Lucca*, Baroni, Lucca, 1914, p.11.

4 Marco Paoli, *I corali della Biblioteca Statale di Lucca*, Leo S. Olschki, Florence, 1977, pp 28–9, 47–50.

5 Enrico Ridolfi, *L'arte in Lucca studiata nella sua Cattedrale*, Canovetti, Lucca, 1882, pp 259–62, 272–4; Clara Baracchini and Antonio Caleca (eds), *Il Duomo di Lucca*, Cassa di Risparmio, Lucca, 1973, p.42; Graziano Concioni, Luigi Ferri and Giuseppe Ghilarducci, *I pittori rinascimentali a Lucca. Vita, opere, committenza*, Rugani Edizioni d'Arte, Lucca, 1988, pp 203–4.

6 Roberto Chiarelli, *I codici miniati del Museo di San Marco a Firenze*, Bonechi, Florence, 1968, p.25.

7 Paoli, *I corali*, p.29.

8 Margaret Fassler, 'The Office of the Cantor in early Western Monastic Rules and Customaries: A Preliminary Investigation', *Early Music History*, no.5, 1985, pp 29–51; Anne Bagnall Yardley, *Performing Piety: Musical Culture in Medieval English Nunneries*, Palgrave MacMillan, New York, 2006, p.43.

9 Arthur Danto, *The Transfiguration of the Commonplace*, Harvard University Press, Cambridge, MA, 1981, pp 52, 68–9, 81–2.

10 Lynda Dennison, 'The Significance of Ornamental Penwork in Illuminated and Decorated Manuscripts of the Second Half of the Fourteenth Century', in Marlene Villalobos Hennessy (ed.), *Tributes to Kathleen L. Scott. English Medieval Manuscripts: Readers, Makers and Illuminators*, Harvey Miller Publishers, Turnhout, 2009, pp 31–64.

11 Sylvie Duval, 'Usages du livre et de l'écrit', in Nicole Bériou, Martin Morard and Donatella Nebbiai (eds), *Entre stabilité et itinérance. Livres et culture des ordres mendiants, xiiie–xve siècle*, Brepols, Turnhout, 2014, pp 215–28, n.47.

12 Jeffrey F. Hamburger, 'La bibliothèque d'Unterlinden et l'art de la formation spirituelle', in *Les dominicains d'Unterlinden*, exh.cat., Musée d'Unterlinden, Colmar, 2 vols, Somogy éditions d'art, Paris et Colmar, 2000, vol.i, pp 144–5.

13 Kira Hall, 'Performativity', *Journal of Linguistic Anthropology*, vol.9, nos 1–2, 2000, pp 184–7.

14 Elsie Payne, 'The Nature of Musical Emotion and its Place in the Appreciative Experience', *British Journal of Aesthetics*, vol.13, no.2, 1973, pp 171–81, p.180.

15 Philip Alperson, 'The Arts of Music', *Journal of Aesthetics and Art Criticism*, vol.50, no.3, 1992, pp 217–30.

EPILOGUE: THE LOST COLOPHON

1 Innocenzo Taurisano, OP, *I Domenicani in Lucca*, Baroni, Lucca, 1914, p.161.

2 See Appendix.

3 Sharon T. Strocchia, 'Naming a Nun: Spiritual Exemplars and Corporate Identity in Florentine Convents, 1450–1530', in William J. Connell (ed.), *Society and Individual in Renaissance Florence*, University of California Press, Berkeley, CA, 2002, pp 215–40, p.234.

4 CSD, t.ii, front list of names.

5 Melissa Moreton, 'Pious Voices: Nun-Scribes and the Language of Colophons in Late Medieval and Renaissance Italy', *Essays in Medieval Studies*, no.29, 2014, pp 43–73, p.43.

6 ibid., p.47.

7 Loretta Vandi, 'Sister Eufrasia Burlamacchi (Lucca, 1478–1548). A Multi-faceted Illuminator within Artistic and Religious Reforms', *Art Herstory*, 20 September 2021.

8 Girolamo Savonarola, 'Epistole', 1497, BNCF, Magl. Cust. D 1, fols 1r, 25v.

9 For Savonarola's large number of publications, see Piero Scapecchi (ed.), *Catalogo degli incunaboli della Biblioteca Nazionale Centrale di Firenze*, Nerbini, Florence, 2017, pp 365–80.

Appendix: Codicological Notes and Colophon

CONVENT OF SAN DOMENICO, LUCCA (NOW DOMINICAN CONVENT, CALIFORNIA)

MS 1 Antiphonarium de Tempore / de Sanctis ab Adventu / usque ad Septuagesimam, sixteenth century

Parchment, folium 54.2 × 38.5 cm (21 ⅜ × 15 ⅛ in), fols II + 313 + II, Gothic script in black ink in line, titles and versicles in red ink, square notes (8 mm; ⅜ in), five red tetragrams per page

Inc. fol.1ʳ: *Dominica prima in adventu.* Exp. fol.313ᵛ: *Mentem sanctam*

Liturgical content: Antiphonary from the first Sunday of Advent to the Septuagesima Sunday

Historiated initials: none

Ornamental initials with acanthus leaves and flowers: 6 (all 9.5 × 8 cm; 3 ¾ × 3 ⅛ in):

fol.1ʳ *Ecce nomen domini*

fol.74ᵛ *Rex pacificus*

fol.80ʳ *Hodie nobis*

fol.125ʳ *Hodie in Iordane*

fol.182ʳ *Unus ex duobus*

fol.193ᵛ *Confessor dei*

Large penwork initials: 6

MS 2 Antiphonarium de / Tempore et de Sanctis / a Septuagesima usque ad Penthecostem, sixteenth century

Parchment, folium 54.2 × 38.5 cm (21 ⅜ × 15 ⅛ in), fols II + 346 + II, Gothic script in black ink in line, titles and versicles in red ink, square notes (8 mm; ⅜ in), five red tetragrams per page

Inc. fol.1ʳ: *Dominica in LXX.* Exp. fol.346ʳ: *Tempore res*

Liturgical content: Antiphonary from the Septuagesima Sunday to Pentecost

Historiated initials: 1

fol.160ʳ *Angelus autem* (14 × 14 cm; 5 ½ × 5 ½ in)

Ornamental initials with acanthus leaves and flowers: 11 (all 8.5 × 8.5 cm; 3 ⅜ × 3 ⅜ in):

fol.1ʳ *Igitur*

fol.156ᵛ *Angelus domini*

fol.211ʳ *Ascendens Christus in altum*

fol.213ᵛ *Post passionem suam*

fol.224ʳ *Tu es pastor ovium* (with stylised bird)

fol.227ʳ *Felix Thomas doctor*

fol.246ᵛ *Orietur sicut sol*

fol.266ᵛ *Diem nove laudis*

fol.293ʳ *Colletetur turba fidelium triumphantis*

fol.308ᵛ *Immortali laude*

fol.335ʳ *Adest dies letitie*

Large penwork initials: 24

MS 3 Antiphonarium de Tempore / Penthecoste usque ad Adventum / et de Sanctis a Penthecoste / usque ad Festum Angelorum, sixteenth century

Parchment, folium 54.2 × 38.5 cm (21 ⅜ × 15 ⅛ in), fols II + 334 + II, Gothic script in black ink in line, titles and versicles in red ink, square notes (8 mm; ⅜ in), five red tetragrams per page

Inc. fol.1ʳ: *In vigilia Penthecostes*. Exp. fol.334ʳ: *triumphavit rex angelorum*

Liturgical content: Antiphonary from Pentecost to the first Sunday of Advent and on Saints from Pentecost to the Feast of the Angels

Historiated initials: 3

fol.206ᵛ *Laudibus excelsis*, L with Mary Magdalene (9 × 8 cm; 3 ½ × 3 ⅛ in)

fol.218ᵛ *Gaude felix parens*, G with Saint Dominic (14.2 × 14 cm; 5 ⅝ × 5 ½ in)

fol.270ᵛ *Vidi speciosam*, V with the Virgin Mary (14.2 × 14 cm; 5 ⅝ × 5 ½ in)

Ornamental initials with acanthus leaves and flowers: 10 (all 8.5 × 8 cm; 3 ⅜ × 3 ⅛ in)

fol.1ʳ *Veni sancte spiritus* (God's hands and Dove)

fol.8ʳ *Dum complerentur*

fol.47ᵛ *Sacerdos in eternum*

fol.48ʳ *O quam suavis est*

fol.125ʳ *Ingresso*

fol.147ʳ *Quem dicunt homines*

fol.151ʳ *Symon Petre*

fol.189ᵛ *Recumbente Iesu*

fol.221ᵛ *Mundum vocans*

fol.283ᵛ *Assumpta est Maria*

Large penwork initials: 30

MS 4 Antiphonarium de Sanctis a / Festo Angelorum usque ad Adventum / et Commune Sanctorum, sixteenth century

Parchment, folium 54.2 × 38.5 cm (21 ⅜ × 15 ⅛ in), fols II + 263 + II, Gothic script in black ink in line, titles and versicles in red ink, square notes (8 mm; ⅜ in), five red tetragrams per page

Inc. fol.1ʳ: *Sancti Michaelis Archangeli*. Exp. fol.263ᵛ: *In te domine speravi*

Liturgical content: Antiphonary of the Saints from the Feast of the Angels to the Advent and the Common of Saints

Historiated initials: 4

fol.1ʳ *Dum sacrum misterium*, D with the Three Archangels (13 × 13 cm; 5 ⅛ × 5 ⅛ in)

fol.91ᵛ *Virgo gloriosa semper*, V with Saint Cecilia (13 × 13 cm; 5 ⅛ × 5 ⅛ in)

fol.120ʳ *Virginis eximie*, V with Saint Catherine of Alexandria (13 × 13 cm; 5 ⅛ × 5 ⅛ in)

fol.132ʳ *Estote fortes in bello*, E with the Saints Peter and Paul (13 × 12.8 cm; 5 ⅛ × 5 in)

Ornamental initials: 2

fol.22ʳ *O quam gloriosum*, O with acanthus leaves and flowers (13 × 13 cm; 5 ⅛ × 5 ⅛ in)

fol.25ʳ *Summe trinitati*, S with acanthus leaves and flowers (8 × 8 cm; 3 ⅛ × 3 ⅛ in)

Large penwork initials: 31

MS 5 Graduale de Tempore et de Sanctis, sixteenth century

Parchment, folium 54.2 × 38.5 cm (21 ⅜ × 15 ⅛ in), fols II + 290 + II, Gothic script in black ink in line, titles and versicles in red ink, square notes (8 mm; ⅜ in), five red tetragrams per page

Inc. fol.1ʳ: *Incipit Graduale de tempore et de sanctis per totum annum*. Exp. fol.176ʳ: *in eternum quia pius es*. fol.176ᵛ: blank. Inc. fol.177ʳ: *Kyrie leyson*. Exp. fol.290ʳ: *Gloria patri et filio et spiritu sancto*

Liturgical content: from the sprinkling of Holy Water outside of Easter time to the Antiphon to the Communion of the Mass for the dead

Historiated initials: 12

fol.7ᵛ *Puer natus est*, P with Nativity (14 × 14 cm; 5 ½ × 5 ½ in)

fol.48ᵛ *Resurrexi et adhuc*, R with Resurrection (14 × 14 cm; 5 ½ × 5 ½ in)

fol.67ʳ *Spiritus domini replevit*, S with Pentecost (14 × 13 cm; 5 ½ × 5 ⅛ in)

fol.71ʳ *Cibavit eos*, C with chalice (14 × 14 cm; 5 ½ × 5 ½ in)

fol.87ʳ *Michi autem*, M with Saint Andrew (14 × 13.5 cm; 5 ½ × 5 ⅜ in)

fol.122ʳ *Protexisti me deus*, P with Peter martyr (14 × 13 cm; 5 ½ × 5 ⅛ in)

fol.135ᵛ *De ventre matris*, D with Saint John the Baptist
(14 × 13 cm; 5 ½ × 5 ⅛ in)

fol.139ʳ *Nunc scio vere*, N with Saint Peter (14 × 13 cm;
5 ½ × 5 ⅛ in)

fol.146ᵛ *Gaudeamus omnes*, G with Mary Magdalene
(14 × 14 cm; 5 ½ × 5 ½ in)

fol.152ʳ *Pie pater Dominice*, P with Saint Dominic (16.5 × 14
cm; 6 ½ × 5 ½ in)

fol.155ʳ *Confessio et pulchritudo*, C with Saint Lawrence
(14 × 13 cm; 5 ½ × 5 ⅛ in)

fol.168ᵛ *Gaudeamus omnes*, G with the Assumption of
Mary (14 × 14 cm; 5 ½ × 5 ½ in)

Ornamental initials: 8

fol.4ʳ *Dominus dixit* (14 × 13 cm; 5 ½ × 5 ⅛ in)

fol.13ʳ *Ecce advenit dominator* (14 × 13 cm; 5 ½ × 5 ⅛ in)

fol.78ʳ *Benedicta sit S. Trinitas* (14 × 13 cm; 5 ½ × 5 ⅛ in)

fol.103ᵛ *Scio cui credidi* (14 × 13 cm; 5 ½ × 5 ⅛ in)

fol.113ʳ *Rorate celi de super* (14 × 13 cm; 5 ½ × 5 ⅛ in)

fol.131ʳ *Benedicite domino* (14 × 13 cm; 5 ½ × 5 ⅛ in)

fol.149ᵛ *In festo sanctissimi Dominici officium* (21 × 14 cm;
8 ¼ × 5 ½ in)

fol.164ᵛ *Gaudeamus omnes* (14 × 13 cm; 5 ½ × 5 ⅛ in)

Large penwork initials: 48, 16 in part 1 and 32 in the Kyrie
part

CONVENT OF SAN DOMENICO, LUCCA (NOW BIBLIOTECA STATALE, LUCCA)

MS 1984 Ritual, c.1500

Parchment, folium 26 × 19 cm (10 ¼ × 7 ½ in), fols
II + 168 + II, of which fols 160ʳ–168ᵛ added later.
Gothic script, black and red ink. Original binding

Inc. fol.1ʳ: *Ianuarius*. Exp. fol.168ᵛ: *Qui vivit et regnat*

Liturgical content: fols 1ʳ–6ᵛ: Calendar; fols 6ʳ–15ʳ: *Modus
inchoandi horas* (with notes); fols 16ʳ–110ʳ: Gradual
Sanctoral (with notes from fol.100ʳ); fols 110ᵛ–133ʳ:
principia antiphonarum (with notes); fols 133ᵛ–138ᵛ: *In
adventu Domini versicula*; fols 138ᵛ–143ʳ: *orationes*; fols
143ᵛ–157ʳ: *Benedictio cerei paschalis* (with notes); fols
157ᵛ–159ᵛ: *formulae generalis*

Historiated initials: 2

fol.16ʳ *Ecce dies veniunt*, E with prophet Jeremiah
(6.8 × 7.6 cm; 2 ⅝ × 3 in)

fol.81ʳ *Deus qui ecclesiam tuam*, D with Saint Dominic
(7.2 × 8 cm; 2 ⅞ × 3 ⅛ in)

Ornamental initials: none

Large penwork initials: 127

CATHEDRAL OF SAN MARTINO, LUCCA (NOW ARCHIVIO STORICO DIOCESANO, LUCCA)

MS 14 Antiphonarium de Tempore, 1496–c.1520

Parchment, folium 62 × 44.5 cm (24 ⅜ × 17 ½ in), fols
II + 155 + II, of which fols 76–83 and 129–55 added
later. Acephalous. Gothic script in black ink in line
under red tetragrams – five for each page – with
square notation. Binding not original

Inc. fol.1ʳ: [. . .] *re nomini tuo altissime*. Exp. fol.128ᵛ:
Benedicamus domino Alleluia alleluia

Liturgical content: Antiphonary Temporal from Saturday
preceding the ninth Sunday before Easter to Palm
Sunday

Historiated initials: none

Ornamental initials: 215, with acanthus leaves, fruits,
flowers and fanciful animals. Eufrasia started
from fol.15ᵛ the completion of the miniatures left
unfinished by Giuliano Amadei. However, not all
the ornamental initials after fol.15ᵛ are by her hand,
since Amadei had already worked on various quires
recomposed when the parchment sheets were bound
together

Large penwork initials: none

MONASTERY OF SAN ROMANO, LUCCA (NOW BIBLIOTECA STATALE, LUCCA)

MS 2649 Liber Missarum de Tempore ab Adventu usque ad Coenam Domini, sixteenth century

Parchment, folium 59.3 × 43.2 cm (23 ⅜ × 17 in), fols
II + 275 + II, Gothic script in black ink in line, titles
and versicles in red ink, square notes (8 mm; ⅜ in),
five red tetragrams per page. Gradual Temporal *per
totum annum*. Perhaps original binding

Inc. fol.1ʳ: *Ad te levavi*. Exp. fol.275ʳ: *Amen*

Liturgical content: Gradual Temporal with the sung parts
of the Mass from the first Sunday of Advent to the
fourth feria after Palm Sunday
Historiated initials: 2
fol.1ʳ *Ad te levavi*, A with God the Father and David
(19 × 17 cm; 7½ × 6¾ in)
fol.49ᵛ *Puer natus est*, P with Nativity (22.7 × 18.2 cm;
8⅞ × 7⅛ in)
Ornamental initials: 3
fol.45ʳ *Lux fulgebit*, L with fanciful animal (14.7 × 14 cm;
5¾ × 5½ in)
fol.41ʳ *Dominus dixit*, D with cornucopias (14 × 13.7 cm;
5½ × 5⅜ in)
fol.58ᵛ *Ecce advenit*, E with fanciful animal (14.5 × 14.5 cm;
5¾ × 5¾ in)
Large penwork initials: 55

*MS 2650 Liber Missarum de Tempore a Coena Domini
usque ad Adventum, sixteenth century*

Parchment, folium 60.5 × 43.3 cm (23⅞ × 17 in), fols
II + 256 + II, Gothic script in black ink in line, titles
and versicles in red ink, square notes (8 mm; ⅜ in),
five red tetragrams per page. Perhaps original binding
Inc. fol.1ʳ: *Nos autem gloriari*. Exp. fol.256ᵛ: *Memento verbi*
Liturgical content: Gradual Temporal with the sung parts
of the Mass from the fifth feria in *coenam domini* to
the twenty-third Sunday after the Saint Trinity
Historiated initials: 4
fol.1ʳ *Nos autem*, N with Crucifixion (19.7 × 19.3 cm;
7¾ × 7⅝ in)
fol.31ᵛ *Resurrexi et adhuc*, R with Resurrection (19 × 17.5 cm;
7½ × 6⅞ in)
fol.87ᵛ *Viri galilei*, V with Ascension (15.3 × 14.8 cm;
6 × 5⅞ in)
fol.99ʳ *Spiritus domini*, S with Pentecost (18.6 × 18.6 cm;
7⅜ × 7⅜ in)
Ornamental initials: 6
fol.36ᵛ *Introduxit nos*, I with leaves and flowers (16 × 12.1 cm;
6¼ × 4¾ in)
fol.40ᵛ *Aqua sapientiae*, A with cock and spike (14.5 × 14.5
cm; 5¾ × 5¾ in)
fol.92ʳ *Exaudi domine*, E with fanciful animal (15 × 14.5
cm; 5⅞ × 5¾ in)

fol.103ʳ *Cibavit eos*, C with chalice (15.2 × 15.3 cm; 6 × 6 in)
fol.106ᵛ *Accepite*, A with flowers (15.3 × 14.5 cm; 6 × 5¾ in)
fol.120ᵛ *Benedicta sit*, B with stem and leaves (15.3 × 14.5
cm; 6 × 5¾ in)
Large penwork initials: 48

THE 'LOST COLOPHON'

'Sia noto a tutte quelle che succederanno di po noi come
questi libri da cantare funno scripto circha li anni del
Signore 1515 per una vilissima serva di Jesu Cristo, el nome
della quale preghate el Signore gli sia di piacere scrivere
in del libro della vita. Se nessuna cosa ci e che stia bene
ringratiatene el Signore largitore di tutti et beni, appresso
il dolcissimo angelo gabriello al quale fu raccomandata
questa opera la quale eccedeva la forza et capacita della
scriptora. El quale preditto angelo se visto ghuardarli
da in numerabili pericoli che accadeno in dello scriverli
et preghovi humiliate mi perdoniate i difetti che ci
troverete. Preghando el Signore che mi perdoni quelli
e tutti li altri in numerabili miei difetti et conduchimi
mediante le vostre sancte orationi a quella felice patria di
vita eterna a cantare per infinita secula seculorum quel
dolce canto *Benedictio et claritas et sapientia et gratiarum
actio. Amen.*'

Bibliography

ELECTRONIC DATABASE

Treccani online

MANUSCRIPT SOURCES

Bibbiena, Arezzo, Archivio del Monastero di Santa Maria del Sasso, 'Chronica di San Domenico di Lucca', 6 vols, 1502–1925

California, Dominican Convent, MSS 1–5, Eufrasia Burlamacchi, 4 Antiphonaries and 1 Gradual, sixteenth century

Florence, Archivio di Stato di Firenze, Corporazioni Religiose Soppresse dal Governo Francese, MS 106, vol.80, ins.1, 'Inventario de Roselli per Suor Maria', 3 March 1525 [but 1526]

—, Corporazioni Religiose Soppresse dal Governo Francese, MS 111, vol.40, Antonio del Ceraiolo, 'Contract for an Altarpiece', 1520

Florence, Biblioteca di San Marco, MS 529, Fra Eustachio, Psalter, c.1505

Florence, Biblioteca Nazionale Centrale di Firenze, Banco Rari 310, Girolamo Savonarola, Breviarium, fifteenth century

—, MS Landau Finaly 21, Marcus Tullius Cicero, *Orationes*, fifteenth century

Lucca, Archivio di Stato, Notari, no.848, Ser Acconcio Nuccorini, 1490

—, Notari, no.761, Ser Benedetto Franciotti, 1491

—, Notari, no.850, Ser Acconcio Nuccorini, 1491

—, Notari, no.856, Ser Acconcio Nuccorini, 1492

—, Notari, i, no.1300, Ser Piero Piscilla, 1509

—, Notari, no.1936, Ser Giuseppe Piscilla, 1523

—, Anziani, Copialettere, no.548, bundle 25, 1543

Lucca, Archivio Storico Diocesano, MSS 1, 7, 8, 9, 10, Martino di Bartolomeo, Graduals, late fourteenth century

—, MS 2, Baldassarre di Biagio del Firenze, Common of Saints, fifteenth century

—, MS 6, Baldassarre di Biagio del Firenze, Antiphonary, fifteenth century

—, MS 14, Giuliano Amadei and Eufrasia Burlamacchi, Antiphonary, fifteenth–sixteenth centuries

—, MS 16, Giuliano Amadei, Antiphonary, fifteenth century

—, Enti Religiosi Soppressi, MS 2498, 'Terrilogio del Monastero di San Domenico, Lucca', 1702

—, Enti Religiosi Soppressi, MS 2620, Fra Michele di Andrea da Firenze, 'Chronica del Monastero di San Giorgio, Lucca', sixteenth century

Lucca, Basilica di San Frediano, Guardaroba, MS F, Giuliano Amadei, Hymnary, fifteenth century

Lucca, Biblioteca Statale, MS 1015, Bartolomeo Baroni, 'Raccolta universale delle iscrizioni sepolcrali, armi e altri monumenti si antichi che moderni esistenti nelle chiese e altri luoghi della città di Lucca fino al presente anno MDCCLX', eighteenth century

—, MS 1108, Giuseppe Vincenzo Baroni, 'Notizie genealogiche delle famiglie lucchesi', eighteenth century

—, MS 1941, Gherardo Burlamacchi, 'Ricordi sulle famiglie nobili lucchesi', sixteenth century

—, MS 1984, Benedetta Arnolfini, Ritual, sixteenth century

—, MS 2415, Girolamo Savonarola, Epistole, sixteenth century

—, MS 2572, Chronica di San Romano, sixteenth century

—, MS 2645, Gradual Sanctoral, sixteenth century

—, MSS 2649–50, Eufrasia Burlamacchi, Graduals, sixteenth century

—, MS 3122, Master of Jean de Boucicaut's Book of Hours, Missal, early fifteenth century

Perugia, Archivio del monastero della Beata Colomba, 'Codice Savonaroliano', sixteenth century

PRINTED SOURCES

Florence, Biblioteca Nazionale Centrale di Firenze, Cinq. Guicciardini 23, 2, 11 [Martin Luther], *Libretto volgare con la dechiaratione de li dieci commandamenti, del Credo, del Pater noster, con una breve annotatione del vivere christiano*, Nicolò di Aristotile detto Zoppino, Venezia, 1525

—, Inc. Magl. N 20, Francesco Berlinghieri, *Geographia*, engravings by Francesco Rosselli, Firenze, Niccolò di Lorenzo della Magna, 1482

—, Inc. Magl. Cust. F 12, Girolamo Savonarola, *De simplicitate christianae vitae*, Impressum Florentiae Anno Domini m.cccc.lxxxxvi Quinto Kalendas Septembris [28 August 1496]

—, Inc. Magl. Cust. F 13, Girolamo Savonarola, *Della semplicità della vita cristiana*, Impresso in Firenze per Ser Lorenzo Morgiani adi ultimo doctobre m.cccc. xxxxvi [31 October 1496]

—, Inc. Magl. Cust. D 1, Girolamo Savonarola, *Epistola a tutti gli eletti di Dio*, Bartolomeo de' Libri, Firenze, 1497

Lucca, Biblioteca Statale, El. ii/2, *Map of Lucca*, sixteenth century

—, El. ii/27, *Lucca Cityscape*, 1757

PUBLICATIONS

Adorni Braccesi, Simonetta, 'Libri e lettori a Lucca tra Riforma e Controriforma: un'indagine in corso', in Biondi and Prosperi (eds), *Libri, idee e sentimenti religiosi nel Cinquecento italiano*, pp 39–46

—, *'Una città infetta.' La Repubblica di Lucca nella crisi religiosa del Cinquecento*, Leo S. Olschki, Florence, 1994

—, 'Lando, Ortensio', *Dizionario Biografico degli Italiani*, 63 (2004), Treccani online

Alpers, Svetlana, 'Art History and its Exclusions: The Example of Dutch Art', in Broude and Garrard (eds), *Feminism and Art History*, pp 183–99

Alperson, Philip, 'The Arts of Music', *Journal of Aesthetics and Art Criticism*, vol.50, no.3, 1992, pp 217–30

Ames-Lewis, Francis, 'Drapery "Pattern"-Drawings in Ghirlandaio's Workshop and Ghirlandaio's Early Apprenticeship', *The Art Bulletin*, vol.63, no.1, 1981, pp 49–62

Anselmi, Valentino (ed.), *Nuovi studi su Matteo Civitali. Il Salvator coronatus di Santa Maria Corteorlandini e la Madonna col Bambino di Colle di Compito*, Maria Pacini Fazzi, Lucca, 2021

Bagnall Yardley, Anne, *Performing Piety: Musical Culture in Medieval English Nunneries*, Palgrave MacMillan, New York, 2006

Banta, Andaleeb Badiee, and Alexa Greist (eds), *Making Her Mark: A History of Women Artists in Europe, 1400–1800*, exh.cat., Baltimore Museum of Art, Baltimore, MD, 1 October 2023–7 January 2024, and Art Gallery of Ontario, Toronto, 30 March–1 July 2024, Fredericton, New Brunswick, Goose Lane Editions, 2023

Baracchini, Clara, and Antonio Caleca, *Il Duomo di Lucca*, Cassa di Risparmio, Lucca, 1973

Barker, Sheila, 'Painting and Humanism in Early Modern Florentine Convents', in Sheila Barker and Luciano Cinelli, OP (eds), *Artiste nel chiostro. Produzione artistica nei monasteri femminili in età moderna*, *Memorie domenicane* special issue, vol.132, no.46, 2015, pp 105–39

—, *Artemisia Gentileschi*, Lund Humphries, London, 2021

— (ed.), *'La grandezza dell'universo' nell'arte di Giovanna Garzoni*, exh.cat., Galleria degli Uffizi, Florence, 28 May–28 June 2020, Sillabe, Livorno, 2020

Berengo, Marino, *Nobili e mercanti nella Lucca del Cinquecento*, Einaudi, Turin, 1965

Bériou Nicole, Martin Morard and Donatella Nebbiai

(eds), *Entre stabilité et itinérance. Livres et culture des ordres mendiants, xiiie-xve siècle*, Brepols, Turnhout, 2014

Bianchi, Ilaria, 'La gloria della serafica Chiara e del suo ordine: suor Dorotea Broccardi copista e miniatrice nel convento di San Lino a Volterra', in Fortunati (ed.), *Vita artistica nel monastero femminile*, pp 106–13

Biondi, Albano, and Adriano Prosperi (eds), *Libri, idee e sentimenti religiosi nel Cinquecento italiano*, Panini, Modena, 1987

Bocci Pacini, Piera, and Anna Maria Maetzke (eds), *Il Museo dell'Accademia Etrusca di Cortona*, Giorgi & Gambi, Florence, 1992

Bollati, Milvia (ed.), *Dizionario biografico dei miniatori italiani: secoli ix–xvi*, Bonnard, Milan, 2004

Borelli, Ernesto, *Nel segno di Fra Bartolomeo. Pittori del Cinquecento a Lucca*, Maria Pacini Fazzi, Lucca, 1984

Bozzoli, Chiara, and Maria Teresa Filieri (eds), *Scoperta armonia. Arte medievale a Lucca*, Edizioni Fondazione Ragghianti, Lucca, 2014

Bratchel, Michael E., *Lucca 1434–1494: The Reconstruction of an Italian City-Republic*, Clarendon Press, Oxford, 1995

Broude, Norma, and Mary D. Garrard (eds), *Feminism and Art History: Questioning the Litany*, Westview Press, Boulder, CO, 1982

Caglioti, Francesco, 'Su Matteo Civitali scultore', in Filieri (ed.), *Matteo Civitali e il suo tempo*, pp 29–77

Calderoni Masetti, Anna Rosa, 'Corali trecenteschi', in Baracchini and Caleca (eds), *Il Duomo di Lucca*, pp 80–85

—, 'Miniatura del Quattrocento a Lucca', in Sesti (ed.), *La miniatura italiana tra gotico e rinascimento*, pp 639–54

—, 'Miniatura a Lucca tra xii e xiii secolo. Prolegomena a un'esposizione', in Bozzoli and Filieri (eds), *Scoperta armonia*, pp 155–76

Caleca, Antonino, 'Pittura del Duecento e del Trecento a Pisa e a Lucca', in Castelnuovo (ed.), *La pittura in Italia*, vol.i, pp 233–64

Callahan, Meghan, 'Antonio del Ceraiolo at La Crocetta and a Note on Lorenzo di Credi's Niece', *The Burlington Magazine*, vol.152, no.1282, January 2010, pp 7–11

Castelnuovo, Enrico (ed.), *La pittura in Italia*, Milan, Electa, 1986

Castiglione, Baldesar, *The Book of the Courtier*, trans. Charles S. Singleton, ed. Edgar Mayhew, Doubleday, Random House, New York, 1959

—, *The Book of the Courtier. The Singleton Translation*, ed. Daniel Javitch, W.W. Norton, New York and London, 2002

Cecchi, Alessandro, 'Sfortuna di Raffaellino del Garbo', in Nuttall et al. (eds), *Filippino Lippi*, pp 347–60

Chiarelli, Roberto, *I codici miniati del Museo di San Marco a Firenze*, Bonechi, Florence, 1968

Coli, Massimiliano, '"La grande et animosa impresa di sancto Georgio." Come e perché il monastero di s. Giorgio di Lucca nacque e crebbe savonaroliano', *Memorie domenicane*, vol.115, no.29, 1998, pp 321–87

—, 'Le grandi famiglie lucchesi e la loro influenza sui monasteri savonaroliani di S. Giorgio e S. Domenico in Lucca', *Memorie domenicane*, vol.33, no.119, 2002, pp 95–129

—, 'Da monastero domenicano a manifattura. Come le monache di S. Domenico di Lucca vissero e raccontarono la perdita del loro monastero finito a pezzi nella Manifattura Tabacchi', *Rivista di archeologia, storia e costume*, vol.33, no.4, 2005, pp 201–33

Collareta, Marco, and Clara Baracchini, 'Grandi maestri e tecniche di riproduzione. Lo spazio dell'oreficeria nell'arte a Lucca tra Quattro e Cinquecento', in Filieri (ed.), *Matteo Civitali e il suo tempo*, pp 191–203

Concioni, Graziano, Luigi Ferri and Giuseppe Ghilarducci, *I pittori rinascimentali a Lucca. Vita, opere, committenza*, Rugani Edizioni d'Arte, Lucca, 1988

Connell, William J. (ed.), *Society and Individual in Renaissance Florence*, University of California Press, Berkeley, CA, 2002

Corsi, Domenico, 'La Biblioteca dei frati domenicani di S. Romano di Lucca nel sec. xv', in *Miscellanea di studi vari in memoria di Alfonso Gallo*, Leo S. Olschki, Florence, 1956, pp 289–302.

Dacos, Nicole, *La découverte de la Domus Aurea et la formation des grotesques à la Renaissance*, The Warburg Institute and Brill, London and Leiden, 1969

Dalli Regoli, Gigetta, 'Corali quattrocenteschi', in Baracchini and Caleca (eds), *Il Duomo di Lucca*, pp 85–95

—, 'I pittori nella Lucca di Matteo Civitali. Da Michele Ciampanti a Michele Angelo di Pietro', in Filieri (ed.), *Matteo Civitali e il suo tempo*, pp 95–141

—, 'Le intersezioni tra le arti: le tipologie elaborate nella miniatura dei secoli xi e xii', in Bozzoli and Filieri (eds), *Scoperta armonia*, pp 133–54

Danto, Arthur, *The Transfiguration of the Commonplace*, Harvard University Press, Cambridge, MA, 1981

De Hollanda, Francisco, *De la pintura antigua por Francisco de Hollanda*, Spanish version, Manuel Denis [1563], ed. E. Tormo, J. Ratés Impresor, Madrid, 1921

—, *On Antique Painting*, trans. Alice Sedgwick Wohl, Pennsylvania State University Press, University Park, PA, 2013

De Marchi, Andrea, 'Identità di Giuliano Amadei miniatore', *Bollettino d'arte*, vol.80, nos 93–4, 1995, pp 119–58

Del Badia, Jodoco, 'La bottega di Alessandro di Francesco Rosselli merciaio e stampatore, 1525', *Miscellanea fiorentina di erudizione e di storia*, no.2, 1984, pp 24–30

Dennison, Lynda, 'The Significance of Ornamental Penwork in Illuminated and Decorated Manuscripts of the Second Half of the Fourteenth Century', in Villalobos Hennessy (ed.), *Tributes to Kathleen L. Scott*, pp 31–64

Desideri Trigari, Marisa, 'Burlamacchi, Pacifico', *Dizionario Biografico degli Italiani*, Società grafica romana, Rome, 1972, pp 451–2

D'Afflitto, Chiara, Franca Falletti and Andrea Muzzi (eds), *L'età di Savonarola. Fra Paolino e la pittura a Pistoia nel primo '500*, Marsilio, Venice, 1996

Di Agresti, Domenico, *Sviluppi della riforma monastica savonaroliana in Lucca*, Leo S. Olschki, Florence, 1980

D'Apuzzo, Mark Gregory, 'Le monache di Savonarola tra arte e committenza', in Fortunati (ed.), *Vita artistica nel monastero femminile*, pp 131–45

—, 'Eufrasia Burlamacchi (?–1548)', in Fortunati (ed.), *Italian Women Artists from Renaissance to Baroque*, pp 96–101

Didron, Adolphe Napoléon, *Christian Iconography or The History of Christian Art in the Middle Ages*, 2 vols, Bohn, London, 1851

Dunn, Marilyn, 'Convent Creativity', in Poska et al. (eds), *The Ashgate Research Companion to Gender and Women in Early Modern Europe*, pp 53–73

Dunn, Marilyn, and Saundra Weddle (eds), *Convent Networks in Early Modern Italy*, Brepols, Turnhout, 2010

Duval, Sylvie, 'Chiara Gambacorta e le prime monache del monastero di san Domenico di Pisa: l'Osservanza domenicana al femminile', in Festa and Zarri (eds), *Il velo, la penna e la parola*, pp 93–112

—, 'Usages du livres et de l'écrit', in Bériou, Morard and Nebbiai (eds), *Stabilité et itinérance*, pp 215–28

Elen, Albert J., and Chris Fischer, *Fra Bartolommeo: The Divine Renaissance*, Museum Boijmans van Beuningen, Rotterdam, 2016

Fantoni, Marcello, Louisa C. Matthew and Sara F. Matthews-Grieco (eds), *The Art Market in Italy (15th–17th Centuries)*, Franco Panini Editore, Modena, 2003

Fassler, Margaret, 'The Office of the Cantor in early Western Monastic Rules and Customaries: A Preliminary Investigation', *Early Music History*, no.5, 1985, pp 29–51

Ferretti, Massimo, 'Domenico Bigordi detto del Ghirlandaio, *Sacra conversazione*', in Filieri (ed.), *Matteo Civitali e il suo tempo*, pp 426–8

Ferri, Claudio, 'Nuove notizie documentarie su autori e dipinti del '400 lucchese', *Actum Luce*, vol.11, nos 1–2, 1982, pp 53–72

—, 'I rapporti tra Lucca, Bruges e le Fiandre dal xv alla metà del xvi secolo, quali emergono dagli atti notarili esistenti nell'Archivio di Stato di Lucca', *Rivista di archeologia, storia e costume*, vol.30, nos 1–2, 2002, pp 9–52

Festa, Gianni, and Gabriella Zarri (eds), *Il velo, la penna e la parola. Le domenicane: storia, istituzioni, scritture*, Nerbini, Florence, 2009

Filieri, Maria Teresa, 'Matteo Civitali e Baldassarre di Biagio *pictores*', in Filieri (ed.), *Matteo Civitali e il suo tempo*, pp 79–93

—, 'Il rinnovamento delle chiese lucchesi alla fine del Quattrocento', in Filieri (ed.), *Matteo Civitali e il suo tempo*, pp 207–35

— (ed.), *Sumptuosa tabula picta. Pittori a Lucca tra gotico e rinascimento*, Sillabe, Lucca, 1998

— (ed.), *Matteo Civitali e il suo tempo. Pittori, scultori e orafi a Lucca nel tardo Quattrocento*, Silvana Editoriale,

Cinisello Balsamo, MI, 2004

Fortunati, Vera (ed.), *Vita artistica nel monastero femminile. Exempla*, Editrice Compositori, Bologna, 2002

— (ed.), *Italian Women Artists from Renaissance to Baroque*, exh.cat., National Museum of Women in the Arts, Washington, DC, 16 March–15 July 2007, Skira, New York, 2007

Freeman Sandler, Lucy, 'The Study of Marginal Imagery: Past, Present, and Future', in *Studies in Manuscript Illumination 1200–1400*, Pindar Press, London, 2008, pp 76–126

Galizzi, Diego, 'Gherardo di Giovanni', in Bollati (ed.), *Dizionario biografico dei miniatori italiani*, pp 258–62

—, 'Monte di Giovanni', in Bollati (ed.), *Dizionario biografico dei miniatori italiani*, pp 798–801

—, 'Francesco Rosselli', in Bollati (ed.), *Dizionario biografico dei miniatori italiani*, pp 914–16

—, 'Vante di Gabriello di Vante Attavanti', in Bollati (ed.), *Dizionario biografico dei miniatori italiani*, pp 975–9

Garrard, Mary D., 'The Cloister and the Square: Gender Dynamics in Renaissance Florence', *Early Modern Women: An Interdisciplinary Journal*, vol.11, no.1, 2016, pp 5–44

—, *Artemisia Gentileschi and Feminism in Early Modern Europe*, Reaktion Books, London, 2020

Garzelli, Anna Rosa, *Miniatura Fiorentina del Rinascimento, 1440–1525. Un primo censimento*, 2 vols, La Nuova Italia, Florence, 1985

Gianeselli, Matteo, 'De Domenico à Ridolfo del Ghirlandaio. Pratiques et fortune d'un atelier familial à Florence entre le xve et le xvie siècles', *ArtItalies*, no.19, 2013, pp 39–46

Gombrich, Ernst H., 'Paintings on Walls: Means and Ends in the History of Fresco Painting', in *The Uses of Images. Studies in the Social Function of Art and Visual Communication*, Phaidon Press, London, 1999, pp 14–47

Greist, Alexa, 'Manuscript Illumination', in Banta and Greist (eds), *Making Her Mark*, pp 194–6

Grivel, Marianne, and Emmanuel Lurin (eds), *The Lettering of Prints. Forms and Functions of Writing in the Printed Image in Sixteenth-Century Europe*, Peter Lang, Bern, 2021

Guidi, Pietro, and Ermenegildo Pellegrinetti, *Inventari del Vescovato, della Cattedrale e di altre chiese di Lucca*, Tipografia Poliglotta Vaticana, Vatican City, 1921

Hall, Kira, 'Performativity', *Journal of Linguistic Anthropology*, vol.9, nos 1–2, 2000, pp 184–7

Hamburger, Jeffrey F., *Nuns as Artists: The Visual Culture of a Medieval Convent*, University of California Press, Berkeley, CA, 1997

—, 'La bibliothèque d'Unterlinden et l'art de la formation spirituelle', in *Les dominicains d'Unterlinden*, exh. cat., Musée d'Unterlinden, Colmar, 2 vols, Somogy éditions d'art, Paris et Colmar, 2000, vol.i, pp 144–5

Herman, Nicholas, 'Excavating the Page: Virtuosity and Illusionism in Italian Book Illumination, 1460–1520', *Word & Image*, vol.27, no.2, 2011, pp 190–211

Holmes, Megan, *Fra Filippo Lippi, the Carmelite Painter*, Yale University Press, New Haven, CT, 1999.

Howard, Peter, *Beyond the Written Word: Preaching and Theology in the Florence of Archbishop Antoninus 1427–1459*, Leo S. Olschki, Florence, 1992

Howard, Peter, and Cecilia Hewlett (eds), *Studies on Florence and the Italian Renaissance in Honour of F.W. Kent*, Brepols, Turnhout, 2016

Jacobs, Fredrika H., 'Woman's Capacity to Create: The Unusual Case of Sofonisba Anguissola', *Renaissance Quarterly*, vol.47, no.1, 1994, pp 74–101

—, *Defining the Renaissance Virtuosa. Women Artists and the Language of Art History and Criticism*, Cambridge University Press, Cambridge, 1997

Labriola, Ada, 'Martino di Bartolomeo (Siena, c.1365/1370–1435)', in Filieri (ed.), *Sumptuosa tabula picta*, pp 202–14

—, 'Martino di Bartolomeo', in Bollati (ed.), *Dizionario biografico dei miniatori italiani*, pp 742–4

Lando, Ortensio, *Forcianes quaestiones, in quibus varia Italorum ingenia explicantur, multaque alia scitu non indigna. Auctore Phylalethe Polytopinsi cive*, Neapoli [but Lyon], 1535

Lazzi, Giovanna, 'Il Cicerone Landau Finaly della Biblioteca Nazionale di Firenze', in Sesti (ed.), *La miniatura italiana tra gotico e rinascimento*, pp 309–27

Leonardi, Claudio (ed.), *Caterina Vigri: la santa e la città*, Sismel-Edizioni del Galluzzo, Florence, 2004

Levi D'Ancona, Mirella, *Miniatura e miniatori a Firenze dal xiv al xvi secolo. Documenti per una storia della miniatura*, Leo S. Olschki, Florence, 1962

—, *The Garden of the Renaissance. Botanical Symbolism in Italian Painting*, Leo S. Olschki, Florence, 1977

Lowe, Kate J.P., 'The Progress of Patronage in Renaissance Italy', *Oxford Art Journal*, vol.18, 1995, pp 147–50

—, *Nuns' Chronicles and Convent Culture in Renaissance and Counter-Reformation Italy*, Cambridge University Press, Cambridge, 2003

Luzzati, Michele, 'Burlamacchi', *Dizionario Biografico degli Italiani*, Società grafica romana, Rome, 1972, pp 433–6

—, 'Burlamacchi, Francesco', *Dizionario Biografico degli Italiani*, Società grafica romana, Rome, 1972, pp 440–46

Macey, Patrick, 'The Lauda and the Cult of Savonarola', *Renaissance Quarterly*, vol.45, no.3, 1992, pp 439–83

Mancini, Augusto, *Storia di Lucca*, Sansoni, Florence, 1950

Mansi, Gerardo, *I patrizi di Lucca. Le antiche famiglie lucchesi ed i loro stemmi*, Titania, Lucca, 1996

Marchese, Vincenzo, *Memorie dei più insigni pittori, scultori e architetti domenicani*, Giusti, Lucca, 1845–6, 2nd edn, 1869

Marcon, Susy, 'Amadei, Giuliano', in Bollati (ed.), *Dizionario biografico dei miniatori italiani*, pp 10–13

Martinelli, Stefano, 'Dalle Fiandre a Lucca: modalità di ricezione e rielaborazione nella pittura lucchese del secondo Quattrocento', in Anselmi (ed.), *Nuovi studi su Matteo Civitali*, pp 65–87

Milanesi, Gaetano (ed.), *Le opere di Giorgio Vasari*, Sansoni, Florence, 1878

Mirollo, James V., *The Poet of the Marvellous: Giambattista Marino*, Columbia University Press, New York, 1963

Moreton, Melissa, 'Pious Voices: Nun-Scribes and the Language of Colophons in Late Medieval and Renaissance Italy', *Essays in Medieval Studies*, no.29, 2014, pp 43–73

Muessig, Carolyn, George Ferzoco and Beverly Mayne Kienzle (eds), *A Companion to Catherine of Siena*, Brill, Leiden and Boston, MA, 2012

Murano, Giovanna (ed.), *Autographa II.1. Donne, sante e madonne (da Matilde di Canossa a Artemisia Gentileschi)*, La Mandragora, Imola, 2018

Murphy, Caroline, 'Plautilla Nelli: Between Cloister and Client. A Study in Negotiation', in Nelson (ed.), *Suor Plautilla Nelli*, pp 57–65

Muzzi, Andrea, 'Eclettismo e devozione a Pistoia nella prima metà del Cinquecento', in D'Afflitto et al. (eds), *L'età di Savonarola*, pp 9–35

Nelson, Jonathan K. (ed.), *Suor Plautilla Nelli (1523–1588): The First Woman Painter of Florence*, Edizioni Cadmo, Florence, 2000

— (ed.), *Plautilla Nelli (1524–1588). The Painter-Prioress of Renaissance Florence*, S.E.I., Florence, 2008

Nochlin, Linda, 'Why Have There Been No Great Women Artists?', in *Women, Art and Power*, Harper & Row, New York, 1988, pp 145–78

Nuttall, Geoffrey, 'Filippino Lippi's Lucchese Patrons', in Nuttall et al. (eds), *Filippino Lippi*, pp 85–118

Nuttall, Paula, *From Flanders to Florence*, Yale University Press, New Haven, CT, and London, 2004

—, 'From Reiteration to Dialogue: Filippino's Responses to Netherlandish Painting', in Nuttall et al. (eds), *Filippino Lippi*, pp 187–207

Nuttall, Paula, Geoffrey Nuttall and Michael W. Kwakkelstein (eds), *Filippino Lippi. Beauty, Invention and Intelligence*, Brill, Leiden, 2020

Padovani, Serena, and Silvia Meloni Trkulija (eds), *Il cenacolo di Andrea del Sarto a San Salvi: guida al museo*, Libreria editrice Salimbeni, Florence, 1982

Palearii Verulani, Aonii, *Orationes ad Senatum populumque Lucensem*, Vincenzo Busdraghi, Lucca, 1551

Paoli, Marco, *I corali della Biblioteca Statale di Lucca*, Leo S. Olschki, Florence, 1977

—, 'Messale di Lorenzo Trenta', in Filieri (ed.), *Sumptuosa tabula picta*, pp 227–9

Parmeggiani, Riccardo, 'Pietro da Noceto', *Dizionario Biografico degli Italiani*, 83 (2015), Treccani online

Payne, Elsie, 'The Nature of Musical Emotion and its Place in the Appreciative Experience', *British Journal of Aesthetics*, vol.13, no.2, 1973, pp 171–81

Polizzotto, Lorenzo, 'When the Saints Fall Out: Women and the Savonarolan Reform in Early Sixteenth-Century Florence', *Renaissance Quarterly*, vol.46, no.3, 1993, pp 486–525

—, *The Elect Nation: The Savonarolan Movement in Florence, 1494–1545*, Clarendon Press, Oxford, 1994

Pope Hennessy, John, 'The Study of Italian Plaquettes', in Alison Luchs (ed.), *Italian Plaquettes*, Studies in the History of Art, no.22, 1989, pp 19–32

Poska, Allyson M., Jane Couchman and Katherine A. McIver (eds), *The Ashgate Research Companion to*

Gender and Women in Early Modern Europe, Ashgate, Farnham, 2013

Pseudo-Burlamacchi, *La vita del beato Ieronimo Savonarola, scritta da un anonimo del sec. xvi e già attribuita a Fra Pacifico Burlamacchi, pubblicata secondo il codice ginoriano*, ed. Principe Piero Ginori Conti, Leo S. Olschki, Florence, 1937

Quaranta, Chiara, 'Paleario, Aonio', *Dizionario Biografico degli Italiani*, 80 (2014), Treccani online

Rebhorn, Wayne A., *Courtly Performances. Masking and Festivity in Castiglione's Book of the Courtier*, Wayne State University Press, Detroit, MI, 1978

Ridolfi, Enrico, *L'arte in Lucca studiata nella sua Cattedrale*, Canovetti, Lucca, 1882

Ridolfi, Roberto, *Le lettere di Girolamo Savonarola*, Leo S. Olschki, Florence, 1933

—, 'La questione dello "Pseudo-Burlamacchi" e della "Vita latina"', in *Opuscoli di storia letteraria e di erudizione. Savonarola, Machiavelli, Guicciardini, Giannotti*, Bibliopolis libreria editrice, Florence, 1942, pp 3–27

Ristori, Renzo, 'Le origini della Riforma a Lucca', *Rinascimento*, vol.3, 1952, pp 227–92

Roberts, Ann, *Dominican Women and Renaissance Art: The Convent of San Domenico of Pisa*, Ashgate, Aldershot, 2008

Roberts, Sean, 'Francesco Rosselli and Berlinghieri's *Geographia* Re-examined', *Print Quarterly*, vol.28, no.1, 2011, pp 4–17

Rudolph, Conrad, *'The Things of Greater Importance': Bernard of Clairvaux's Apologia and Medieval Attitude toward Art*, University of Pennsylvania Press, Philadelphia, PA, 1990

Salmi, Mario, 'Piero della Francesca e Giuliano Amadei', *Rivista d'Arte*, vol.24, nos 1–2, 1942, pp 26–44

Sancti Antonini Archiepiscopi Florentini Ordinis Praedicatorum Summa Theologica, Verona, Augustus Caratonius, 1740; repr. Akademische Druck – Universitäts Verlagsanstalt, Graz, 1959

Savonarola, Girolamo, *Prediche sopra i salmi*, ed. Vincenzo Romano, A. Belardetti, Rome, 1969–74

Scapecchi, Piero (ed.), *Catalogo degli incunaboli della Biblioteca Nazionale Centrale di Firenze*, Nerbini, Florence, 2017

Seidel Menchi, Silvana, 'Le traduzioni italiane di Lutero nella prima metà del Cinquecento', *Rinascimento*, series ii, vol.28, no.17, 1977, pp 31–108

—, *Erasmo in Italia: 1520–1580*, Bollati Boringhieri, Turin, 1987

Sesti, Emanuela (ed.), *La miniatura italiana tra gotico e rinascimento*, Leo S. Olschki, Florence, 1985

Silva, Romano, *La Basilica di san Frediano in Lucca. Urbanistica, architettura, arredo*, Maria Pacini Fazzi, Lucca, 2010

Speranza, Laura, 'Antonio del Ceraiolo', in Bocci Pacini and Maetzke (eds), *Il Museo dell'Accademia Etrusca di Cortona*, pp 155–9

Steinberg, Ronald M., *Fra Girolamo Savonarola, Florentine Art, and Renaissance Historiography*, Ohio University Press, Athens, OH, 1977

Strocchia, Sharon T., 'Naming a Nun: Spiritual Exemplars and Corporate Identity in Florentine Convents, 1450–1530', in Connell (ed.), *Society and Individual in Renaissance Florence*, pp 215–40

—, 'Savonarolan Witnesses: The Nuns of San Jacopo and the Piagnone Movement in Sixteenth-Century Florence', *Sixteenth Century Journal*, vol.38, no.2, 2007, pp 393–418

—, *Nuns and Nunneries in Renaissance Florence*, Johns Hopkins University Press, Baltimore, MD, 2009

—, 'Begging for Favours: The "New" Clares of S. Chiara Novella and their Patrons', in Howard and Hewlett (eds), *Studies on Florence and the Italian Renaissance*, pp 277–94

Tamborino, Alessandra, 'Considerazioni sull'attività di Antonio del Ceraiolo e proposte al suo catalogo', *Proporzioni. Annali della Fondazione Roberto Longhi*, nos 2–3, 2001–2, pp 104–22

Taurisano, Innocenzo, OP, *I Domenicani in Lucca*, Baroni, Lucca, 1914

Tazartes, Maurizia, 'Ipotesi di percorso per Agostino Marti', *Ricerche di Storia dell'Arte*, nos 43–4, 1991, pp 149–64

—, *Fucina lucchese. Maestri, botteghe, mercanti in una città del Quattrocento*, Edizioni ETS, Pisa, 2007

Thomas, Anabel, *Art and Piety in the Female Religious Communities of Renaissance Italy. Iconography, Space, and the Religious Woman's Perspective*, Cambridge University Press, Cambridge, 2003

Tommasi, Girolamo, *Sommario della storia di Lucca*

dall'anno MIV all'anno MDCC, G.P. Vieusseux, Florence, 1847

Tozzi, Ileana, 'I corali miniati di Suor Eufrasia Burlamacchi, fondatrice del monastero di san Domenico a Lucca', *Arte cristiana*, vol.829, no.4, 2005, pp 217–22

—, 'Suor Eufrasia Burlamacchi. I corali del monastero di San Domenico a Lucca', *Alumina*, vol.3, no.11, 2005, pp 20–25

Tugwell, Simon, et al. (eds), *Letters of Bede Jarrett*, Downside Abbey & Black Friars Publications, Bath and Oxford, 1989

Turrill Lupi, Catherine, 'Parenti, clienti e cognoscenti: The Nun-Artisans of Santa Caterina da Siena and Their Clients', in Fantoni et al. (eds), *The Art Market in Italy*, pp 95–103

—, 'Pursuing a Savonarolan Thread: Patrons, Painters, and *Piagnoni* in S. Caterina in Cafaggio', in Dunn and Weddle (eds), *Convent Networks in Early Modern Italy*, pp 85–114

Van Buren, Anne H., and Sheila Edmunds, 'Playing Cards and Manuscripts: Some Widely Disseminated Fifteenth-Century Model Sheets', *The Art Bulletin*, vol.56, no.1, 1974, pp 12–30

Vandi, Loretta, 'Carte da gioco e manoscritti. Note sul rapporto tra miniatura quattrocentesca e incisione in area romagnola', *Studi Romagnoli*, vol.49, 1998, pp 123–38

—, *La trasformazione del motivo dell'acanto dall'antichità al xv secolo. Ricerche di teoria e storia dell'ornamento*, Peter Lang, Bern, 2002

—, *Il Manoscritto Oliveriano 1. Storia di un codice boemo del xv secolo*, STIBU, Urbania, PU, 2004

—, 'The Eternal Flame. Eufrasia Burlamacchi and Savonarolan Art in the Lucchese Convent of San Domenico', in Loretta Vandi, *Four Essays*, Umeå University Press, Umeå, 2007, pp 19–53

—, 'Sister Eufrasia Burlamacchi and the Art of the Wayside', *Memorie domenicane*, vol.132, no.46, 2015, pp 87–102

—, 'Eufrasia Burlamacchi', in Murano (ed.), *Autographa ii.1*, pp 114-15

—, 'Re-forming Images through Lettering. Savonarola's Heritage in a Corpus of Sixteenth-Century Woodcuts in the Biblioteca Statale, Lucca', in Grivel and Lurin (eds), *The Lettering of Prints*, pp 119–41

—, 'Sister Eufrasia Burlamacchi (Lucca, 1478–1548). A Multi-faceted Illuminator within Artistic and Religious Reforms', *Art Herstory*, 20 September 2021

— (ed.), *Suor Eufrasia Burlamacchi (1478–1548). Scrivere, miniare, cantare nella Lucca del Cinquecento*, exh.cat., Biblioteca Statale, Lucca, 23 September–15 December 2023, Maria Pacini Fazzi, Lucca, 2023

Vasari, Giorgio, *Le vite de' più eccellenti architetti, pittori et scultori italiani, da Cimabue insino a' tempi nostri*, ed. Luciano Bellosi and Aldo Rossi, Einaudi, Turin, 1986

Verde, Armando Felice, OP, *Il Breviario di frate Girolamo Savonarola. Postille autografe trascritte e commentate*, SISMEL-Edizioni del Galluzzo, Florence, 1999

Verdon, Timothy, *Fra Angelico*, Brepols, Turnhout, 2020

Villalobos Hennessy, Marlene (ed.), *Tributes to Kathleen L. Scott. English Medieval Manuscripts: Readers, Makers and Illuminators*, Harvey Miller Publishers, Turnhout, 2009

Vinay, Valdo, 'Il piccolo catechismo di Lutero come strumento di evangelizzazione fra gli italiani dal xvi al xx secolo', *Protestantesimo*, vol.25, 1970, pp 65–84

Vitruvius, *De architectura*, ed. F. Granger, Harvard University Press, Cambridge, MA, 1985

Zabeo, Laura, 'L'ultimo Amadei a Lucca', *Rivista di storia della miniatura*, no.24, 2020, pp 109–23

Zambrano, Patrizia, and Jonathan K. Nelson, *Filippino Lippi*, Electa, Milan, 2004

Zeri, Federico, *Pittura e Controriforma. L'arte 'senza tempo' di Scipione da Gaeta*, Neri Pozza Editore, Vicenza, 1997 (1st edn Einaudi, Turin, 1957)

—, 'Antonio del Ceraiolo', *Gazette des Beaux-Arts*, vol.109, no.70, 1967, pp 139–54

Zucker, Mark J., 'Savonarola Designs a Work of Art. The Crown of the Virgin in the Compendium of Revelations', in Vincenzo De Nardo and Christopher Fulton (eds), *Machiavelli Studies*, vol.5, 1996, pp 119–45

Image Credits

Courtesy of the Archivio Fotografico Diocesano di Lucca: figs 27, 39, 65

Courtesy of the Archivio Storico Diocesano di Lucca: figs 13, 22, 23, 26, 28, 29, 30, 31

Baltimore Museum of Art. On loan from the archives of the Dominican convent, California. Photo: Mitro Hood: fig.75

Biblioteca Medicea Laurenziana, Florence. Courtesy of the Ministry of Culture. Photo: Loretta Vandi: fig.3

Biblioteca Nazionale Centrale, Florence. Courtesy of the Ministry of Culture: figs 52, 53

Biblioteca Statale, Lucca. Courtesy of the Ministry of Culture. Photo: Federico Caruso, Margherita Montanari and Chiara Mazzanti: figs 4, 5, 6, 7, 8, 10, 11, 14, 16, 17, 18, 20, 21, 25, 32, 42, 63, 64, 67, 70, 71, 74, 76, 77, 79, 80

Dominican convent, California: figs 1, 2, 15, 19, 24, 33, 34, 35, 37, 38, 40, 41, 44, 45, 46, 50, 54, 57, 58, 60, 61, 62, 69, 73, 78

Photo: Loretta Vandi: fig.9

Kunsthistorisches Institut in Florenz - Max-Planck-Institut: photo – Paolo Bacherini: fig.36; photo – Roberto Sigismondi: fig.49

Museo Nazionale del Bargello, Florence. Courtesy of the Ministry of Culture. Photo: Loretta Vandi: figs 47, 66

Courtesy of the San Martino cathedral, Lucca: fig.56

Courtesy of Santa Maria del Sasso Monastery, Bibbiena, Arezzo. Photo: Loretta Vandi: fig.12

Sant'Agostino Order Photo Archives, Florence. Photo: Albino Todeschini: fig.55

Tuscany Regional Museums Directorate, Florence. Courtesy of the Ministry of Culture: figs 48, 51, 59, 68, 72

Index

Note: italic page numbers indicate figures; page numbers followed by n refer to notes; Eufrasia Burlamacchi is abbreviated to EB in headings and subheadings.